New Directions in East Asian History

This series addresses the ways in which history influences the political, economic and social development of East Asia, a region which now plays a pivotal role in our world's multipolar international system. The series provides new perspectives on East Asia's distinctive economic and political situation through the lens of 20th century history, with a particular focus on Pre-War and Cold War periods. It argues the need to re-examine the history of East Asia and provide new historical approaches to a vibrant and constantly changing region.

Highlighting that history is at the root of many modern day conflicts in Asia, this series provides a global forum for rigorous academic research and timely debate by scholars worldwide, and showcases significant new research on East Asian history and politics in the contemporary era.

The series will appeal to specialists in the history and politics of Asia; international history; scholars of modern and contemporary Japan, Chinese and Korea as well as international relations.

NOW INDEXED ON SCOPUS!

Christopher Perkins

The Tokyo University Trial and the Struggle Against Order in Postwar Japan

palgrave
macmillan

Christopher Perkins
University of Edinburgh
Edinburgh, UK

ISSN 2522-0195 ISSN 2522-0209 (electronic)
New Directions in East Asian History
ISBN 978-981-99-7042-1 ISBN 978-981-99-7043-8 (eBook)
https://doi.org/10.1007/978-981-99-7043-8

Cover credit: Three Lions/Getty images

This Palgrave Macmillan imprint is published by the registered company Springer Nature Singapore Pte Ltd.
The registered company address is: 152 Beach Road, #21-01/04 Gateway East, Singapore 189721, Singapore

Paper in this product is recyclable.

Preface

All Japanese in this book are transliterated using the modified Hepburn system. Japanese names are given in Japanese order except in cases where the person is well known and generally referred to using the Western order.

Legal terms, where possible, have been translated according to the Japanese Ministry of Justice Japanese Law in Translation dictionary. The University of Tokyo is referred to in most materials examined in this book by the shorthand *Tōdai*. As such, and for ease of reading, I have referred to the University of Tokyo as Tokyo University throughout.

Edinburgh, UK Christopher Perkins

Acknowledgments

While writing this book I have been lucky to share my ideas and receive feedback at various stages with colleagues at several conferences and workshops. Thanks go to Mara Vodopivec for the kind invitation to the University of Leiden at which I first started to put my thoughts together; Ferran de Vargas and his colleagues and students at the Autonomous University of Barcelona; Helen Macnaughtan for the invitation to speak at the Japan Research Centre at the School of African and Oriental Studies; Fujino Hanako at the Europe Japan Research Centre (Oxford Brookes); Giulio Pugliese, Roger Goodman, and the staff and students at the Nissan Institute at the University of Oxford; and Daniel Laqua and the other participants in the wonderful workshop at the University of Northumbria on campus based activism.

I am indebted to the support and advice of William Marotti, Matthias Zachmann, Richard Weisman, Ferran de Vargas, Till Knaut, Anna Vittinghoff, Holly Stephens, Aaron Moore, Helen Parker, Yoko Matsumoto-Sturt, and Mark McLeister. All mistakes are of course my own.

Special thanks to Daniel Hammond.

Cassandra Lord's help in securing materials from the National Diet Library was invaluable.

I would not have been able to complete this book without the support of my friends and family, chief among them Joey, Zach, and Biscuit.

Contents

List of Tables

CHAPTER 1

Introduction: Disorder in the Courts

On a hot and humid day in July 1969 journalists and spectators took their places in court to watch the next episode in the tumultuous Tokyo University trials. Six months had passed since the events had taken place for which the defendants were accused. Between the 18th and 19th of January 1969, in the deep chill of winter, after a battle between hundreds of students and thousands of riot police at Tokyo University, around 600 student activists had been arrested. Those students found themselves separated and distributed across prisons in the Tokyo area. Students were, in the most part, charged with the crimes of failing to disperse when ordered to by the police, obstructing police business, and assembling with weapons (stones, pipes, concrete, and Molotov cocktails) with the intent to do harm. Of this number, around a third, who became known as the 'Repentant Group' (*hanseigumi*), opted to be tried separately (*bunkatsu kōhan*). Their cases were resolved quickly, with the students mostly receiving suspended sentences. The remaining students, however, held out for a unified trial (*tōitsu kōhan*).

On this day in July, it was the turn of 'Yasuda Group 18', named after Tokyo University's famous Yasuda Auditorium in which they had been arrested, to have their day in court. The room was swollen to capacity; two prosecutors sat at their table waiting for proceedings to begin. The defendants and their lawyers, however, were nowhere to be seen. At just

C. Perkins, *The Tokyo University Trial and the Struggle Against Order in Postwar Japan*, New Directions in East Asian History,
https://doi.org/10.1007/978-981-99-7043-8_1

past 10am, with the defendants still absent, the presiding judge declared the start of the trial. Amid calls from the gallery for the judge to justify opening proceedings in absence of the defendants, the judge called for a report on the situation in the detention centres. 'Defendant I' reported the courtroom attendant 'stripped himself naked, soaked his clothes in water, and clung onto the base of the sink in his cell. Stubbornly refusing to appear in court he yelled: "I demand a unified trial! I have submitted my reasoning to the courts in writing!"' The attendant repeated the same report for the other defendants.

A call from the gallery: 'Their reasons for not appearing in court are legitimate, aren't they?' The judge: 'the spectator who just said that, stand!'

Three guards rushed to where the offending spectator sat and tried to jostle him to his feet. 'He won't stand…' they reported back to the judge.

'Eject him from the courtroom' ordered the judge. As the guards did so the courtroom erupted into noise, calls of 'down with absentee trials' echoed around the walls. Five more spectators were taken bodily from the courtroom.

Next, defendants who were on bail were admitted to the courtroom. Emblazoned on their shirts in marker pen were the slogans 'do not allow trials in absentia!' and 'repeal legal fascism!' One student tore of his shirt to reveal the same slogans written all across his body.

Their lawyers were now also present but had no intention of complying with the trial. 'We have come here to demand a single unified trial,' they responded when addressed by the judge. 'We do not intend on engaging in legal activities in this group trial courtroom.'

The prosecutors began to present their case, starting with the argument that under Article 286 section 2 of the Code of Criminal Procedure, should defendants fail to appear in court without a legitimate reason to do so it was legally possible to hold trials without the defendants present. At this the courtroom erupted once more and the presiding judge called a recess to confer with his two colleagues who were seated to either side. Returning to the courtroom the judge stated they agreed with the prosecution: Article 286 section 2 would be applied, and the trial would continue. The lawyers rushed towards the bench, demanding an explanation. The spectators shouted their disapproval.

At 10:55 the presiding judge called in the riot police, who had been stationed close by and who quickly bundled away two thirds of the spectators. Only twenty people, mostly families of the accused, were left in the gallery. 'As they have hampered the management of this courtroom, I order the removal of the defendants from the courtroom'.

'Now we have peace,' the judge remarked as he asked the prosecutor to continue, drawing wry smiles from journalists. Indeed, the room was now so silent the that journalists could easily hear the thrum of the air conditioner as it fought against the heat of the Japanese summer. And with the proper atmosphere secured, the prosecution began to make their case.

This brief account of one episode of the Tokyo University trial, drawn from a longer piece that appeared in 1969 in the magazine Shūkan Asahi, raises a number of questions that are central to this book.[1] What led to such a huge indictment of students? What spurred the acrimony between the courts and students? Why were the students' lawyers so adamant they would not comply with the trial process? What was the outcome of holding trials with the defendants and their lawyers absent? And what provoked the wry smiles from the journalists when the judge had finally secured peace in the courtroom? In seeking to answer these and other questions, this book offers an account of the Tokyo University trial, the processes that shaped it and the impact the battle in the courtroom had on the protagonists and their communities. The story of the trial that emerges in one about the management of order (in Japanese *chitsujo*) in postwar Japan—social, legal, and emotional—efforts to naturalise that order in Japanese institutions, and the work of New Left students, their lawyers, and their allies to breach that order through their radical praxis. But it is also about the cost of that battle and the impact it had in ultimately shoring up the very order it tried to challenge.

This book contributes to the growing literature on New Left student activism in Japan in the late 1960s. Since the publication of Oguma Eiji's historical overview of Japan's 1968 there has been a steady stream of scholarly investigations of Japan's New Left movement to which the following discussions in this book is indebted.[2] But when the Tokyo University trial is mentioned in the historiography on this period it is usually as a side note to the transition of the student movement away from the campus struggles of 1968/69 and towards the domestic and international action of New Left political factions in the early to mid-1970s. Furthermore, other than some early discussions in Japan, the trial is almost absent from scholarship on Japan's legal system.[3] The exception to this rule is the work of Patricia Steinhoff, who has discussed the Tokyo University trial in the context of New Left activism in the late

1960s and 1970s and the development of the *Kyūen renraku sentā* (Relief Contact Centre, Kyūen), a clearing house which coordinated relief efforts for students on trial during this period of mass arrest. As Steinhoff has argued, through its publications and the leg work of its volunteers, which at the organisation's peak numbered in the tens of thousands, Kyūen played a crucial role in coordinating activist resistance to police interrogation, worked hard to block the authorities from co-opting students' families into their efforts to break down student resistance, and were instrumental in supporting defendants and devising courtroom strategies to tie up state resources. Support organisations also played an important role in connecting the student movement to the wider Japanese public through their information campaigns and fundraising efforts.[4] Steinhoff's work has been invaluable in documenting the range of the work done by support groups during the late 1960s and into the 1970s and has helped with understanding the challenges they faced and the emotional toll that work took.[5] The approach taken in this book, however, differs from that taken by Steinhoff in two main respects.

First, rather than placing the Tokyo University trial within the many trials that followed the mass arrests of New Left activists that took place between 1968 and 1972, this book focusses on the Tokyo University trial itself, and in particular on events leading up to the first verdict in late 1969. In doing so this book does not intend to downplay nor intentionally ignore other university struggles, which were wide, geographically dispersed, and various. Neither does it wish to suggest that by virtue of being centred on Tokyo University—the most elite of elite Japanese universities—this trial has some sort of exalted status and as such is representative of the whole. With these caveats in place, however, it is the case that the Tokyo University trial deserves attention because it was the first truly mass arrest, indictment and detention of students in the period.[6] As such, and perhaps unsurprisingly, when examining the materials produced by the students, their support groups and their lawyers, the letters of students in detention awaiting trial, as well as the documents produced by the prosecution and the courts, it became clear that in early 1969 questions of intention, process, and tactics on all sides in response to this new form of mass trial had yet to be worked out. Examining the trial on its own terms allows for analysis to examine the social, political, and legal forces entangled in the decisions taken by the students (who themselves were far from a homogenous body), their lawyers and the courts in a situation that was new to all involved. With legal doctrine clashing with the theory and practice of students and their legal representation there were no clear answers about how to proceed, and legitimacy of the whole trial process could not be taken for granted. It is therefore important to understand the processes through which the trial came to take the form that it did, and how that form contested and legitimised.

Second, and related, this book argues for the Tokyo University trial in particular being an important moment in the complex and again contested development of the Japanese state's postwar approach to the management of domestic order. The collapse of the Japanese Empire, and the institutional reconfiguration of Japan under the Allied Occupation, presented Japan's conservative elite with the challenge of managing domestic order without the institutional and legislative techniques, and the ideological justifications for those techniques, that had been used so successfully to crack down on dissent before the war. As Ogino Fujio has argued, however, within the context of Cold War fears of international communism the Japanese state was remarkably successful in rebuilding its security apparatus in the name of securing order as a prerequisite for the new democracy.[7] The late 1940s and 1950s saw a war of attrition waged on left-wing social movements as successive laws were passed in the name of securing order to close down spaces in which counter hegemonic practices—namely left-wing politics—could occur. As the state cracked down on left-wing political mobilisation, however, those battles moved into the courts where the judiciary demonstrated their newfound independence in rulings that hampered the state's efforts to gain hegemony over the articulation of the sociolegal order. In response to these riotous courtroom battles—the 1952 May Day trial chief among them—the state introduced new legislation for maintaining order in the courts, and the Supreme Court advocated strongly for that legislation's use. Importantly, this legislation was designed to secure a certain form of atmosphere in courtrooms—one of peace and solemnity—the maintenance of which was articulated with the legitimacy and authority of the law.

The mass national protests—spearheaded by student radicals—over the renewal of the Japan-US Security Treaty (known in Japan as Anpo) between late 1959 and 1960 brought about a sense in Japan that its fledgling democracy was on the brink of collapse. Afterwards, the ruling Liberal Democratic Party (LDP) moved into the 1960s with a focus on economic growth, as well as securing social order through the careful inculcation within the populace of a 'proper' understanding of the importance of respect for the forces of law and order in securing the 'bright society' of the future. While Japan performed its economic miracle, however, contradictions within this new society—chief among them that the same order that secured prosperity also meant alignment with the US in the increasingly bloody war in Vietnam—prompted a resurgence of student unrest. As student action became more unified and organised, Japan's security apparatus began to see them as a significant threat to their view of order and called for increasingly more proactive and punitive approaches to policing. The Shinjuku Riots Incident of 1968, in which the students' sense of outrage threatened to spread to bystanders, solidified in the minds of state security agencies, police, and prosecutors, that student radicalism presented a significant threat to public order which threat would likely escalate to untold levels in 1970 with the renewal of the Anpo.

Thus, by the time the occupation of Tokyo University came to a head in January 1969, the state was set to make an example. Indeed, the rhetoric from conservative politicians and prosecutors was of the future of Japan at stake. At the height of student unrest across Japan, for example, Japan's Prosecutor General Imoto Daikichi made the following assessment of Japan's development since the end of the Second Word War (WWII), in which he spoke of the moral imperative to secure order:

> Japan's recent economic growth has been remarkable, ranking second in the free world's GNP, just behind the United States. Currently, it can be considered an industrialized nation, but it seems that a post-industrial society is not far off. There are said to be four distinctive industries in such a society: the information industry, symbolized by the development of computers; the marine industry, centred around the continental shelf, which accounts for about 80% of our territory; the materials industry, represented by plastics and others; and industries associated with the growth of megalopolises. While the development of these industries is noteworthy, I believe that such economic growth is based on the maintenance of law and order, which we all work tirelessly to uphold. Without the preservation of law and order, we cannot expect individuals to thrive freely, and it would be easy to see that economic development cannot be achieved.[8]

In fact, for Imoto Japan had been on the path to such greatness almost a century before, when after the 1868 Meiji Restoration the nation made economic, social, and political gains that took the entire world by surprise. In his analysis, however, this incredible progress had been destroyed by the unlawful acts of the military who, through insubordination, murder, and ultimately the failed coup d'etat by young military officers of the Imperial Way Faction on 26th February 1936, plunged Japan into chaos and destroyed any vestiges of democracy. The February 26th Incident, Imoto argued, could have been avoided had defence lawyers not drawn-out previous cases, and had the courts been allowed to try two of the principal actors—officers Kurihara Yasuhide and Muranaka Takaji—who had been involved in a prior incident but whose prosecution had been suppressed by the military. The military's inability to secure order, according to Imoto, also led to the murder of General Mori Takeshi at the Imperial Palace in August 1945 in an attempt to prevent Japan from accepting the terms of the Potsdam declaration and as such ending the war. It was in this context that Imoto characterised student unrest:

> Since the first Haneda Incident in the fall of 1967 until September 1968, around 2,400 individuals have been charged with assault, injury, and obstruction of public duties in Tokyo, Osaka, Nagasaki, and elsewhere. Among them, more than 600 have been sentenced, while over 1,800 remain unresolved. People seem to think that a trial in the first instance is over with the prosecutor's indictment, but this is an urgent matter requiring correction. That is to say, more prompt and appropriate trials must be conducted. In today's Japanese society, student unrest incidents are symbolic. If law and order can be maintained through these incidents, it can be said that law and order have been generally maintained. If this breaks down, Japan's economy would also collapse, just as the once-powerful Japanese military did.[9]

Imoto's analysis of the parallels between Japan's descent into war and the tumultuous politics of the late 1960s was emblematic of thinking amongst Japan's conservative elite on the threat of student unrest and the barriers they saw towards its effective policing. In their eyes, like the young officers of the Imperial Way Faction, students were seen as coddled by the legal establishment, who saw something to be admired in their youthful adherence to their ideals. Judges were too lenient. Defence lawyers were apt to employ strategies that held up the course of justice. And like those officers who attempted to block the acceptance of the Potsdam declaration, which paved the way to Japan's return to democracy, students were through their actions destroying the foundations of Japan's economic, social, and political progress. In this regard the policing of student unrest in the late 1960s was for Imoto both a new challenge and a ghost come back to haunt Japan from the darkest days in living memory: a re-emergence of a test for the robustness of Japan's democracy that it had once before failed.

The approach taken in the courts during the Tokyo University trial, however, was not one of simple punishment of students for reckless acts. From the writings of prosecutors and judges it is clear that their aim was rather to make distinctions between those students for whom redemption in the eyes of the national community (for which prosecutors and the judiciary claimed to speak) was possible, and those who could only serve as symbolic of the outcome of transgressing the rules governing the actions appropriate to young people, and students in particular.[10] The distinction hinged on compliance with the trial process, and through it expressions of remorse. In this regard the courts were engaged in what legal scholar Richard Weisman calls the 'moral regulation of social life'.[11] For Weisman, an important function of the law is eliciting remorse from the offender regarding the wrongdoings that have been committed and in so doing communicating to the national community the rules of feeling to be associated with certain acts.[12] In this sense expressions of remorse are performative acts that demarcate, or when lacking fail to demarcate, a distinction between the self that committed the offence and the new self that now joins the national community in condemning the act committed. If remorse is expressed and accepted, the offender successfully establishes their new remorseful self as their true self. In the eyes of the law, they now have the potential to move on with their lives. But when there is no performance of remorse, or that performance is deemed inauthentic, the crime comes to define who the offender is: it becomes their 'essence' and means they can never be successfully reintegrated into the national moral community.[13]

And the nation was watching. Indeed, the trial took place under extreme media scrutiny across the legal press, intellectual magazines, weeklies, daily newspapers, and even television. During 1969, not a single day passed without the press reporting on the latest developments in the sensational trial. Pages were filled with open discussions, roundtables, and reportage. In this regard, the trial represented what Douglas Kellner refers to as a 'media spectacle,' which he defines as those 'phenomena of media culture that embody society's fundamental values, initiate individuals into its way of life, and dramatize its controversies, struggles, and modes of conflict resolution.'[14] The media coverage, however, did not all go in favour of the prosecutors and the courts. The defence team's strategy for the students was to actively promote such a spectacle in an attempt to erode the court's hegemony over legal process and moral rectitude, and bring the court battle to the masses. As tensions grew, the trial risked undermining the judiciary's legitimacy as final arbiters of proper conduct, prompting them to leave the sanctity of their courtrooms and violate a core principle of judiciary "never explaining" (*saibankan wa benmei sezu*) their positions.[15] This approach by the defence, however, was also subject to fierce criticism as a violation of legal ethics and a betrayal of their student clients.

This brings us to another theme of the book: the role of lawyers in Japanese society, their status within the Japanese legal system, and the question of legal ethics. Prior to WWII, under the Meiji inquisitorial legal system, lawyers held a lower status in the legal hierarchy than judges and prosecutors and established their place in society by advocating for social movements in politically charged cases. The postwar Constitution and 1949 Attorney's Act (*Bengoshi-hō*) elevated the status of lawyers, but their role in the judicial process remained a subject of debate. In the new adversarial system ushered in by the Allied occupation after the war, during detention and interrogation defence lawyers were now expected to uphold the rights of the accused as stipulated by the Constitution, and during the trial submit evidence that called into question the prosecutor's version of events. The new emphasis on human rights and the right to counsel within an adversarial legal system was to expand the scope of and demand for legal representation, and professionalisation secured independence. The current literature on legal defence in Japan, however, agrees that in practice the adversarial model only went so far. As characterised by Murayama Masayuki, defence lawyers have instead tended to act as 'caretakers' through the legal process, whose job is to help the client tell the truth and make reparations to secure the most lenient outcome possible.[16] Thus, despite being constitutionally required to defend their clients, lawyers are pressured to expedite trials by collaborating with judges and prosecutors. Instances in which lawyers resisted cooperation, such as during the 1952 May Day Trial, were criticized not only by the state but also by their own professional associations as unethical. By the late 1960s, the debate about the appropriate role of lawyers in the legal system had reached a critical point, with loud voices on the right arguing that the judiciary was succumbing to left-wing influences through its relationship with organisations such as the Young Lawyers Association (*Seinen hōristuka kyōkai*). Within this context the defence team for the students in the Tokyo University trial, who identified strongly with the anti-establishment thought of their clients, became increasingly at odds with the legal system itself—the courts, the prosecutors, and progressively their own community of lawyers and legal associations.

As legal anthropologists have shown the legitimacy of trials is bound up with their orderly conduct. 'For a hearing or trial to function,' observes Justin Richland 'the parties must tacitly agree to participate—they have to consent to the game's rules. There's significant cooperation involved in this respect.'[17] As long as such cooperation persists, the question of the proceedings' legitimacy remains tacit. When cooperation is no longer assumed, however, the issue of legitimacy shifts from being a latent concern to a prominent feature of the trial. This stage, in the words of Winnifred Sullivan, is when 'the trial itself begins to be on trial… the legitimacy of the proceedings becomes a persistently present question.'[18] Precisely this outcome transpired during the Tokyo University trial. The students and lawyers who constituted the "unified group" refused to comply with the legal process entirely, arguing against the caretaker view of the defence lawyer, and maintaining that as the courts were now functioning as a tool for suppressing the movement they were now illegitimate. The lawyers further argued that the law's emphasis on individuals and their rights, so central to the reformulation of Japan's postwar Consitutitonal order after WWII was being weaponsied against communities and value systems that opposed the hegemonic order of the state. They believed that the ability to speak, as guaranteed by the postwar Constitution, was meaningless if the students were forced to express themselves only as individuals before the judge, rather than as part of the community that gave their words and actions meaning. And by refusing to cooperate with the trial process, the students and their lawyers transformed the trial into a debate in the courtroom on the moral legitimacy of the law itself.

A brief look at the previous work of lead lawyer defence lawyer Yamane Jirō demonstrates this approach did not come out of the blue. Born in 1935, Yamane was a graduate of Chūō university who had already made a name for himself as a provocative advocate willing to take on cases that asked uncomfortable questions about Japan's postwar status-quo. In 1968, for example, Yamane had been part of a team representing Kim Hiro, a second-generation Japanese Korean who in February of that year shot dead two organized crime members to whom he owed money.[19] Kim had then escaped to Senzu in Shizuoka, where he occupied the Fujimiya Inn and took 16 hostages. In the resultant standoff with police, punctuated with sporadic gunfire and blasts of dynamite from the Inn, Kim demanded police apologise for the attitude they took towards Koreans in Japan. During the siege Kim held press conferences with the mass media, who had flocked to the scene, even going so far as to phone into a television variety show (*waido shō*) to forward his claims that his crimes were a product of systematic prejudice against Koreans in Japan.[20] After the 88-hour siege, and two televised apologies by the Shizuoka Prefectural Police Chief for use of discriminatory language, Kim was eventually arrested and put on trial for the two murders.[21]

The Kim Hiro incident (*Kimuhiro jiken*), as it became known, has some telling similarities with the Tokyo University trial. In one sense Kim's case was cut and dry. Kim had killed two loan sharks and had repeatedly confessed to the murders. But much like the events that would play out in 1969, although Kim acknowledged his crime, he refused to attend his trial until he felt the court was ready to discuss the case in the context of Japanese racial prejudice towards Korean residents.[22] In effect, Kim and his defence team aimed to use the trial to examine the history of discrimination towards Koreans in postwar Japan; as Yamane's legal team put it, the case had brought to light the 'significant problem of race in Japan' and it was now incumbent on the court to 'closely examine the causes and meaning of [Kim's] actions'.[23] To do so the defence ushered in sources of authority from different fields of social practice, and like the Tokyo University trial, Kim's siege and the trial that followed became a media-spectacle that threatened to breach the legal sanctity of the courtroom. The penetration of the media sphere into the legal sphere was part of Kim's defence: one of the conditions set by Kim for his appearance in court was appointment of Korean Japanese literary figures as 'special council' (*tokubestu bengonin*).[24] And here the Kim Hiro incident presaged another concern found in the Tokyo University trial: namely the status and character of 'truth' (*shinjitsu*) within the criminal justice system. As noted, the truth of Kim's actions was not disputed—he did what he did and admitted as much. But for Kim and his legal team this truth was inherently limited as it did not address the potential structural causes for his actions. These structural 'truths' had no status within the epistemology and processes of the legal system, which on the defence's view was interested only in the truth of guilt or innocence with respect to charges against the accused. Ushering in voices from outside the courts pushed at the boundaries of legal epistemology. Those voices were a threat. These questions about which category of truth belongs in the court would become core to the Tokyo University trial as well.

Finally, offers new insight into the experiences of students held in detention while awaiting trial. For the students, continued defiance of the courts meant long detention with minimum contact with others inside and outside prison walls. But moving forward with their lives was predicated on accepting the legitimacy of the trial, the procuracy's narrative reconstruction of their actions, and that they offer an apology in the courts: an act that resonated painfully with the prewar phenomenon of apostasy known as *tenkō* (lit. turning) which saw progressive and radical political actors recanting their views in the face of repressive state power. To borrow the words of Robert Weisman once again, for the students to take this option would be to:

> ... acquiesce to a version of their crime that negates its moral content, as well as to shift allegiances from a moral community that views the act as justifiable to a moral community for whom the act cannot be justified. For the unremorseful offender, the price of continued defiance is the risk of continued loss of liberty. The cost of compliance, however, is the repudiation of one's declared moral allegiances as well as the betrayal of the moral community that supported those allegiances.[25]

To explore how students dealt with the tensions of life in detention I draw upon a substantial collection of letters from the students that were collated and edited by supporters on the outside and published as the "Prison Letters" (*Gokuchū shokanshū*). This publication served a dual purpose: facilitating communication between the detainees and the outside world, and promoting conversations among the detainees themselves, who were kept apart from one another. From the letters emerges a picture of a highly regulated life in which the students struggled to maintain the emotions that drove their actions as part of the movement. Trapped in a continual cycle of monotonous routines, they longed for political discourse not only in terms of revolutionary theory but also as a source of excitement and comfort that provided them with a sense of belonging. For many of the students, the experience of detention was a struggle to maintain "our language" (*wareware no kotoba*) not just as simple words but as a way of life intertwined with activities, emotions, and methods of relating within their moral community. However, the letters also demonstrate tensions within the detainee community and between the detainees and the movement on the outside, as some detainees on the inside began to question the motivations of the publication committee, who framed the letters as emotional and linguistic resources for the movement.

The structure of the book largely mirrors the discussion above. The students and their lawyers conceptualised their struggle as one against Japan's bourgeois order and how that manifested in the legal system. Therefore, to provide necessary context for their view of the trial, Chapter 2 discusses state approaches to the question of order between 1945 and 1960, with a particular focus on the legal legacies produced by approaches to the management of troublesome students and riotous courts. Chapter 3 uses documents from the ruling Liberal Democratic Party (LDP), Japanese Public Safety Intelligence Agency (PSIA) and Cabinet Office reports, and examples from the popular and legal press to place the Tokyo University struggle within the context of rising state alarm over student radicalism in the lead up to the 1970 renewal of the Anpo security treaty. During this time political elites called for harsher punishments for students and exerted pressure on the judiciary to cooperate more closely with prosecutors in the policing of student unrest, while prosecutors struggled to find a balance between meeting the demands of politicians and adopting an effective method of policing that would not escalate the threat of radical student action. Chapter 4 surveys the initial aftermath of the battle for the university, detailing changing prosecutorial and judicial policy towards students and mobilisation by the students' support groups and lawyers to challenge these new approaches. Chapter 5 is dedicated to the battle between the courts and the students' lawyers over process. This chapter shows how the question of unified vs small group trials was in fact a distillation of two radically opposed views on the scope and function of the trial: views that framed fundamental questions about rights, responsibility, the collective versus the individual, and ultimately the meaning of truth within the courts.

Chapter 6 details the trials themselves using first person accounts of proceedings, documents produced by the courts and the students' lawyers, and the wide-ranging media coverage. While the courts attempted to manage order in the courtroom students and their supporters continued to resist the trial process. However, I also show how as the trial progressed, and it became increasingly clear that the judiciary had no qualms about using Article 268 section 2 to try the students in absentia, cracks began to develop between groups of student detainees over the continued efficacy of trial refusal. The result was the permanent splitting of the 'unified' student support group in 1970. Chapter 7 uses a large collection of letters written by students in detention to investigate the conditions in which they were held, and impact those conditions had on the students, their methods of resistance, and how they came to view their movement from prison. As indicated above, I also show how students worried over becoming symbols of the movement—fetishized sources of inspiring language at the expense of securing their freedom. The epilogue traces the outcome of the trial for students, their lawyers, and Japan's approaches to managing domestic security.

Notes

1. "Rupo tōdai saiban," *Shūkan Asahi*, no. 2637 (August 8, 1969): 16–18.
2. Oguma Eiji, *1968: wakamono-tachi no hanran to sono haikei* (Tokyo: Shin'yōsha, 2009). Some key texts on Japan's New Left movement and 1968 include: Ando Takemasa, *Japan's New Left Movements: Legacies for Civil Society* (Abingdon: Routledge, 2014); Kosugi Ryōko, *Tōdaitōsō no katari: shakai undō no yoji to senryaku* (Tokyo: Shin'yōsha, 2018); Setsu Shigematsu, *Scream from the Shadows: The Women's Liberation Movement in Japan* (University of Minnesota Press, 2012); William Marotti, *Money, Trains, and Guillotines Art and Revolution in 1960s Japan* (Durham and London: Duke University Press, 2013); Gavin Walker, ed., *The Red Years: Theory, Politics, Aesthetics in the Japanese'68* (London: Verso, 2020). Earlier, but still valuable accounts are Guy Thomas Yasko, "The Japanese Student Movement 1968–70: The Zenkyoto Uprising" (1997); Donald Frederick Wheeler, "The Japanese Student Movement: Value Politics, Student Politics and the Tokyo University Struggle" (1974); Kurata Kazunari, *Shinsayoku undō zenshi* (Tokyo: Ryūdō shuppan, 1978); Kōji Takazawa, *Rekishi toshite no shinsayoku* (Tokyo: Shinsen-sha, 1996).
3. For example, see Odanaka Toshiki, *Gendai shihō no kōzō to shisō* (Tokyo: Nihon hyōron-sha, 1973), 207–16.
4. Patricia G. Steinhoff, ed., *Going to Court to Change Japan: Social Movements and the Law in Contemporary Japan* (Michigan: The University of Michigan, 2014).
5. See for example: Patricia G. Steinhoff, "Doing the Defendant's Laundry: Support Groups as Social Movement Organizations in

Contemporary Japan," *Japanstudien* 11, no. 1 (January 27, 2000): 55–78; Patricia G. Steinhoff, "Emotional Costs of Providing Social Support to Political Prisoners," *Contemporary Japan* 31, no. 2 (2019): 1–18; Steinhoff, *Going to Court to Change Japan: Social Movements and the Law in Contemporary Japan*. William Andrews has also written about support organisations, see William Andrews, "Trial Support Groups Lobby for Japanese Prisoner Rights, Fight to Rectify Injustices," *The Asia–Pacific Journal: Japan Focus* 12, no. 21 (2014): 1–10, https://apjjf.org/-William-Andrews/4120/article.pdf.

6. Mass arrest of students had taken place in 1968, for example at Nihon University and after the October 1968 Shinjuku riots, but the even in these cases the numbers of those arrested were far smaller than at Tokyo University and indictment ratios were extremely low. See Chapter 4.
7. Ogino Fujio, *Sengo chian taisei no kakuritsu* (Tokyo: Iwanami shoten, 1999).
8. Imoto Daikichi, "Hō to chitsujo to," *Tsumi to Batsu* 7, no. 1 (October 1969): 2.
9. Ibid., 4.
10. In this there are clear parallels with the management of 'bad youth' in modern prewar Japan. See David Ambaras, *Bad Youth: Juvenile Delinquency and the Politics of Everyday Life in Modern Japan* (Berkeley and Los Angeles: California University Press, 2006).
11. Richard Weisman, "Being and Doing: The Judicial Use of Remorse to Construct Character and Community," *Social & Legal Studies* 18, no. 1 (2009): 48.
12. Ibid.
13. Richard Weisman, *Showing Remorse: Law and the Social Control of Emotion* (London: Routledge, 2014), 9.
14. Douglas Kellner, *Media Spectacle* (London: Routledge, 2003).
15. According to former Chief Justice of Japan's Supreme Court, Tanaka Kōtarō, this principle requires that "judges must remain silent and demonstrate their position through the verdict itself," regardless of the criticism or dissatisfaction they may face. See Tanaka Kōtarō, "Hō no shihō to saiban" (Tokyo: Yuhikaku, 1960).
16. Murayama Masayuki, "The Role of the Defense Lawyer in the Japanese Criminal Justice System," in *The Japanese Adversary*

System in Context: Controversies and Comparisons, ed. Malcolm Feeley and Setsuo Miyazawa (Basingstoke: Palgrave, 2001), 42–66.
17. Robert Burns et al., "Analyzing the Trial: Interdisciplinary Methods," *PoLAR: Political and Legal Anthropology Review* 31, no. 2 (2008): 318.
18. Ibid., 319.
19. "Kim no bengonin kimaru," *Yomiuri Shimbun*, February 25, 1968.
20. Masataka Kondō, "Gozonjidesuka? 2-gatsu 20-nichi wa kinhirō jiken ga okotta hi desu," *Bunshun Onrainu*, Winter 2, 2018, https://bunshun.jp/articles/-/6272.
21. "Hi Ro Kim Makes Court Appearance," *The Japan Times*, August 22, 1968.
22. "Saiban mo furikaisu," *Yomiuri Shimbun*, June 25, 1968.
23. Ibid.
24. Kim was eventually convicted and sentenced to life imprisonment in 1975. In 1999 he was released and returned to Korea, where in 2000 he was arrested on suspicion of attempted murder. Kim died in 2010 at the age of 81. Kondō, "Gozonjidesuka? 2-Gatsu 20-Nichi Wa Kinhirō Jiken Ga Okotta Hi Desu."
25. Weisman, *Showing Remorse: Law and the Social Control of Emotion*, 86.

References

Ambaras, David. *Bad Youth: Juvenile Delinquency and the Politics of Everyday Life in Modern Japan*. Berkeley and Los Angeles: California University Press, 2006.

Ando, Takemasa. *Japan's New Left Movements: Legacies for Civil Society*. Abingdon: Routledge, 2014.

Andrews, William. "Trial Support Groups Lobby for Japanese Prisoner Rights, Fight to Rectify Injustices." *The Asia-Pacific Journal: Japan Focus* 12, no. 21 (2014): 1–10. https://apjjf.org/-William-Andrews/4120/article.pdf.

Burns, Robert, Marianne Constable, Justin Richland, and Winnifred Sullivan. "Analyzing the Trial: Interdisciplinary Methods." *PoLAR: Political and Legal Anthropology Review* 31, no. 2 (2008): 303–29.

Imoto, Daikichi. "Hō to Chitsujo To." *Tsumi to Batsu* 7, no. 1 (October 1969): 2–4.

Kellner, Douglas. *Media Spectacle*. London: Routledge, 2003.

Kondō, Masataka. "Gozonjidesuka? 2-Gatsu 20-Nichi Wa Kinhirō Jiken Ga Okotta Hi Desu." *Bunshun Onrainu*, Winter 2, 2018. https://bunshun.jp/articles/-/6272.

Kosugi, Ryōko. *Tōdaitōsō no katari: shakai undō no yoji to senryaku*. Tokyo: Shin'yōsha, 2018.

Kurata, Kazunari. *Shinsayoku undō zenshi*. Tokyo: Ryūdō shuppan, 1978.

Marotti, William. *Money, Trains, and Guillotines Art and Revolution in 1960s Japan*. Durham and London: Duke University Press, 2013.

Mouffe, Chantal. *On the Political*. Abingdon: Routledge, 2005.

Murayama, Masayuki. "The Role of the Defense Lawyer in the Japanese Criminal Justice System." In *The Japanese Adversary System in Context: Controversies and Comparisons*, edited by Malcolm Feeley and Setsuo Miyazawa, 42–66. Basingstoke: Palgrave, 2001.

Odanaka, Toshiki. *Gendai shihō no kōzō to shisō*. Tokyo: Nihon hyōron-sha, 1973.

Ogino, Fujio. *Sengo chian taisei no kakuritsu*. Tokyo: Iwanami shoten, 1999.

Oguma, Eiji. *1968: Wakamono-tachi no hanran to sono haikei*. Tokyo: Shin'yōsha, 2009.

"Rupo tōdai saiban." *Shūkan Asahi*, no. 2637 (August 8, 1969): 16–23.

Shigematsu, Setsu. *Scream from the Shadows: The Women's Liberation Movement in Japan*. University of Minnesota Press, 2012.

Steinhoff, Patricia G. "Doing the Defendant's Laundry: Support Groups as Social Movement Organizations in Contemporary Japan." *Japanstudien* 11, no. 1 (January 27, 2000): 55–78.

———. "Emotional Costs of Providing Social Support to Political Prisoners." *Contemporary Japan* 31, no. 2 (2019): 1–18.

———, ed. *Going to Court to Change Japan: Social Movements and the Law in Contemporary Japan*. Michigan: The University of Michigan, 2014.

Takazawa, Kōji. *Rekishi toshite no shinsayoku*. Tokyo: Shinsen-sha, 1996.

Tanaka, Kōtarō. *Hō no shihō to saiban*. Tokyo: Yuhikaku, 1960.

The Japan Times. "Hi Ro Kim Makes Court Appearance." August 22, 1968.

Walker, Gavin, ed. *The Red Years: Theory, Politics, Aesthetics in the Japanese '68*. London: Verso, 2020.

Weisman, Richard. "Being and Doing: The Judicial Use of Remorse to Construct Character and Community." *Social & Legal Studies* 18, no. 1 (2009): 47–69.

———. *Showing Remorse: Law and the Social Control of Emotion*. London: Routledge, 2014.

Wheeler, Donald Frederick. "The Japanese Student Movement: Value Politics, Student Politics and the Tokyo University Struggle," 1974.

Yasko, Guy Thomas. "The Japanese Student Movement 1968–70: The Zenkyoto Uprising," 1997.

Yomiuri Shimbun. "Kim no bengonin kimaru." February 25, 1968.

Yomiuri Shimbun. "Saiban mo furikaisu." June 25, 1968.

CHAPTER 2

Contesting Order in Postwar Japan

Japan's defeat in the Second World War (WWII) and the ensuing occupation by the Allies led to a radical transformation of Japan's political, legal, and institutional structures. These changes, which can be characterised as a drive towards dilution of state power through decentralisation of key functions, and towards emphasizing individual freedom and respect for fundamental human rights, occurred against the backdrop of Japan's devastated economy and political institutions: a landscape in which a variety of left-wing actors were empowered to engage in increasingly confrontational actions against Allied Occupation and state policies. Particularly concerning for Japanese elites were the activities of the Japan Communist Party (JCP). The rise in the JCP's status and influence with the electorate in the immediate postwar, which was a result of their leadership's resistance to the prewar system and adoption in 1945 of a 'friendly' democratic platform, was by the late 1940s placed within the emerging Cold War paradigm. As that paradigm solidified, the actions of the JCP, which were perceived by Japanese elites and the Allied Occupation as intentionally destabilising, enabled the Japanese state to rollback many of the Allies' domestic security reforms.[1] Yet in the absence of the spectrum of repressive techniques available to the state prior to WWII, and the legitimising power derived from enacting those techniques in the emperor's name to protect the sacred 'national body' (*kokutai*), conservative elites

C. Perkins, *The Tokyo University Trial and the Struggle Against Order in Postwar Japan*, New Directions in East Asian History,
https://doi.org/10.1007/978-981-99-7043-8_2

invoked the concept of order (*chitsujo*) as a prerequisite for democracy to legitimise their actions.

On the streets, in campuses, and in courtrooms, maintaining order for the sake of democracy became the rationale for managing the 'riotous' behaviour of those whose political practices conflicted with state objectives. However, the state did not have an easy task, as social movements sought to challenge the emerging order, and the newly independent courts showed their willingness to rule against prosecutors in cases that pushed the boundaries of state power. Two trials that commenced in 1952, almost immediately after Japan regained its formal independence from Allied occupation, were particularly significant in setting the stage for the Tokyo University trial. The first was the Poporo Incident trial, which examined the limits of university autonomy and academic freedom, the legitimacy of police presence and intervention on university campuses, and the position of students within university the community. The second, and arguably most consequential trial followed the 1952 Bloody May Day Incident. Due to its highly confrontational nature, this trial heralded the development of new techniques for maintaining order in the courtroom. In response to this and other courtroom battles, the Supreme Court asserted that the authority of the courts—and indeed their credibility within the international community—hinged on their ability to preserve a proper, 'solemn' (*seishuku*) atmosphere, arguing that judges should play an active role in regulating emotions in the courtroom. However, while judges were granted new powers to manage their courtrooms, the memory of Japan's prewar inquisitorial courtrooms made them reticent to exercise these powers. As will be shown in later chapters, it would not be until the Tokyo University trial that these techniques were employed in earnest.

Prewar Legacies in the Management of Order and the Transition to Democracy

Although this chapter focusses on the late 1940s and 1950s, it is important to sketch out some of the features of Japan's pre-war legal system. There are a number of reasons for doing so. First, as Ogino Fujio and Max Ward have argued, rather than the end of WWII representing a complete break with past approaches to law and order, there was a remarkable amount of continuity in personnel involved in, and ideological orientation to, the management of social order.[2] Furthermore, memories of the interwar period, in which judges and procurators worked together closely in the management of public order within an oppressive 'thought control' regime, went on to shape the terms of discourse on the proper role of the courts within Japan's new postwar democracy. Resistance to the intended outcome of that regime, namely the process of recantation and reintegration into the national community known as *tenkō* (lit. turning), became the postwar index of dedication to progressive political principles. Also important to the story is the ambiguous position of lawyers within the Meiji legal system, who were constructed within that system as a lesser counterpart to their procurator and judicial counterparts. Lawyers' self-identification in opposition to the arbitrary exercise of state power in this period became a lasting point of contention in the postwar, as lawyers, legal societies, and the various Bar Associations struggled to reconcile their position as advocates against state power with their goal of obtaining recognition by the establishment as a mode of legal practice equal in worth with the judiciary and the prosecutor's office.

Japan's modern legal system was created by the Meiji state soon after it was established in 1868. The Judicial code of 1872 established a system of courts and procurators, overseen by the Ministry of Justice Court, and allowed for advocates (*daigennin*) to represent plaintiffs in civil cases (there was no provision for representation in criminal matters at this time). This system, however, was far from independent, not least because the Minister of Justice headed up the Ministry of Justice Court and had the power to appoint and remove judges at will. Although incremental steps were taken over the next 20 years towards greater independence and professionalisation it was not until 1889 that, in response growing public outcry at the arbitrary exercise of state power within the context of Japan's rapidly developing economy, a new Meiji Constitution was promulgated in Japan that enshrined a system of 'rule by law.' Modelled after the German principle of *Rechtsstaat*, which 'assumes the superiority of administrative power over the people and controls this superior administration through legislative statutes', the Meiji Constitution guaranteed individuals the right to know the law and how it would be applied but took the fundamental stance that rights and duties were given to the people by the state.[3] In turn the administrative functions of the state were to be governed by statute, but there was no limitation on the content of those statutes (as might be the case should there be provision in the Constitution for fundamental human rights for example). Importantly the Meiji Constitution was framed as a gift to the people from the Meiji emperor, who had ultimate supremacy over parliament and through the constitution made allegiance to his person a requisite duty.[4]

Within the rule by law framework of the 1889 Meiji Constitution, the judiciary were given independent power to adjudicate in legal matters, which they did in the name of the emperor. Before assuming their position, judges were required to undertake professional training, take national examinations, and work as an apprentice to the court for three years. Appointments, when made, were for life. The same standards were applied to the procuracy, who took the same examination as candidates for the judiciary and undertook the same post-qualification training.[5] Lawyers too saw their social position rise in the wake of the Meiji Constitution, although not to the same extent as judges and procurators. Knowledge of the legal system, tested by exam, was made a prerequisite for practice, but that test was different in content—and perceived as easier—than exams for public office. There was also no requirement for further post-exam training. Therefore, despite lawyers (now termed *bengoshi*) being officially recognised as a profession, they were seen as substantially lower in the legal pecking order than judges and procurators. This perception continued throughout the prewar period, even after the national law examinations were merged into one exam for all legal professionals.[6] Cognisant of this disparity in status and power, many prewar lawyers found their vocation defending individuals in politically charged cases and were often involved in progressive political movements.[7]

Proceedings operated under the inquisitorial principle (*shokken shugi*), whereby the procurator was an overseer to proceedings and judges were actively involved in the investigative process. As Miyazawa Setsuo puts it, under this principle 'evidence was collected and interrogations were conducted through the exercise of judicial power. Moreover, the defendant was not clearly recognized as a subject in proceedings.'[8] It is also worth noting that Meiji bureaucrats, always wary of diluting their administrative power, limited the scope of judicial power to civil and criminal cases. Legal challenges to the exercise of administrative power, which had the potential to bring the courts into conflict with the state, were excluded from the scope of the courts. To maintain the outward appearance of rule by law promised by the Constitution, provision was made for Japanese subjects to bring administrative cases to a special Administrative Court (*gyōsei saiban*). This court, however, was in essence an extension of the bureaucracy rather than part of the judiciary and acted only to strengthen and legitimise bureaucratic power.[9]

While the Meiji period laid the foundation for Japan's modern legal system, it was during the Taishō period (1912–1926) that the problem of managing social order became more acute and new techniques its management were formulated by the state. In the context of the 1917 revolution in Russia, increased labour disputes between 1919 and 1920, the growing radicalization of students in universities, the re-emergence of old socialists into public attention, and the emergence of discontent in rural regions all pointed to an intensification of social unrest.[10] The reaction to this intensification of social turmoil was what would become the centrepiece of Japan's interwar public security framework: the Peace Preservation Law (*Chian iji hō*).[11] Enacted in 1925 the law outlawed any organisation that threatened either the kokutai (national body) or the system of private property. The law was enforced by the Special Higher Police (*tokkō*), also known as the 'Thought Police' (*shisō keiji*) which had been established in 1911 to investigate social movements and suppress radicals 'spreading dangerous foreign ideologies' and was prosecuted by specialist 'Thought Procurators' (*shisō kenji*).[12]

While the Japan Communist Party (JCP), which had been founded in 1923, was the primary target of the new law, it was first used against student members of the National Federation of Students (Gakuren) at Kyoto University in 1925, who were suspected of spreading destabilising communist propaganda. Although the students were initially released, their freedom was short-lived. Viewing this incident as a test case for the new law, the police redoubled their efforts and arrested the students once again. A year later, the Gakuren students were convicted under the Peace Preservation Law of conspiring to change the fundamental social and economic structure of Japan and to establish a communist society in its place.[13] The Gakuren incident, however, was only a taste of things to come. On 15 March 1928, procurators carried out a mass roundup of suspected JCP members, involving thousands of police spread across Japan in what would become known as the March 15 Incident. Over 1600 suspects were arrested and 500 were prosecuted including many in the higher echelons of the JCP.[14] In the wake of these arrests, officials were alarmed at the level of student involvement in communist activity, especially at Tokyo Imperial University, the designated breeding ground of Japan's bureaucratic elite. The Ministry of Education introduced stricter measures against leftist professors, and educators were urged to help their students understand the meaning and significance of the kokutai and to monitor the infiltration of foreign thought into the student body.[15]

With the 15 March Incident the JCP was dealt a blow that it would not recover from until the end of the WWII. But rather than rest on their laurels the Japanese thought crime apparatus continued to expand. This was because the Peace Preservation Law was more than a simple mechanism for suppression of leftist organisations. As Richard Mitchell and more recently Max Ward have both argued, the Peace Preservation Law, with its language of protecting the emotionally imbued kokutai, was in fact an 'integrative device designed to rally a divided leadership and society around the emperor.'[16] With the Manchurian Incident of 1931 and the beginning of Japan's war in China, the integrative functions of the Peace Preservation Law expanded to include individuals and groups espousing any foreign ideology with the potential to destabilise the kokutai. While repressive violence and imprisonment were well-established tools in the Thought Polices' toolkit, along with this expansion of its remit, the state invested considerable effort in bypassing the penal system to manage ideological dissidents. Procurators and the judiciary exercised selective leniency in applying the Peace Preservation Law in an administrative capacity through suspended sentences with the aim of rehabilitating and reintegrating thought criminals into the kokutai. This process of recantation and reintegration became known as tenkō. From 1936, the Thought Criminal Protection and Supervision Law standardised the process of tenkō through a network of criminal protection and supervision centres that administered re-education courses. The stages of tenkō were codified, starting with recalcitrant communists at one end of the scale and the born-again worshipers of the emperor at the other. The results were stark: by the end of the early 1940s, nearly 66,000 radicals, including a large number of communists, had recanted their views, and returned to the national fold. Those who continued to dissent, mainly the few remaining communists, either left Japan or languished in prison. Meanwhile, the goal of spiritual purity embodied in the idea of tenkō became state policy for all Japanese as Japan continued to fight its increasingly unwinnable war in the Pacific.[17]

Amidst the ruins of a defeated German in July 1945, the Allies issued to Japan the Potsdam Declaration, which contained the terms for Japan's unconditional surrender. The document set out the basis of the Allies' vision for postwar Japan as a liberal democracy. In particular Article 10 made clear that Japan's political system would be subject to dramatic change. 'The Japanese Government shall remove all obstacles to the revival and strengthening of democratic tendencies among the Japanese people,' it read. 'Freedom of speech, of religion, and of thought, as well as respect for the fundamental human rights shall be established.'[18] The slew of directives that followed Japan's defeat in August made good on this promise. The 4th October 1945 Memorandum on 'Removal of Restrictions on Political, Civil, and Religious Liberties' (SCAPIN-93, known in Japanese as the *jiken shirei*, Civil Liberties Directive) abolished the Peace Preservation Law and 14 associated laws, called for the immediate release of all persons detained under those laws, and 'abolished all organisations or agencies' created to implement these laws, including all secret police agencies, the Home Ministry, departments of the Thought Police and those agencies charged with 'protection and surveillance and control of thought, speech, religion, or assembly'.[19] The most sweeping changes, however came with the Postwar Constitution, which was promulgated in 1946 and came into effect in 1947. Based on the principles of sovereignty of the people, respect for fundamental human rights, and in Article 9 the renunciation of war, the Constitution enacted a new structure for the government, with a bicameral legislature, the Diet, and clearly defined the separation of powers. The emperor, who had renounced his divine status in January 1946, was re-positioned as the symbol of the state and the unity of the people, without powers related to government. All Japanese citizens were guaranteed freedom of thought and conscience (Article 19), freedom of expression (Article 21), and explicitly guaranteed academic freedom (Article 23).[20]

The new Constitution and the 1947 Courts Act (*Saibansho-hō*) also made explicit the independence of the Judiciary and ushered in a system of rule of law.[21] Judicial power was vested entirely in the Supreme Court of Japan and its inferior courts, all forms of extraordinary court, such as the prewar administrative courts were outlawed, and the independence of judges was enshrined. Along with structural reform came a rebalancing of the relationship between judges, the procuracy and lawyers. The inquisitorial principle of the Meiji system was replaced with the adversarial principle (*tōjisha shugi*). This shift severed the formal link between prosecutors and judges in the examination of cases: rather than active involvement in investigation, judges were now to adopt the position of 'passive and impartial adjudicator' who examined the evidence presented by both prosecutor and defence lawyer in the context of the charges brought by the prosecution.[22] In this way, as guarantors of the rights granted to Japanese citizens by the post-war Constitution, the courts were made completely independent of the institution with the greatest power to trample on those rights: the state. To further cement this separation, all administrative functions of the law were transferred to the courts, including the appointment of new judges (Articles 77 and 80). The 1947 Judges' Council Law (*saibankan kaigi*) established judges' councils in all courts (Supreme Court, High Court, and District Court) whose role was to manage all administrative functions of the court. All judges working in the court were automatically members of that court's council, and the presiding judge *(sōkatsu saibankan)* of the court—responsible for the general supervision of administrative matters—was elected by the council and served as its chairman. This system was designed to promote local self-government and to foster a community of legal research and scholarship within the courts. The unification of training for prosecutors, judges and lawyers was intended to foster a culture within the legal community of fundamental commitment to human rights. To further empower citizens, mechanisms were put in place to enable ordinary Japanese to petition for the impeachment of judges if they believed that those individuals were not living up to the spirit of the Constitution. Judges themselves, to help bridge the gap between the legal bureaucracy and the people, were guaranteed freedom of association and expression.[23]

With regards to legal representation the Constitution guaranteed the 'immediate privilege to counsel' for anyone arrested or detained on suspicion of an offence (Article 34) and maintained that right to counsel through the trial process (Article 37). Defendants were also explicitly protected from self-incrimination, and any confession 'made under compulsion, torture or threat, or after prolonged arrest or detention shall not be admitted in evidence' (Article 38). Within the context of these provisions, the Attorneys Act (*Bengoshi-hō*) of 1949 entrusted lawyers 'with the mission of protecting fundamental human rights and achieving social justice', while also requiring that they perform their 'duties in good faith and endeavour to maintain the social order and improve the legal system' (Article 1).[24] The Attorney's Act also set out qualification expectations for practicing lawyers, established the postwar Bar Association, and detailed processes for disciplinary action. Legal training for lawyers, which within the Meiji system was broadly criticised, was revised such that prospective lawyers were now required to enrol in the Legal Training and Research Institute of Japan (*Shihō-kenshū-jo*, LTRI), which had been established in 1947, along with judges and prosecutors. Importantly, with the establishment of the Bar Association came the professionalisation of legal practice; it also secured the independence of lawyers from Ministry of Justice oversight.[25]

The Allies also radically reformed Japan's police force in order to dilute state power as part of its democratisation programme. With the dissolution of the Home Ministry in 1947, and with it the dismantling of the thought police system, came a new Police Law (*Keisatsu-hō*) which mandated the decentralisation and shrinkage of the police force and restricted to purely civil policing their previously wide-ranging administrative remit. The vast majority of Japan's standing police force—95,000 out of a total of 125,000 officers—was placed under the authority of public safety commissions in local communities, with the aim of transforming 'the police from agents of the state to servants of the people.'[26] The state's central authority was restricted to a small (30,000) 'national rural' police force which was associated with a new National Public Safety Commission.[27] Supreme Commander for the Allied Powers (SCAP) Douglas MacArthur made clear that he wanted no channels of command between the national and local police forces. As Aldous and Leishman put it, '[s]trict separation of the two police forces was deemed necessary to prevent the re-emergence of a repressive, authoritarian pattern of policing—the dominant paradigm in Imperial Japan.'[28]

Yet, while there is no denying significance of the depth and scope of these changes to Japan's legal institutional structure, there was disjuncture between the new legislation and facts on the ground. Anticipating widespread civil unrest, a strengthening labour movement, and the rise of the Japanese Communist Party as a force in Japanese politics, the Japanese state made a concerted effort to maintain pre-war police and prosecutorial structures. This was made possible in part by the limitations of Allied reforms, which, by targeting headline legislation such as the Peace Preservation Law and concentrating purges on mid- to high-ranking thought police officials, let slip through the net lesser pre-war public security laws (*chian hōrei*) and thought prosecutors whose knowledge and orientation would shape the new security structures. Even the much-vaunted purge of the thought police was only moderately successful: once removed from office, it was common for thought police to suddenly appear in an adjacent police force, and in the end restrictions on their participation of in public life were eventually lifted.[29]

The Occupation's decision to govern through existing political structures and GHQ's ambiguous views on civil unrest also enabled Japanese officials to undermine efforts to reform the national security apparatus. The new Police Law was a case in point—as soon as the law was passed the Japanese government undermined the new local safety commissions by purposely mishandling their funding.[30] GHQ were adamant that Japan's new civil police force would be responsible for policing Japan, and that if it remained lawful, all protest would be allowed. But GHQ also charged the Japanese with managing any disturbance that impacted the implementation of GHQ reforms and the intelligence branch of GHQ, G2, made liberal use of former Thought Police in their efforts to monitor social activism.[31] Significantly, in an act of foresight in 1945, the Police Bureau of the Home Ministry had established a new Public Security Section (*Kōan-ka*), which by 1946 was mirrored in local police departments throughout Japan. Even after the dissolution of the Home Ministry in 1947, these public security sections continued to operate and were again staffed by many former thought police and thought prosecutors.[32] Therefore, while the formal structures that supported prewar policing of undesirable social elements had by 1947 been abolished, the informal vestiges of that system—its ideological orientation, practical techniques of policing and prosecuting including reliance on observation and information gathering, and indeed many personnel, survived.[33]

Nevertheless, Japanese elites could no longer outwardly use kokutai ideology to justify their public security efforts. Instead, they began very early in the Occupation period to approach democratic reform via the mediating concept of order (*chitsujo*). While not denying the necessity (or indeed inevitability) of Japanese democratisation, Japanese officials argued that democracy could only be established on a foundation of order and as such a robust system for securing domestic security was necessary. As early as 18 October 1945, Japanese officials announced their intention, using distinctly pre-war language, to maintain 'peace and order' (*an'nei chitsujo no iji*) in the face of the inevitable mass movements (*taishū undō*) unleashed by the Civil Liberties Directive.[34] This language was soon ameliorated once it became clear just how far-reaching Occupation reforms would be. But between 1945 and 1947 increasingly virulent labour unrest in the context of rampant inflation threatened to undermine the Occupation's plans to restructure the Japanese economy, and Japanese police with the backing of Occupation MPs progressively intervened in the actions of organised labour.[35] Tensions mounted such that, when a series of rallies in May 1946 over food, wages and governance culminated in 250,000 protestors participating in a sit-down strike outside the Prime Minister's residence, General MacArthur warned sternly that should 'minor elements' be unable to exercise self-restraint he would be forced 'to take the necessary steps to remedy such a deplorable situation'.[36] Demonstrating SCAPs conflicted stance, however, MacArthur took a dim view of the treatment of one protester, JCP organiser Matsushima Matsutarō, who was arrested and prosecuted for displaying a placard containing derogatory remarks against the emperor.[37] 'If the citizens are not able to express themselves as they wish,' MacArthur proclaimed, 'democracy will not survive.'[38]

Emboldened by MacArthur's statement in opposition to the May Day protests, however, the Japanese government issued their own statement on the 'The maintenance of social order' (*shakai chitsujo hoji ni kansuru seifu seimei*) one month later, which set out restrictions on protest and specifically the act of production control (*seisan kanri*). In the statement the language of democracy, economics and order were fully entangled:

> Our country is currently undergoing a revolutionary phase in its development into a democratic state. Moreover, food shortages, intensifying inflation, increasing unemployment and other phenomena that are destroying people's lives are becoming increasingly serious. To overcome these immediate diverse problems and achieve the great task of building a democratic Japan, it is absolutely essential to increase production and stabilise people's lives, and to maintain social order [*shakai chitsujo*] by respecting democratic laws. However, recently there is a tendency among some people to ignore social order in the name of democracy, to disregard laws and regulations and to make incendiary affirmations. This is truly worrying.[39]

The issue for the police was that because information collection activities had ceased with the dissolution of the thought police, their actions against those who 'ignored social order' could only be reactive. But with GHQ's attitude towards mass movements hardening, the Japanese police force in June 1946 applied to GHQ for permission to widen their activities to include data gathering and analysis activities on potential threats to order. GHQ agreed to this expansion. Although fascists and ultranationalists were the nominal targets of these activities, information gathering extended to trends in public sentiment towards Allied reforms and the 'factual situation and developments on various fronts concerning pressing economic, social, political or other problems that may be the cause of riots or disturbances or that are extremely agitating to people's feelings.'[40]

Said deplorable economic conditions, however, remained. With discontent at government policy reaching fever-pitch, in January 1947 all major labour unions united under the banner of the National Trade Union Council (*Zenkoku rōdō kumiai renraku kaigi*, Zenrōren). And when negotiations with the government broke down on 30 January it looked as if a General Strike on 1st February mobilising as many as four million workers across all sectors was inevitable. Yet it was not to be. Making good on his warning in May the previous year, MacArthur directly ordered the leaders of the coalition to call off the strike, stating that he would not allow 'the use of so deadly a social weapon'.[41] The strike was called off. It did, however, bring down the Yoshida government, which was replaced by a coalition led by the Socialist Katayama Tetsu. While the Socialists were in power revision of Japan's security apparatus slowed, however the tempo would once again pickup after first Katayama's downfall then the wholesale collapse of the coalition amidst continuing economic pain, Katayama's weak leadership, and Japan's first postwar political corruption scandal.[42]

The second iteration of the Yoshida Government took power in January 1949. Yet although Yoshida's conservatives had won with an outright majority, due in part to the left–right split in the Socialist party after the collapse of the government, the JCP had captured 34 seats themselves and boasted a base of support numbering around a million individuals.[43] It was clear to Allied General Headquarters (GHQ) that should inflation continue the JCP would capitalise on the resultant unrest, which was unacceptable if the US was to rely on Japan as a stable ally and base of operations in the coming Cold War against the USSR. Furthermore, by 1949 the Japanese and GHQ were increasingly starting to view the JCP as a threat to national security.[44] In particular a series of attacks on Japan's railways in 1949 were attributed the JCP guerrillas by the Japanese government and GHQ intelligence. Although the veracity of that assessment is contested, these incidents convinced the authorities that the JCP were on the way to becoming a violent revolutionary force.[45] The response was two-fold. First was economic reform in the shape of a stringent new counter inflationary policy, dubbed the 'Dodge-line' after the Detroit banker who devised it. Second new ordinances were passed to manage social unrest. In response on 4th April the Yoshida government, with SCAP approval, issued the *Associations Control Ordinance* (*Dantai nado kiseirei*).

> To ensure the healthy fostering and development of pacifism and democracy, the purpose is to make the contents of political organisations available to the public and to prohibit the formation and leadership of secret, militarist, extreme nationalist, violent and anti-democratic organisations, as well as such acts by organisations and individuals.[46]

Militarists and nationalists were no longer the real concern however: it was 'anti-democratic' organisations—namely the JCP—that were the main target. The JCP were forced to report details of their membership, which made it easier for Japan's public security apparatus to identify and track communist activities.[47] Indeed the first legal crackdown on communists was in Yamagata city for failure to register their membership and activities.[48] Under continued onslaught from the Yoshida government, again with MacArthur's backing, the JCP began to see its gains in membership and influence falter. What followed was the 'Red Purge' of communists from Japan's workforce, which resulted in roughly 27,000 workers across both the public and private sectors.[49]

In 1950, fortunes for the JCP went from bad to worse. That year the JCP was heavily criticised by the Soviet Union Comintern, who ordered the party to adopt a more militant strategy. The criticism, which was wholly out of the blue, set in motion an internal struggle between factions within the party, which would end in the JCP proclaiming a new revolutionary agenda on January 19th. With the commencement of the Korean War in June of the same year MacArthur wrote to Prime Minister Yoshida demanding members of the Central Committee of the JCP be banned from public office. The language was again of order as prerequisite for democracy: the JCP, argued MacArthur had 'hurled defiance at constituted authority, shown contempt for the process of law and order, and contrived by false and inflammatory statements and other subversive means to arouse through resulting public confusion that degree of social unrest which would set the state for the eventual overthrow of constitutional government in Japan by force'.[50] With this the JCP were once again forced to go underground.

Troublesome Students and University Autonomy

As the Allied occupation, the Japanese State, and labour movements and the JCP pushed and pulled at the Japan's new constitutitional framework, students too were reassessing their place and purpose within the democratic Japan. In this regard students found that as they worked to define their own autonomous position and political agenda, the state, the JCP, and later GHQ, all attempted in different ways to restrict the sorts of politics in which they could engage. For the JCP this took the form of maintaining its hegemony over student thought and disciplining strictly those who ventured beyond their agenda. The state also attempted to limit student activity to their view of a democratic politics suitable for students, which they defined as separate from the labour movement. The Poporo Incident and subsequent trial tested the limits of state intervention on campus and set important precedents for the Tokyo University trial regarding students' role in university self-governance.

Even before Constitutional guarantees of freedom of expression had been put in place student politics had made a resurgence, with students placing themselves in the vanguard of the democratisation of Japan. An editorial published in Tokyo University's *University Newspaper* (*daigaku shinbun*) in October 1945, for example, called for a restoration of a nationwide student movement that would guard against the resurgence of militarist, governmental and capitalist 'liars and opportunists' who would pervert the course of democracy in Japan for their interests.[51] While it was easy to see the fruits of disarmament, students argued, democracy was the 'stuff of thought' and as such was far more difficult to secure. As such the anonymous authors argued stridently that the only way to secure democratic change in Japan was to *do democracy* through appropriate democratic organisations. Democratic action, not simply thought, was key for embedding democracy in Japan; not just formally, but as intrinsic to Japanese national political subjectivity. And in their estimation students were compelled to take their historically mandated role in the vanguard of this movement.[52] It was this commitment to direct action that would characterise the student movement from this point on.

Yet while students saw for themselves a leadership role in safeguarding the promise of postwar Japan, the Japanese Communist Party (JCP) viewed the student movement as a natural extension of their influence. Thus, while JCP-sponsored cells soon sprang up on school and university campuses across Japan, the JCP disagreed with the students' assessment of their social position as vanguard of the revolution (this position was reserved for urban workers and rural peasants) and was intolerant of students who transgressed party orthodoxy. Students, however, did not simply accept this top-down assessment of their position, nor did they simply acquiesce to JCP directives.[53] The shared experience of the effects of inflation in the late 1940s helped students to position themselves within the wider labour movement opposed to government policies. The impetus within the student movement was firmly towards unification under a national body. But the JCP, concerned about its control over the movement, was opposed to the creation of a new centre of power that might run counter to the party's commitment to democratic action. In the end, it was the Katayama government that provided the final push towards a unified student movement. In February 1948, Katayama's education minister announced a tripling of tuition fees at public universities. Then, in March, GHQ proposed a US-style governance structure for Japan's universities, centred on a board of trustees. Students across Japan's universities responded to these decrees first by withholding their fees and then, as negotiations with the Ministry of Education (Monbushō) stalled, by going on national strike. To coordinate this national campaign, students recognised the need for a national umbrella organisation for the student movement, and at a three-day founding conference in September 1948, the All-Japan League of Student Self-Government Associations (Zengakuren) was formed.[54] Despite the evident tension between the students and the JCP, however, Zengakuren was still dominated by the JCP.

As the late 1940s unfolded, GHQ's appraisal of student politics also changed. While up to 1947 student action and the study of Marxism on campus was viewed by GHQ as relatively benign, and student communist activity on campus seen as insignificant, with the reverse course GHQ and the Japanese state began to take an increasingly dim view of communist influence on campus. In universities the anti-communist policy was fronted by American educationalist Walter C. Eells, who from 1949 gave speeches at universities across Japan on the threat of communism to democratic freedom of thought, and urged communist faculty be dismissed (and who was often greeted by angry Zengakuren students).[55] But perhaps less remarked upon is how the Monbushō also attempted to use the concept of order to delimit the modes of political activity allowed on campus and how those limits would be tested in the courts.

Shortly after the formation of Zengakuren, the Vice-Minister of Education sent a notice to all public and private universities, technical colleges and teacher education schools entitled 'With regard to the political activities of students'.[56] The guidance, which was framed as helping define the acceptable limits of student political activity (*seiji undō no genkai*), hinged on an interpretation of the Article 8 of the Fundamental Law on Education (FLE), which reads as follows:

> Article 8 (Political Education) The political knowledge necessary for intelligent citizenship shall be valued in education. (2) The schools prescribed by law shall refrain from political education or other political activities for or against any specific political party.

The guidelines on student politics, while they appeared to echo the FLE's Article 8, notably redefined its terms. Instead of broadly endorsing political education for intelligent citizenship, the guidelines confined freedom to 'research and criticism', only insofar as these facilitated responsible voting. The Monbushō then introduced the concept of 'order' to justify the prohibition of on-campus political action, arguing it was necessary to maintain political neutrality. In essence, they used order to reinterpret the clause's ban on partisan political education as a ban on all political activities that could disrupt campus neutrality. The guidelines further detailed students' social status and permissible political associations, implicitly targeting the JCP while acknowledging students' right to form independent organizations. They insisted that universities had to prevent the establishment of student groups supporting outside political entities to uphold political neutrality and academic autonomy. Political activities were allowed only if sanctioned by university officials, considering students' political responsibility. The guidelines also distinguished students from workers, arguing that students' involvement in workers' movements was inappropriate due to their different social roles and responsibilities. In essence the Monbushō outlined the boundaries of acceptable student politics, asserting that Japan's democracy encouraged cooperation and consensus over strong-willed minority domination.

The principles of the 1948 notice and the limits of policing on campus were then put to the test in what became known as the Poporo Incident. On 20th February the Tokyo University Poporo drama group (*Gekidan poporo*) staged a production based on the events surrounding the controversial 1949 Matsukawa train derailment, for which members of the National Railway Workers Union were standing trial.[57] During the performance, which took place in a room on campus that had been formally requested by the group, members of the troop noticed three plainclothes policemen sitting in the audience and loudly pointed them out while shouting 'spies!' A scuffle ensued when the policemen tried to leave the room during which students detained the policemen and demanded they produce their police notebooks. When the students examined the notebooks, they found detailed observations of the campus activities of left-wing students and staff. These revelations, which brought back painful memories of pre-war thought police activities on campus, soon spread across the university, and caused uproar.[58]

The Poporo incident proved so significant that the National Diet opened a public hearing into the event. At the hearing Tokyo University President Yanaihara Tadao made an impassioned plea in support of the students' actions for academic freedom as guaranteed by the new Constitution. Yanaihara's argument rested on three main pillars. First, he positioned the university within the framework of the national polity, and as such governed by the Japanese Constitution, which guaranteed freedom of thought and expression. It was therefore incumbent on the university to guarantee this freedom. Second, he argued that government guidance and convention stated that it was the universities' responsibility to maintain order on campus under the principle of self-governance, and presence on campus of plainclothes police officers broke with this convention. Yanaihara was at pains to remind the committee that this division of labour had been codified in a Monbushō Notice in July 1950, issued to educational institutions in response to a Tokyo Metropolitan Government ordinance passed early that month that required any organisation planning to activities in public to apply for permission from the local Public Safety Commission (*Kōan i'inkai*).[59] The Monbushō notice made clear that group activities on campus that had obtained university permission were not required to register with the Public Safety Commission, and that police were only to intervene in university activities at the request of the university administration. There was, therefore, no reason for the police to be there in the first place and indeed their presence destabilised order on campus. And anyway, while it was unfortunate there had been an altercation, and students may have to be disciplined within the university's structure, the notebooks had been returned.[60]

In the end Yanaihara's defence of university autonomy did not stop the police arresting three students in connection with the incident. The students, however, were not charged for obstructing the police or for theft of the notebooks. Instead, they found themselves indicted under the 1926 *Law on the Punishment of Acts of Violence* (*Bōryoku kōi nado shobatsu ni kansuru hōristu*), a vague law established in the shadow of the 1925 Peace Preservation Law that stipulated punishments for equally vaguely defined groups accused of committing violence, and which had not been taken off the books by the Civil Liberties Directive.[61] The indictment, which was forensically detailed in its description of students ruffling in pockets and plucking at coat buttons was evidently designed to avoid admission that the police were at the performance in an official capacity: in effect it was worded to render the case as one of simple assault. Yet, despite the prosecution's protestations that the policemen were at the performance in a personal capacity, and that they had sustained significant injuries at the hands of the students, the courts found the students innocent on all charges. In their summation the district court judges found no evidence that the three students charged had either committed a violent act or conspired to do so as part of a group.[62]

Undeterred, the prosecution appealed the decision and took the case to the Tokyo High Court. This time the prosecution took a different tack, arguing that the police were within their rights to be on campus to collect information about activities that had the *potential* to disturb the peace. The fact the performance took place the day before 'Anti-Colonialism Day' (and as such could be viewed as part of the anti-colonial movement), the appearance on campus of a subversive poster, and the presence on campus of a JCP cell all indicated, they argued, that such a disturbance was likely. Furthermore, in response to Yanaihara's invocation of the Monbushō's own guidance regarding police presence on campus, the prosecution argued that due to the factors noted above, the university was clearly unable to maintain order on campus and therefore it was right and proper for the police to intervene. Again, however, the courts ruled in favour of the students. In an extremely lengthy verdict, the court argued that the prevention of a hypothetical disturbance of the peace did not constitute sufficient reason to intervene in campus life. Indeed, in a clear rebuke to police authorities the courts judged the police action as potentially threatening the freedom to study guaranteed under the Constitution and the Fundamental Law on Education.[63]

In 1963, six years after the second trial found in favour of the defendants and eleven years after the original incident, the Poporo verdict was appealed for a final time in Japan's Supreme Court. Significantly for later cases of police interventions on campus, the outcome was a complete reversal of the original verdicts. According to the Supreme Court, the district courts had made a fundamental mistake in their interpretation of the scope and application of the freedoms guaranteed in Article 23 of the Constitution, which guarantees academic freedom and autonomy. In contrast to the lower court rulings, the Supreme Court interpreted the text of Article 23 as only applying to the conduct and dissemination of academic research (*gakumon*) by professors and other researchers. Consequently, for students, protection from state interference was restricted only to the ability of students to learn from their professors unhindered. As such, activities that fell beyond those directly related to research and teaching were seen by the Supreme Court as ineligible for special consideration by state authorities other than with regards to the general protections under the Constitution.

In the view of the Supreme Court judges, the fact that the Poporo drama group's performance was open to the public, was based on investigations into political events, and was collecting funds for the upcoming 'anti-colonialism day' meant that Poporo's activities fell outside the category of academic pursuits and into a broader category of 'social and political activities' (*seijiteki shakaiteki katsudō*). As such it was not illegal for the police to attend the performance. With the questions of academic freedom and university autonomy now defined beyond the scope of the case, the question now boiled down to whether the defendants had committed violent acts (*bōryoku kōi*), which in 1965, after the Supreme Court returned the case, the Tokyo High Court found they had. But a further important outcome of the Poporo Incident Trials related to the status of students within the governance structure of universities. Again, building on the principle that academic freedom and autonomy rested with researchers insofar as it related to scholarly pursuits, the Court argued that 'university facilities and students, as effects of these freedoms and autonomy, are to be managed autonomously by the university authorities, and students are also allowed the freedom of learning and the use of facilities.' Students were thus positioned not the as subjects of university autonomy but as public 'facility users.'[64] As will be seen in later chapters, this question of the subject of autonomy within the university was a key point of contention at Tokyo University in 1968.

Bloody May Day and Order in the Courts

In September 1951, Japan signed two documents: the San Francisco Peace Treaty, which formally ended the war and with it the Allied Occupation, and the Treaty of Mutual Cooperation and Security between the United States and Japan, known in Japan as Anpo. These agreements, particularly Anpo, were shaped by the US's growing concerns over the spread of communism in East Asia within the rapidly solidifying Cold War framework. International events intensified this concern. In 1949, the Chinese Revolution concluded with the People's Liberation Army's victory and the establishment in mainland China of the communist People's Republic. A year later, in 1950, the simmering hostilities between communist North Korea and the US-aligned South Korea escalated into all-out war, with the North backed in the conflict by Communist China and the South supported by UN troops. The Anpo treaty, forced upon Japan as a precondition for ending the Occupation, encapsulated these geopolitical developments. The US saw Japan as a vital regional base of operations, and the treaty provisions reflected this strategic importance. It granted the US the right to maintain military bases on Japanese soil, provided US soldiers with extraterritorial privileges, and allowed the US military to intervene in cases of domestic unrest in Japan. Emblematic of the colonial nature of the treaty was the continued US military occupation of the Ryūkū Islands, including the island of Okinawa. When both documents came into effect in April 1952, Japan regained its formal independence. However, the US military presence remained substantial, with over 260,000 servicemen stationed across 2,824 facilities throughout Japan.[65]

In addition, in preparation for independence, the Yoshida government had established a new National Police Reserve (NPR) to fill the gap in policing capacity creating by US troop deployment in Korea and proposed a new public security law—the Subversive Activities Prevention Act (*Hakaikatsudō bōshi-hō*, Habōhō)—to replace the now defunct *Associations Control Ordinance*, which had been used to control 'anti-democratic' organisations since 1949. Like the Control Ordinance before it, the Habōhō made provisions for monitoring, limiting, and preventing the work of organisations deemed to be engaging, planning, or inciting any one of a range of 'violent destructive actions' (*Boryokushugiteki hakaikatsudō*). The law, argued the Public Security Intelligence Agency (PSIA), was necessary due to the increasing threat posed by armed guerrilla organisations that proclaimed the 'legitimacy and necessity of overthrowing the constitutional government of Japan' and that were backed by 'organisations with international connections.'[66]

While a lack of specifics within the Anpo regarding timelines for withdrawal of US troops from Japanese soil, and the humiliating clauses on extra-territoriality and US right to intervene in domestic disturbance, troubled the Japanese right, there was broad agreement in conservative circles with Japan's alliance with the US as part of an anti-communist pact. For the left, however, Anpo, the Habōhō and the NPR were all seen as mutually reinforcing components of Japan's new conservative order: an order which connected international and domestic security arrangements into one 'Anpo system'.[67] The position for many on the left was rejection of the notion that Japan had to pick sides in the ensuing Cold War conflict, arguing that the destruction wrought on Japan by past militarism had demonstrated that the best course of action was to steer a path of absolute peace as emblemised by Article 9 of the postwar Constitution. There was also the fear, evidenced by the Habōhō bill, that Japan's conservative elite were capitalising on the geopolitical conditions to re-establish centralised, authoritarian control over the populace.

One of the most ardent critics of the left in this regard was Chief Justice of Japan's Supreme Court, Tanaka Kōtarō who was appointed to the position in 1950, and who would play a major role in shaping the culture of Japan's courts over the next decade. Tanaka, a Tokyo University trained legal scholar, devout Catholic, and internationalist had from 1917 to 1944 been a professor of commercial law at the Tokyo Imperial University. His work on commercial law led him to believe in the promise of a World Law that could bring about positive social change in world (and national) society. Despite remaining a high profile academic, Tanaka's views on World Law were increasingly seen by state security as coming into conflict with the establishment *kokutai* view of the law in which the force of the law emanated from the body of the emperor.[68] After the war, Tanaka became Minister for Education in 1946 in the first Yoshida Cabinet, and in which position he drafted the basic plan for the Fundamental Law of Education. Tanaka continued to hold onto his globalist outlook and saw in the United Nations a model for the realisation of World Law. As the Cold War began, however, he began to see the international system in Manichean terms as a battle between the proponents of peace and order as codified in the United Nations Charter (the democratic west) and the menace of 'red imperialism' (the USSR, the

Peoples Republic of China and their satellites) who would pull the international system into anarchy.[69] This view of order and chaos extended to his appraisal of what he described as the 'discourse of total peace' as it manifested amongst Japan's left wing 'intelligentsia'. If they were really committed to peace, Tanaka argued in his 1952 New Years Address, rather than attacking the Anpo they should 'turn their criticism towards the ideals of communism and the reality of the nations that adopt them.' Salvation for Japan would only come from putting all of the nation's energy behind the new Constitution and the ideals of the United Nations, which Tanaka viewed as inextricably linked.[70]

Notwithstanding Tanaka's arguments, an anti-Habōhō coalition of all the major trade unions, the JCP and Zengakuren students formed around the General Council of Trade Unions of Japan. Demonstrations against both Anpo and the Habōhō were planned for May Day. In defiance of a court order to the contrary, the state banned demonstrators from entering the Imperial Palace Plaza. However, when the demonstrators were provoked into entering the Plaza, they were met by riot police armed with batons and tear gas. Two demonstrators were killed in the ensuing violence, including Hōsei University student Kondō Hiroshi.[71] In the aftermath police arrested 1,232 protesters of whom 261 were indicted and charged with the crime of rioting (*sōjōzai*), a remnant of the Meiji Penal Code introduced in 1908 to criminalise individuals or groups who disturbed the peace through threats (*kyōhaku*) or acts of violence (*bōkō*).[72] The 'Bloody May Day' trial that followed, and Tanaka's response to it, would have profound implications for the Tokyo University trial almost 20 years later.

To deal with such an unprecedented number of cases, the Tokyo District Court split the defendants into eight groups, and the trial began in September 1952. In response to the small-group trial approach adopted by the court, the defence pushed for a unified trial (*tōitsu kohan*). The trial ground to a halt as the defendants and their lawyers argued for a unified trial whenever they were called to speak. Newspapers reported that over a hundred detained defendants went on hunger strike in protest at the court's small group approach to the trial, and in extreme cases defendants stripped naked and refused to appear in court altogether. The legal team also engaged in strategic defiance. The unified defendants were represented by lawyers from the Japan Lawyers Association for Freedom (Jiyū hōsōdan, JLAF), an organisation with a long history of involvement in politicised trials dating back to the labour struggles of the 1920s. Unlike the state-appointed lawyers who represented the minority of defendants who opted for the small group trials, JLAF lawyers refused to attend all but one of the trials, arguing that to do so would be to bow to the will of the court. The JLAF was also quick to draw attention to what they saw as the naked exercise of power in the courtroom, such as the handcuffing of defendants who did not leave the room when ordered to do so. Accounts of the early days of the trial painted a picture of bedlam in the courtroom. According to the colourful account of one courtroom reporter:

> Although the trial had opened in the sense that the doors of the courtroom were open and the judge was in the courtroom, the courtroom, surrounded by a whirlwind of shouting and screaming, was in a state of uncontrollable chaos.

Young defendants wearing white headbands with 'akahata' (red flag) emblazoned upon them were described as hurling abuse at the judge, while spectators in the public gallery stood up to demand a unified trial. A well-dressed man who introduced himself as a lawyer from the Tokyo Bar Association told the journalist: 'This is a revolution, isn't it? This is revolutionary progress'.[73] The cleavages in Japan wrought by the entanglement of the Cold War and Japanese domestic political legacies had manifested in the courtroom.

It was the courts that blinked first. By 1953 the Tokyo District Court, citing the complete lack of progress with the trial acquiesced to the demands of the defence and allowed, for those defendants who wish for it, a unified trial.[74] Due to the impossibility of catering in one room for over one hundred defendants, their lawyers, spectators, prosecutors, and court attendants, the hearings were attended by representatives of the unified trial group. Even so, this meant in practice upwards of 60 defendants in attendance at any one time.[75] And as the trial continued, observers in the legal press remarked that the judges seemed unable to control the courtroom to the detriment of the courts obligation to secure an expedient trial. Writing in the popular legal journal *Hōritsu no hiroba*, one observer remarked that:

> The exchanges between the plaintiff and the defendant at the evidentiary stage, centred on objections, are, so to speak, like a sporting contest fought in the courtroom. The two sides use all their secret techniques to wage a war of aggression, but this war must be a correct offensive and defensive

> battle that adheres to the rules. If the rules are violated, the referee, the judge, must immediately declare a foul. The foul must be declared in a timely manner, but the judges at the May Day trial seemed reluctant to make a quick and clear decision. This led to a tendency for objections and exchanges of arguments to be unnecessarily heated, which wasted valuable time and seemed to be the cause of court congestion.[76]

The events of the May Day trial had a number of outcomes for future approaches to courtroom governance as courtroom order became a matter of immediate significance for both prosecutors and the Supreme Court. The first was proposed legislation that would give judges new powers to manage courtroom unrest entitled Maintenance of Order in Courtrooms Bill (*Hōtei nado chitsujo ni kansuru hōan*), which was submitted to the Diet for consideration in June 1952. Framed to 'preserve the dignity of judicial decisions in order to ensure the authority of the law in a democratic society', the law provided for penalties (financial and custodial) for those who interfered with the performance of the court's duties or seriously undermined the dignity of the court. As a companion to this law, courts were to be given the power to limit the number of spectators allowed into the gallery, conduct searches of belongings, and to expel spectators who obstructed proceedings.[77]

During their deliberations on the bill defence lawyers sitting on the Judicial Affairs Committee (*Shugi'in homu i'inkai*) identified a number of concerns, including the scope for abuse of the law by judges and the extent to which the law should be applied to lawyers themselves. The new law, the lawyers argued, would allow judges to arrest, try and convict people in court, and therefore risked concentrating too much power in their hands. Judges were human after all, they argued, and if they allowed their emotions to take over in difficult courtroom circumstances, it was conceivable that they might use the law inappropriately to maintain order. There was also concern that if the law were to be applied to defence lawyers, it might interfere with their ability to represent their clients. In both cases, however, the government representatives on the panel maintained that such concerns could be mitigated by proper selection and training of the individuals involved. The government representative on the panel argued that:

> I understand that one of your concerns is that the judges may become emotionally involved, but I would ask the court to be very careful in

> the application of this law, even after it is enacted, so that there are no such mistakes. The idea behind this law is that we appoint good people as judges, trust them and leave the matter to them.

Worries that the law would be applied to defence lawyers were dealt with in a similar way. The law, the Supreme Court member of the committee was assured, would not be used against lawyers engaged in 'legitimate defence activities' (*seitō naru bengoken no kōshi*), and clear instructions to this effect would be sent to all judges.[78] Of course, this statement begged the question of what exactly constituted legitimate defence activities—a question that would be answered definitely in the Tokyo University trial.

Despite these concerns, the Maintenance of Order in Courtrooms Act (*Hōtei nado chitsujo ni kansuru hō*) was passed into law in July. Chief Justice Tanaka told the National Congress of Criminal Judges that 'judges shall, if necessary, apply this law to those who undermine the order and prestige of the court' and that judges must 'have the courage to strictly apply the force of the law'.[79] Yet despite the passage of these laws Tanaka soon became frustrated that they were not being used liberally enough. 'Regardless of the left or right,' he told assembled journalists in September, 'I think the principle of amity that has been extended to individuals and groups who bring disorder to the courtroom has reached its limit. Judges should take all measures permitted by law'.[80] This he followed up in January 1953 with an article entitled 'Issues regarding the maintenance of court order' (*hōtei chitsujo iji no shomondai*) in which he argued that communists and other likeminded activists were using the rights and freedoms granted by democracy to 'destroy the foundations of constitutional politics.' Tanaka concluded that:

> As long as the court is tasked with the mission of maintaining the rule of law, it must aim for a fair and strict application of substantive law related to the content of the case. At the same time, it goes without saying that a strict and purposeful application of procedural law is also expected. For this to be possible, the court must restrain the arbitrary and excessive use of the parties' own will or extreme interests and maintain the authority to proceed with hearings smoothly and expeditiously, exercising its authority purposefully. If the court makes a mistake in this regard, even if the judgment is substantively perfect, it will damage the court's credibility and undermine the authority of the law, making it unworthy of the trust of the people as defenders of the law.[81]

It was not only the state and Chief Justice Tanaka who expressed concern about the ferocity of the May Day trial and the need for restraint on behalf of lawyers. In an opinion piece published in their organisational publication *Jiyū to seigi*, the Japan Federation of Bar Associations (JFBA) made clear its disdain for how the trial was being conducted. Stating that the order and authority of the courts was a clear prerequisite for a functioning democracy, the JFBA criticised the judges for being too passive in their management of the defendants and spectators, and thus failing in their duty to ensure order in the courtroom. But while the JFBA was keen to reiterate that it was the judges who had the ultimate authority over the courtroom, it directed most of its criticism at the JLAF lawyers. Since the ideological views of the JLAF and the spectators seemed to coincide, the Bar Association argued, the JLAF were in a unique position to call for calm, and by not doing so they had failed in their responsibility as one of the three constituent elements of the Japanese legal system. Indeed, the JLAF lawyers' refusal to attend the various courtrooms, even as state-appointed lawyers were present, was a clear dereliction of duty for the JFBA. The JLAF lawyers' lack of respect for judges also came under fire. In a judgement that demonstrated anxiety over the impact the JLAF lawyers might have on the profession's standing within the legal system, the JFBA argued that lawyers' questioning of judges' rulings and raising fears of violence in the courtroom was action that 'sullied the dignity of defence lawyers' and as such their 'responsibility must be questioned'.[82]

In a response to the JFBA the pre-war civil rights lawyer and co-founder of the JLAF, Fuse Tatsuji, argued that the Bar Association's assessment of the 'courtroom chaos' completely overlooked the historical significance of the case. Notwithstanding the fact that the strategies employed by the JLAF lawyers had been successful in achieving a unified trial, Fuse argued, the Bar Association's dogmatic focus on courtroom order had blinded itself to the significance of the trial in what amounted to a 'deplorable lack of historical awareness and narrow formalism'. This historical significance lay in the relationship between the trial and the development of Japan's legal framework for public order. In this regard, Fuse argued that the Bar Association had fundamentally misunderstood the relationship between the courts, the dignity of the law and the Japanese people. According to the JFBA, the dignity of the law was a prerequisite for a functioning democracy, and all those involved in the legal process—including lawyers—were responsible for upholding that dignity. For Fuse, however, this reasoning was backwards: the authority of the courts could only be upheld if the defendants were satisfied with the process and the people supported it. But in his evaluation the cooperative tripartite system had failed to adequately address the steady encroachment of legislation that had facilitated the Reverse Course and exposed the authority of the law as an illusion. Recourse to empty concepts such as 'dignity' and 'authority' to legitimise proceedings could therefore only be the source of courtroom chaos, never its solution. The implementation of group trials was a case in point. According to the JLAF lawyers, the reason for a single trial was simple: there was one crime committed and there should be one indictment. But the prosecution filed 148 separate indictments and the courts proceeded on that basis. This, Fuse argued, made it easier for the prosecution to use coerced confessions, as they were less likely to be challenged, and that the JLAF's actions were therefore legitimate.[83]

The final direct outcome of the May Day Trial with significance for the Tokyo University trial was a small but important amendment to the Code of Criminal Procedure. In reaction to the phenomenon of courtroom refusal, the Code was amended in 1953 to include provision for trials to be conducted in absentia. Article 286 of the Code, which previously prohibited the opening of a hearing without the defendant present, was supplemented with a new clause that read as follows:

> When the court cannot be convened without the appearance of the accused, and the accused, who is under detention has been summoned for the trial date but refuses to appear without a justifiable reason, and it is extremely difficult for the officials of the penal institution to bring the accused to the court, the court may commence the proceedings of the trial without the appearance of the accused.[84]

This provision for trial in absentia would prove pivotal for the Tokyo University trial and was connected to perhaps most significant overall legacy of the May Day trial: its extreme length. As well as guaranteeing the right to counsel and to examine witnesses, Article 37 of the postwar Constitution guaranteed the right to a 'speedy and public trial by an impartial tribunal.' In the end, however, the May Day trial took 17 years and 9 months to reach its first verdict. Even at the seven-year mark, commentators argued that the large number of defendants and complexity of the case did not excuse the extremely drawn-out proceedings.[85] Sixteen defendants died over the course of the trial, and for the rest the trial hung over them in the homes and their workplaces. As a reporter put it in 1970, there was a sense that the trial had got the balance wrong between its two functions of 'seeking truth' and 'assessing guilt or innocence.' In the eyes of commentators, the former had won out over the latter at the expense of the defendants' right to have their day in court and to move on with their lives.[86] As will be discussed in later chapters, in the Tokyo University trial the pendulum swung in the opposite direction, as expediency became the watchword for guaranteeing human rights in the courts.

That the intended scope of these new provisions for maintaining courtroom order went beyond obstructive outbursts and acts of violence, however, was soon made clear during the Suita Incident trial at the Osaka District Court in July 1953. The trial was of protesters arrested in 1952 for rioting (*sojōzai*) at a demonstration in Osaka to mark the second anniversary of the beginning of the Korean War. During proceedings defendants asked permission of the presiding Judge Sasaki Tetsuzō to conduct a round of applause for the ceasefire in the Korean war and observe a moment of silence for those who had died in the conflict. Sasaki responded that he would maintain the court's neutrality by neither denying nor supporting the action, which went ahead. In a notice issued to all courts in September Tanaka signalled his anger at Sasaki's interpretation of neutrality in no uncertain terms. 'The maintenance of order in the courtroom is one of the most important issues of our judiciary at present,' the notice stated flatly, and as such 'we deplore the fact that the attitude of the judges presiding over the Court can undermine the prestige of the Court, shake the people's respect for the law, and lead to a loss of authority of the law.'[87] Indeed Sasaki faced impeachment for his (in)action, and while proceedings against him ended in a deferred verdict, the signal sent by the Supreme Court was unambiguous. Neutrality was the result of the active regulation of the atmosphere and emotions within the courtroom, and it was up to judges to secure such an atmosphere.

In fact, the Sasaki incident foreshadowed moves to further centralise the courts under the administrative authority of the Supreme Court. In 1955, the rules governing the appointment of district court presiding judges were changed so that nominations were no longer sought from the Judicial Council but were based on the opinions of the presidents of the High and District courts. At the same time, the Supreme Court introduced a rigorous system for evaluating the performance of judges based on a number of factors, including the accuracy and speed of individual judges' decisions, their legal knowledge, and their personal qualities.

These evaluations were carried out at a local level by the presiding judge, who was in turn evaluated by the presidents of their respective courts, effectively co-opting the presiding judge into the machinery of the judicial bureaucracy. From 1958, as the caseload and the complexity of cases increased, more day-to-day administrative functions were transferred from the Judges' Councils to the Standing Administrative Committees (*jōchi i'inkai*), and key powers over the employment of general court staff were also transferred. All this was framed as facilitating the speedy resolution of disputes by freeing the judiciary from administrative burdens. And while it was undoubtedly the case that an increasingly overburdened judiciary had little time to deal with such administrative matters, the result was a shift of power over judges and their conduct from local self-government to the Secretariat of the Supreme Court.[88]

Decentralisation of the police had also by now been reversed. Since 1951 the Police Law had been revised to allow for towns and villages to relinquish control over their local police forces and place them under the jurisdiction of the National Rural Police, which over 1000 did. Then in 1954 the Police Law was revised to create a two-tiered system of prefectural-national police. While this system retained the veneer of decentralisation, within it the National Police Agency (NPA) retained key powers over budget and high-ranking personnel. National security policing was also centralised with the NPA and the Metropolitan Police Board (MPB) becoming the primary agencies. In response to the 1952 May Day incident a national Riot Police (*kidōtai*) programme was also established in 1954, although numbers of riot police remained relatively low until the mid to late 1960s.[89] The Public Safety Commissions, which had been established under the Occupation as part of their decentralisation efforts, were recalibrated to become conduits for the transmission of government policy.[90] However, while the recentralisation of the courts and police continued, it was clear that district court judges could still make decisions in cases of social unrest with the potential to shake the status-quo. This next blow to Japan's conservative elite came in the form of a ruling in the long-running dispute over the constitutionality of the US military bases at Sunagawa on the outskirts of Tokyo. The proposed expansion of a US military base at Sunagawa served as a lightning rod for Japan's anti-nuclear and anti-base expansion movements, including Zengakuren students who flocked to the proposed site to block survey attempts.

In fact, by the late 1950s groups within Zengakuren were becoming increasingly disillusioned with the JCP. The roots of this disenchantment came from the fate of the JCP's militant line, which it had adopted in 1949 in response to the Cominform's criticism. Shouldering the burden of this new strategy, between 1951 and 1955 students from various university organisations took the prefectures to rouse farmers and workers into armed revolution. They were, however, met with at best puzzlement and at worst outright hostility. Although the students had some success organising construction workers, they suffered in the face of mounting police crackdowns and subsequent arrests. The nail in the coffin then came at the JCP's Sixth National Party Congress (Rokuzenkyō) when on 28 July 1955 the JCP leadership denounced the militant line as 'leftist adventurism' and returned the JCP to loveable tactics to attract mainstream Japanese to the cause. For the students who had dedicated five years of their lives to the militant line this declaration amounted to betrayal. The JCP, it appeared, was a fickle beast that assumed students would toe the ever-changing party line.[91] The socio-political location of students was that of an expendable resource; a view that contrasted strongly with the identity narratives of students, who located themselves front and centre of the movement.

By 1956 a new faction of students within Zengakuren began questioning the nested hierarchy that located student activism within a left-wing community dominated by the JCP. As the JCP sponsored cultural events, these students found new causes protesting a further tuition fee hike and, significantly at Sunagawa. At the request of local groups opposed to the expansion, who themselves felt betrayed by their established Socialist and Union representation, Zengakuren mobilised and transported thousands of students to Sunagawa, where between 12 and 13 October they clashed violently with police and the survey teams. While fierce local opposition to the base expansion had been ongoing since 1955, it reached a crescendo in October 1956. At its peak, on 12–13 October, a full-scale battle raged between 2,000 armed riot police and a coalition of 21 organisations, including Zengakuren activists, involving 6,000 people and resulting in some 500 injuries and 4 arrests. The scale and force of the resistance pushed the government to announce the cancellation of the survey two days later, much to the delight of the assembled protesters.[92] For the Zengakuren students, this victory was vindication of their active political line and signalled just how out of touch the JCP was with Japan's postwar political reality.[93]

The battle then moved to the courts when, in 1957, the government prosecuted seven members of the anti-expansion organisation for violating Article 2 of the Special Criminal Law of the Security Treaty by destroying the fences around the base and trespassing on US base territory. The defence argued that the presence of the bases was in fact a violation of Article 9 of the Constitution, and as the supreme law of the land, this fact invalidated the prosecution's case. In May 1959, with the Kishi government embroiled in negotiations over the renewal of Anpo, presiding judge Date Akio sent shockwaves through the conservative establishment by finding all the defendants not guilty. Accepting the defence's arguments, Date stated in his verdict that:

> The fact that Japan allows the stationing of the United States armed forces for the purpose of using them in self-defence against external armed attack, whether or not they have command authority and whether or not they are obliged to use them, must be said to constitute the stationing of land, sea, air and other forces prohibited by the first sentence of Article 9, Paragraph 2 of the Constitution of Japan, and therefore it must be said that the presence of the United States armed forces in Japan is not permitted under the Constitution.[94]

As Naoko Koda has shown, this decision worried not only Kishi but also Japan's US partners. Indeed, in the wake of the decision, Ambassador to Japan Douglas MacArthur II arranged a meeting with Japan's Foreign Minister Fujiyama Aiichiro in which he urged the Japanese to bypass the Court of Appeals and appeal directly to the Supreme Court, not only to overturn the Date ruling but also to finally put to rest the question of the constitutionality of the Anpo treaty. Whether as a result of MacArthur's intervention or not, the Japanese government did just that. Putting all other cases on hold, the Supreme Court delivered its verdict in December.[95] In its ruling, the Supreme Court held that 'foreign forces over which Japan does not exercise command and control, even if stationed in Japan, do not constitute 'forces of war' under Article 9(2) of the Constitution'. The court ruled that the question of the constitutionality of the treaty was beyond its jurisdiction, setting a precedent that continues to the present day.[96] But while the immediate shock of the Date ruling had been mitigated, it had once again reinforced for LDP policymakers the threat that an independent judiciary, especially in the lower courts, posed to the political decision-making process. Indeed, while the

Supreme Court ruling had removed the immediate threat to Anpo, it had also served to lend legal legitimacy to the anti-treaty movement, which at its peak attracted over a million protesters from all walks of life to the streets and led to a constitutional crisis that threatened the 1955 system. Now the question for Japan's political elite was how best to deal with the trend of "young judges with a tendency to rush ahead with theory without understanding the actual conditions of society".[97]

Meanwhile tensions within Zengakuren between students aligned with the JCP's strategy of engagement with the masses and students in support of a more direct political struggle with the state continued to mount. On 1 June 1958, the JCP decided to assert its authority over Zengakuren by admonishing the rebellious faction at party headquarters in Yoyogi. The reprimand, however, turned into an argument that devolved into a fistfight. The next day the JCP, via its official publication, denounced the student representatives. After it became clear at the Seventh Party Congress in July 1958 that the JCP remained unrepentant for the events that transpired at Yoyogi, activists high up in Zengakuren resolved to start their own party to wrestle control of the organisation from the JCP. In December 1958, galvanized by a successful a campaign against the introduction by the left's *bête noire* Prime Minister Kishi Nobusuke of further revisions to the Police Law that would have granted greater powers to police to crack down on protests, 45 students founded the Communist League (*Kyōsanshugisha domei*), known colloquially as the Bund (*Bunto*): a 'new' left vanguard party divorced from traditional communist and socialist parties.[98] The Bund were committed to class-struggle, mass struggle (which included students within the masses), antiauthoritarianism, and sense of 'bright' optimism and energy. These characteristics did not amount to a fully-fledged platform, and indeed contained within them a number of contradictions. But that did not matter as above all else the Bund were committed to action. And a focal point for that action was just around the corner in the form of the renewal of Anpo in 1960.[99]

The mass protests against the renewal of Anpo were one of the defining political moments of postwar Japanese history—indeed for some historians it is seen as *the* defining moment in the course of postwar Japanese politics.[100] The struggle pitted Kishi, who was attempting the renegotiate and renew the treaty, against an alliance of left-wing organisations operating under the aegis of the People's Council for Preventing Revision of the Security Treaty (*Anpo Jōyaku Kaitei Soshi Kokumin Kaigi* Citizen's Council), who saw the treaty (and Kishi) as symbolic of Japan's gradual return to prewar fascism and militarism. At its peak, the Citizen's Council mobilised 5.8 million people against renewal of the treaty and the grassroots citizen's organisations that formed as a result went on establish a tradition that would shape development of Japanese civil society for decades to come.[101] Zengakuren were part of the Citizen's Council, although the factional splits in the student organisation meant they did not act as one coherent force. While JCP affiliated students within Zengakuren opted to target symbols of the US imperialism in Japan, the Bund set their sights on the Japanese government itself. On 27 November 1959 students breached the Japanese Diet compound, and on 16 January 1960 students occupied Haneda airport to prevent Kishi flying to the US to sign the Security Treaty. Although this action failed to prevent Kishi leaving, it drew even more attention to the Anpo struggle. When Kishi had resistant socialist lawmakers removed forcibly from the Diet debating chamber to pass the revised Treaty on 19 May there was a further explosion of protest in what seemed like the dissolution of Japanese democracy. On 15 June, just days before the Treaty would be automatically ratified, the Bund once again targeted the Diet compound. This time, however, the clashes with police that ensued resulted in over a thousand casualties and the death of Bund activist Kanba Michiko. The ferocity of this confrontation promoted all seven major newspapers in Japan to publish on 16 June a joint statement calling for the return of parliamentary democracy.[102] The next day, 80,000 students again took to the streets around the Diet, but the there was nothing they could do now to stop the Treaty becoming law. A month later, at the Bund's Fifth Conference, the Bund leadership were subject to harsh criticism and after offering no defence, shattered into opposing factions.[103]

Notes

1. Ogino Fujio, *Sengo chian taisei no kakuritsu* (Tokyo: Iwanami shoten, 1999).
2. Ibid.; Max M. Ward, *Thought Crime: Ideology and State Power in Interwar Japan* (Durham: Duke University Press, 2019), chap. Epilogue.
3. Urabe Noriho, "Rule of Law and Due Process: A Comparative View of the United States and Japan", *Law and Contemporary Problems* 53, no. 1 (1990): 61.
4. Ibid.

5. Hattori Takaaki, "The Legal Profession in Japan: Its Historical Development and Present State", in *Law in Japan*, ed. Arthur von Mehren (Cambridge, Mass: Harvard University Press, 1963), 113.
6. Ibid., 129. Kahei Rokumoto, "The Present State of Japanese Practicing Attorneys: On the Way to Full Professionalization?", in *Lawyers in Society*, ed. Richard L Abel and Philip Lewis (Berkeley: University of California Press, 1996), 129.
7. Ibid., John Owen Haley, *The Spirit of Japanese Law* (Athens: University of Georgia Press, 2006), 53.
8. Miyazawa Setsuo, "Introduction: An Unbalanced Adversary System—Issues, Policies, and Practices in Japan, in Context and in Comparative Perspective", in *The Japanese Adversary System in Context: Controversies and Comparisons*, ed. Malcom Feeley and Setsuo Miyazawa (Basingstoke: Palgrave, 2002), 1.
9. Matsui Shigenori, *The Constitution of Japan: A Contextual Analysis*, Constitutional Systems of the World (Hart Pub., 2011), 120–21. Hideo Wada, "The Administrative Court Under the Meiji Constitution", *Law Japan*, 1977, 5.
10. Peter Duus, "Liberal Intellectuals and Social Conflict in Taisho Japan", in *Conflict in Modern Japanese History: The Neglected Tradition*, ed. Tetsuo Najita and Victor Koschmann (Ithica, New York: Cornell University Press, 2005), 425.
11. See for example: Ward, *Thought Crime: Ideology and State Power in Interwar Japan*. Richard H Mitchell, *Thought Control in Prewar Japan* (Ithaca: Cornell University Press, 1976).
12. Ibid., 25.
13. Takakuwa Suehide, Ogura Joji, and Sumiya Etsuji, *Nihon gakusei shakai undō-shi: kyōto o chūshin ni* (Kyoto: Dōshishadaigaku shuppan-bu, 1953), 124–38.
14. Mitchell, *Thought Control in Prewar Japan*, 86.
15. Ibid., 92.
16. Ibid., 184.
17. Ward, *Thought Crime: Ideology and State Power in Interwar Japan*, chap. 5.
18. "Potsdam Declaration" (1945), https://www.ndl.go.jp/constitution/e/etc/c06.html; K Kawai, "Mokusatsu, Japan's Response to the Potsdam Declaration", *Pacific Historical Review* 19, no. 4 (1950): 409–414; B L Villa, "The US Army, Unconditional

Surrender, and the Potsdam Proclamation", *The Journal of American History* 63, no. 1 (1976): 66.

19. Supreme Commander for the Allied Powers Directives to the Japanese Government (SCAPINs), "Memorandum for: Imperial Japanese Government. Through: Central Liaison Office, Tokyo. Subject: Removal of Restrictions on Political, Civil, and Religious Liberties (SCAPIN-93)" (1945), https://www.ndl.go.jp/modern/e/img_r/M003/M003-001r.html.
20. "The Constitution of Japan", 3 November 1946, https://japan.kantei.go.jp/constitution_and_government_of_japan/constitution_e.html.
21. The concept of rule of law is not expressed directly in these documents, but is manifested in the framing of the Constitution as the Supreme Law of Japan (Chapter 10), that governmental actions must be governed by the Constitution (Article 98), that fundamental human rights are inviolable and guaranteed (Chapter 3), requirement for due process (Article 31), investment of all judicial power in the Supreme Court (Article 76) and establishment of a process of judicial review (Article 81). See Urabe, "Rule of Law and Due Process: A Comparative View of the United States and Japan", 64–65.
22. Miyazawa, "Introduction: An Unbalanced Adversary System—Issues, Policies, and Practices in Japan, in Context and in Comparative Perspective", 1.
23. Odanaka Toshiki, *Gendai shihō no kōzō to shisō* (Tokyo: Nihon hyōron-sha, 1973), 109.
24. "Attorneys Act (Act No. 205 of 1949)" (1949), https://www.japaneselawtranslation.go.jp/ja/laws/view/3636.
25. Hattori, "The Legal Profession in Japan: Its Historical Development and Present State".
26. Peter J. Katzenstein and Yutaka Tsujinaka, *Defending the Japanese State: Structures, Norms and the Political Responses to Terrorism and Violent Social Protest in the 1970s and 1980s*, Cornell East Asia Series (East Asia Program, Cornell University, 1991), 53–54.
27. Christopher Aldous and Frank Leishman, "Policing in Post-War Japan: Reform, Reversion and Reinvention", *International Journal of the Sociology of Law* 25, no. 2 (1997): 138.
28. Aldous and Leishman, "Policing in Post-War Japan: Reform, Reversion and Reinvention". As Aldous and Leishman show, this

democractisation programme was opposed by the Public Safety Division of the Civil Intelligence Section (G-2), who advocated for a more incrementalist approach to decentralisation.

29. Ogino, *Sengo chian taisei no kakuritsu*, 47.
30. Aldous and Leishman, "Policing in Post-War Japan: Reform, Reversion and Reinvention", 139.
31. Ogino, *Sengo chian taisei no kakuritsu*, 31.
32. Ward, *Thought Crime: Ideology and State Power in Interwar Japan*, 180–81. Ogino, *Sengo chian taisei no kakuritsu*, 348.
33. Ibid., 27.
34. Ibid., 21.
35. Christopher Aldous, *The Police in Occupation Japan: Control, Corruption and Resistance to Reform* (Routledge, 1997).
36. Ibid., 90. See also Oppler Christian Alfred, *Legal Reform in Occupied Japan: A Participant Looks Back* (Princeton, NJ: Princeton University Press, 2015), 197.
37. This incident is discussed in detail in William Marotti, *Money, Trains, and Guillotines Art and Revolution in 1960s Japan* (Durham and London: Duke University Press, 2013), 47–49.
38. Nagai Kenichi and Toshitani Nobuyoshi, eds., "Purakādo jiken fukei-zai kyakka ni kansuru makkāsā seimei", in *Shiryō: Nihon Kenpō 1* (Tokyo: Sanseido, 1986), 150–51.
39. Asai Kiyonobu, Kataoka Noboru, and Tsunetō Takeji, eds., "Shakai chitsujohoji ni kansuru seifu seimei", in *Rōdō-Hō: Shiryō* (Tokyo: Hōritsu bunka-sha, 1957).
40. Ogino, *Sengo chian taisei no kakuritsu*, 44.
41. Rodger Swearingen and Paul Fritz Langer, *Red Flag in Japan: International Communism in Action, 1919–1951* (Cambridge, MA.: Harvard University Press, 1952), 156–57.
42. Yong Wook Lee, "The Origin of One Party Domination: America's Reverse Course and the Emergence Of The Liberal Democratic Party in Japan", *The Journal of East Asian Affairs*, 2004, 389.
43. Robert Anthony Scalapino, *The Japanese Communist Movement, 1920–1966* (Berkeley: California University Press, 1967), 71.
44. Thomas William French, *National Police Reserve: The Origin of Japan's Self Defense Forces* (Global Oriental, 2014), chap. 2.
45. Ibid.

46. Ogino, *Sengo chian taisei no kakuritsu*, 85. The Ordinance was not in fact new, but a revision of an Ordinance issued in response to the Potsdam declaration *Prohibition of the formation of political parties, associations and other organisations*, etc. (Imperial Decree No. 101 of 23 February 1946).
47. Kumano Ruriko, "Anticommunism and Academic Freedom: Walter C. Eells and the "Red Purge" in Occupied Japan", *History of Education Quarterly* 50, no. 4 (8 October 2010): 521.
48. Ogino, *Sengo chian taisei no kakuritsu*, 95.
49. John Dower and Tetsuo Hirata, "Japan's Red Purge: Lessons from a Saga of Suppression of Free Speech and Thought", *The Asia–Pacific Journal: Japan Focus* 5, no. 7 (12 July 2007), https://apjjf.org/-Hirata-Tetsuo--John-W--Dower/2462/article.pdf.
50. Douglas MacArthur, "Douglas MacArthur's Letter to Prime Minister", 6 June 1950, Japan, National Diet Library, https://www.ndl.go.jp/modern/e/img_l/M009/M009-001l.html.
51. Tokyo Imperial University reverted to its original name, Tokyo University, in 1947.
52. Chris Perkins, "University Newspaper Editorial: The Starting Point of the Student Movement", *Asiatische Studien - Études Asiatiques* 71, no. 2 (2017): 683–95.
53. Hasegawa Kenji, *Student Radicalism and the Formation of Postwar Japan* (Singapore: Palgrave Macmillan, 2019).
54. Yamanaka Akira, *Sengo gakusei undō-shi* (Tokyo: Aoki shinsho, 1969), 45–56. Hasegawa, *Student Radicalism and the Formation of Postwar Japan*, 68–69.
55. Kumano, "Anticommunism and Academic Freedom: Walter C. Eells and the "Red Purge" in Occupied Japan"; Hans Martin Krämer, "Just Who Reversed the Course? The Red Purge in Higher Education during the Occupation of Japan", *Social Science Japan Journal* 8, no. 1 (30 March 2005): 1–18, https://doi.org/10.1093/ssjj/jyi011; Tetsuo Hirada, *Reddo Pāji No Shiteki Kyūmei* (Tokyo: Shin Nihon shuppansha, 2002).
56. Yamanaka, *Sengo gakusei undō-shi*, 61.The notice itself, as noted in the preamble to the document, was a codification of a radio broadcast by the Minister for Education. See Monbu jikan, "Gakusei no seiji undō ni tsuite", 8 October

1949, http://kohoken.chobi.net/cgi-bin/folio.cgi?index=sch&query=/notice/19481008.txt.

57. The Matsukawa incident, which resulted in three deaths, had become a significant point of public interest after investigations into the derailment found evidence of sabotage, and members of the Railway Workers Union (*Kokutetsu rōdō kumiai*) had been indicted. Throughout this period questions proliferated around the charges and use of evidence, and strong suspicion emerged on the left that the railway workers had been set up. Media interest was also intense. The 1953 trial found twenty members of *kokurō* guilty (of whom five received the death sentence). The case was eventually tried five times, ending in acquittal for all the defendants in the high court in 1958. See Kevin M. Doak, *Tanaka Kōtarō and World Law, Rethinking the Natural Law Outside the West* (Basingstoke: Palgrave, 2019), 98–99.
58. Chida Kenzō, *Poporo jiken zenshi* (Tokyo: Nihon hyōronsha, 2008), 59–64.
59. "Shūkai, shūdan kōshin oyobi shūdan jii undō ni kansuru jōrei" (1950), https://www.reiki.metro.tokyo.lg.jp/reiki/reiki_honbun/g101RG00002205.html.
60. For a full account of Yanaihara's address to the Diet and examples of questions asked by the committee see Chida, *Poporo jiken zenshi*, 84–98.
61. "Bōryokukōi tōshobatsu ni kan suru hōritsu" (1926), https://elaws.e-gov.go.jp/document?lawid=215AC0000000060.
62. Chida, *Poporo jiken zenshi*, 228–33.
63. Ibid., 294–309.
64. Nakamura Mutsuo, "Kokuritsu daigaku no hōjin-ka to daigaku no jichi", *Hokkaigakuendaigaku Hōgaku Kenkyū* 43, no. 3 · 4 (March 2008): 531–33.
65. Justin Jesty, "Tokyo 1960: Days of Rage and Grief", *MIT Visualizing Cultures*, n.d., https://visualizingcultures.mit.edu/tokyo_1960/anp2_essay01.html.
66. Seki Itaru, *Hakai katsudō bōshi-hō to sono un'yō* (Tokyo: Shin Nihon keizai-sha, 1952), 7.
67. For an example of this argument see Hiroshi Miyauchi, "Anpo taisei to chian seisaku" (Tokyo: Rōdō junpō-sha, 1966).
68. Doak, *Tanaka Kōtarō and World Law, Rethinking the Natural Law Outside the West*, chap. 3.

69. Kotaro Tanaka, "Peace and Justice: Japan's Place in the Family of Nations", *American Bar Association Journal* 38, no. 8 (1952): 663.
70. Nagai Kenichi and Toshitani Nobuyoshi, eds., "Tanaka Kōtarō saikō saiban chōkan no shin'nen no kotoba", in *Shiryō: Nihon Kenpō 2* (Tokyo: Sanseido, 1986), 193–94.
71. Yamanaka, *Sengo Gakusei Undō-Shi*, 168.
72. *Sōjōzai* (騒擾罪) is often referred to as *sōranzai* (騒乱罪), and this is how the law now appears. This is because before digital printing the character 擾 was not readily available for typesetters. For the purposes of this discussion, I treat the two as interchangeable.
73. Bunta bunya, "Mēdē kōhan hōtei kisha seki", *Hōritsu No Hiroba* 5, no. 12 (1952): 19–20.
74. Mēdē jiken saiban tōsō-shi' henshū iinkai, ed., *Mēdē jiken saiban tōsō-shi* (Tokyo: Shiraishi shoten, 1982).
75. Matsuda Kaiko, "Mēdē kōhan bōchō-ki", *Shin'nihon Bungaku* 13, no. 4 (1958): 79–80.
76. Qb, "Mēdē kōhan", *Hōritsu No Hiroba* 7, no. 5 (1954): 20.
77. Sōgō hōki kenkyūjo, ed., *Genkō hōki* (Tokyo: Kōbunsha, n.d.).
78. Kanesu Tashio, "'Areru hōtei' to 'hōtei chitsujo iji-hō' ni kansuru shomondai', *Jiyū to Seigi* 11, no. 12 (December 1960): 2–9.
79. Ogino, *Sengo chian taisei no kakuritsu*, 240.
80. "Shasetsu: hotei chitsujo iji no tame ni", *Yomiuri Shimbun*, 26 September 1952.
81. Tanaka Kōtarō, "hōtei chitsujo iji no shomondai", *Hōsō Jihō* 5, no. 1 (January 1953): 30.
82. Nihon bengoshi rengōkai, "Mēdē sōjō jiken no hōtei konran ni taisuru iken-sho", *Jiyū to Seigi* 4, no. 2 (February 1953): 44–49.
83. Fuse Tatsuji, "Mēdē kōhan no hōtei konran ni kansuru iken-sho o yonde", *Jiyū to Seigi* 4, no. 5 (May 1953): 44–47.
84. "Code of Criminal Procedure (Part I and Part II)" (1948), https://www.japaneselawtranslation.go.jp/ja/laws/view/3364#je_pt2ch3sc1at23.
85. Minami Kazeko, "Mēdē kōhan", *Hōristsu No Hiroba*, 1959, 20.
86. Atsumi Katsuhiko, "Shihō kisha no me: mēdē saiban to tōdai saiban", *Hanrei Jihō*, no. 508 (February 1970): 16.
87. Kenichi Nagai and Toshitani Nobuyoshi, eds., "Hōtei no ishin ni kansuru saikōsai tsūtatsu", in *Shiryō: Nihon Kenpō 2* (Tokyo: Sanseido, 1986), 272.

88. Odanaka, *Gendai shihō no kōzō to shisō*, 116.
89. In 1957 there were 1,800 riot police officers organised into 5 divisions. This was a reduction in size from 2,350 officers in 7 divisions, caused by public reaction to heavy handed policing of protestors at the Sungawa military base. See Katzenstein and Tsujinaka, *Defending the Japanese State: Structures, Norms and the Political Responses to Terrorism and Violent Social Protest in the 1970s and 1980s*, 60.
90. Aldous and Leishman, "Policing in Post-War Japan: Reform, Reversion and Reinvention", 141.
91. Hasegawa Kenji, "In Search of a New Radical Left: The Rise and Fall of the Anpo Bund, 1955–1960", *Stanford Journal of East Asian Affairs* 3, no. 1 (17 May 2003): 76.
92. Hasegawa, *Student Radicalism and the Formation of Postwar Japan*, 195.
93. Hasegawa, "In Search of a New Radical Left: The Rise and Fall of the Anpo Bund, 1955–1960", 76.
94. Date Akio, "Dai-Ichiban hanketsu: sunagawa jiken", 3 March 1959, para. 8, https://www.cc.kyoto-su.ac.jp/~suga/hanrei/96-1.html.
95. Naoko Koda, *The United States and the Japanese Student Movement, 1948–1973: Managing a Free World* (Lanham: Lexington Books, 2020), 90–91.
96. Saikōsaibansho dai hōtei, "Nipponkoku to amerikagasshūkoku to no aida no anzen hoshōjōyaku daisanjō ni motozuku gyōsei kyōtei ni tomonau keiji tokubetsu-hō ihan", 30 March 1959, https://www.courts.go.jp/app/hanrei_jp/detail2?id=55816.
97. Odanaka, *Gendai shihō no kōzō to shisō*, 117–18.
98. Hasegawa, "In Search of a New Radical Left: The Rise and Fall of the Anpo Bund, 1955–1960", 83.
99. Ibid., 87.
100. For example, Nick Kapur, *Japan at the Crossroads: Conflict and Compromise after Anpo* (Harvard University Press, 2018), https://cir.nii.ac.jp/crid/1130000797100971392.
101. Simon Avenell, *Making Japanese Citizens: Civil Society and the Mythology of the Shimin in Postwar Japan*, University of California Press (University of California Press, 2010); Sasaki-Uemura Wesley, *Organizing the Spontaneous: Citizen Protest in Postwar Japan* (Honolulu: University of Hawaii Press, 2001).

102. Ibid., 50–51.
103. Hasegawa, "In Search of a New Radical Left: The Rise and Fall of the Anpo Bund, 1955–1960", 89–90. For an account of these splits see Kōji Takazawa, *Rekishi toshite no shinsayoku* (Tokyo: Shinsen-sha, 1996), 21–34.

References

Aldous, C., and F. Leishman. "Policing in Post-War Japan: Reform, Reversion and Reinvention". *International Journal of the Sociology of Law* 25, no. 2 (1997): 135–154.

Aldous, Christopher. *The Police in Occupation Japan: Control, Corruption and Resistance to Reform*. Routledge, 1997.

Asai, Kiyonobu, Noboru Kataoka, and Takeji Tsunetō, eds. "Shakai chitsujo-hoji ni kansuru seifu seimei". In *Rōdō-Hō: Shiryō*. Tokyo: Hōritsu bunka-sha, 1957.

Attorneys Act (Act No. 205 of 1949) (1949). https://www.japaneselawtranslation.go.jp/ja/laws/view/3636.

Avenell, Simon. *Making Japanese Citizens: Civil Society and the Mythology of the Shimin in Postwar Japan*. University of California Press. University of California Press, 2010.

Bōryokukōi tōshobatsu ni kan suru hōritsu (1926). https://elaws.e-gov.go.jp/document?lawid=215AC0000000060.

bunya, Bunta. "Mēdē kōhan hōtei kisha seki". *Hōritsu No Hiroba* 5, no. 12 (1952): 19–20.

Chida, Kenzō. *Poporo Jiken Zenshi*. Tokyo: Nihon hyōronsha, 2008.

Christian, Oppler, Alfred. *Legal Reform in Occupied Japan: A Participant Looks Back*. Princeton, NJ: Princeton University Press, 2015.

Code of Criminal Procedure (Part I and Part II) (1948). https://www.japaneselawtranslation.go.jp/ja/laws/view/3364#je_pt2ch3sc1at23.

Date, Akio. "Dai-Ichiban Hanketsu: Sunagawa Jiken", 3 March 1959. https://www.cc.kyoto-su.ac.jp/~suga/hanrei/96-1.html.

Doak, Kevin M. *Tanaka Kōtarō and World Law, Rethinking the Natural Law Outside the West*. Basingstoke: Palgrave, 2019.

Dower, John, and Tetsuo Hirata. "Japan's Red Purge: Lessons from a Saga of Suppression of Free Speech and Thought". *The Asia-Pacific Journal: Japan Focus* 5, no. 7 (12 July 2007). https://apjjf.org/-Hirata-Tetsuo--John-W--Dower/2462/article.pdf.

Duus, Peter. "Liberal Intellectuals and Social Conflict in Taisho Japan". In *Conflict in Modern Japanese History: The Neglected Tradition*, edited by

Tetsuo Najita and Victor Koschmann. Ithica, New York: Cornell University Press, 2005.

French, Thomas William. *National Police Reserve: The Origin of Japan's Self Defense Forces*. Global Oriental, 2014.

Haley, John Owen. *The Spirit of Japanese Law*. Athens: University of Georgia Press, 2006.

Hasegawa, Kenji. "In Search of a New Radical Left: The Rise and Fall of the Anpo Bund, 1955–1960". *Stanford Journal of East Asian Affairs* 3, no. 1 (17 May 2003): 75–92.

———. *Student Radicalism and the Formation of Postwar Japan*. Singapore: Palgrave Macmillan, 2019.

Hattori, Takaaki. "The Legal Profession in Japan: Its Historical Development and Present State". In *Law in Japan*, edited by Arthur von Mehren, 111–52. Cambridge, Mass: Harvard University Press, 1963.

Hirada, Tetsuo. *Reddo pāji no shiteki kyūmei*. Tokyo: Shin Nihon shuppansha, 2002.

Jesty, Justin. "Tokyo 1960: Days of Rage and Grief". *MIT Visualizing Cultures*, n.d. https://visualizingcultures.mit.edu/tokyo_1960/anp2_essay01.html.

Monbu jikan. "Gakusei no seiji undō ni tsuite", 8 October 1949. http://kohoken.chobi.net/cgi-bin/folio.cgi?index=sch&;query=/notice/19481008.txt.

Kanesu, Tashio. "'Areru hōtei' to 'hōtei chitsujo iji-hō' ni kansuru shomondai". *Jiyū to Seigi* 11, no. 12 (December 1960): 2–9.

Kapur, Nick. *Japan at the Crossroads: Conflict and Compromise after Anpo*. Harvard University Press, 2018.

Katsuhiko, Atsumi. "Shihō kisha no me: mēdē saiban to tōdai saiban". *Hanrei Jihō*, no. 508 (February 1970): 16.

Katzenstein, Peter J., and Yutaka Tsujinaka. *Defending the Japanese State: Structures, Norms and the Political Responses to Terrorism and Violent Social Protest in the 1970s and 1980s*. Cornell East Asia Series. East Asia Program, Cornell University, 1991.

Kawai, K. "Mokusatsu, Japan's Response to the Potsdam Declaration". *Pacific Historical Review* 19, no. 4 (1950): 409–414.

Kenichi, Nagai, and Nobuyoshi Toshitani, eds. "Tanaka Kōtarō saikō saiban chōkan no shin'nen no kotoba". In *Shiryō: Nihon Kenpō 2*, 193–94. Tokyo: Sanseido, 1986.

Sōgō hōki kenkyūjo, ed. *Genkō hōki*. Tokyo: Kōbunsha, n.d.

Koda, Naoko. *The United States and the Japanese Student Movement, 1948–1973: Managing a Free World*. Lanham: Lexington Books, 2020.

Krämer, Hans Martin. "Just Who Reversed the Course? The Red Purge in Higher Education during the Occupation of Japan". *Social Science Japan Journal* 8, no. 1 (30 March 2005): 1–18. https://doi.org/10.1093/ssjj/jyi011.

Kumano, Ruriko. "Anticommunism and Academic Freedom: Walter C. Eells and the "Red Purge" in Occupied Japan". *History of Education Quarterly* 50, no. 4 (8 October 2010): 513–37.
Lee, Y. W. "The Origin of One Party Domination: America's Reverse Course and the Emergence of the Liberal Democratic Party in Japan". *The Journal of East Asian Affairs*, 2004.
MacArthur, Douglas. "Douglas MacArthur's Letter to Prime Minister", 6 June 1950. Japan. National Diet Library. https://www.ndl.go.jp/modern/e/img_l/M009/M009-001l.html.
Marotti, William. *Money, Trains, and Guillotines Art and Revolution in 1960s Japan*. Durham and London: Duke University Press, 2013.
Matsuda, Kaiko. "Mēdē kōhan bōchō-ki". *Shin'nihon Bungaku* 13, no. 4 (1958): 79–80.
Matsui, Shigenori. *The Constitution of Japan: A Contextual Analysis*. Constitutional Systems of the World. Hart Pub., 2011.
Mēdē jiken saiban tōsō-shi' henshū iinkai, ed. *Mēdē jiken saiban tōsō-shi*. Tokyo: Shiraishi shoten, 1982.
Minami, Kazeko. 'Mēdē kōhan'. *Hōristsu No Hiroba*, 1959, 20.
Mitchell, Richard H. *Thought Control in Prewar Japan*. Ithaca: Cornell University Press, 1976.
Miyauchi, Hiroshi. "Anpo taisei to chian seisaku". Tokyo: Rōdō junpō-sha, 1966.
Miyazawa, Setsuo. "Introduction: An Unbalanced Adversary System—Issues, Policies, and Practices in Japan, in Context and in Comparative Perspective". In *The Japanese Adversary System in Context: Controversies and Comparisons*, edited by Malcom Feeley and Setsuo Miyazawa. Basingstoke: Palgrave, 2002.
Nagai, Kenichi, and Toshitani Nobuyoshi, eds. "Hōtei no ishin ni kansuru saikōsai tsūtatsu". In *Shiryō: Nihon Kenpō 2*, 272. Tokyo: Sanseido, 1986.
Nagai, Kenichi, and Nobuyoshi Toshitani, eds. "Purakādo jiken fukei-zai kyakka ni kansuru makkāsā seimei". In *Shiryō: Nihon Kenpō 1*, 150–51. Tokyo: Sanseido, 1986.
Nakamura, Mutsuo. "kokuritsu daigaku no hōjin-ka to daigaku no jichi". *Hokkaigakuendaigaku Hōgaku Kenkyū* 43, no. 3 · 4 (March 2008): 523–62.
Odanaka, Toshiki. *Gendai shihō no kōzō to shisō*. Tokyo: Nihon hyōron-sha, 1973.
Ogino, Fujio. *Sengo chian taisei no kakuritsu*. Tokyo: Iwanami shoten, 1999.
Perkins, Chris. "University Newspaper Editorial: The Starting Point of the Student Movement". *Asiatische Studien - Études Asiatiques* 71, no. 2 (2017): 683–95.
Potsdam Declaration (1945). https://www.ndl.go.jp/constitution/e/etc/c06.html.
Qb. "Mēdē kōhan". *Hōritsu No Hiroba* 7, no. 5 (1954).
Nihon bengoshi rengōkai. "Mēdē sōjō jiken no hōtei konran ni taisuru iken-sho". *Jiyū to Seigi* 4, no. 2 (February 1953): 44–49.

Rokumoto, Kahei. "The Present State of Japanese Practicing Attorneys: On the Way to Full Professionalization?" In *Lawyers in Society*, edited by Richard L Abel and Philip Lewis, 128–69. Berkeley: University of California Press, 1996.

Saikōsaibansho dai hōtei. "Nipponkoku to amerikagasshūkoku to no aida no anzen hoshōjōyaku daisanjō ni motozuku gyōsei kyōtei ni tomonau keiji tokubetsu-hō ihan", 30 March 1959. https://www.courts.go.jp/app/hanrei_jp/detail2?id=55816.

Scalapino, Robert Anthony. *The Japanese Communist Movement, 1920–1966*. Berkeley: California University Press, 1967.

(SCAPINs), Supreme Commander for the Allied Powers Directives to the Japanese Government. Memorandum for: Imperial Japanese Government. Through: Central Liaison Office, Tokyo. Subject: Removal of Restrictions on Political, Civil, and Religious Liberties (SCAPIN-93) (1945). https://www.ndl.go.jp/modern/e/img_r/M003/M003-001r.html.

Seki, Itaru. *Hakai katsudō bōshi-hō to sono un'yō*. Tokyo: Shin Nihon keizai-sha, 1952.

Shūkai, shūdan kōshin oyobi shūdan jii undō ni kansuru jōrei (1950). https://www.reiki.metro.tokyo.lg.jp/reiki/reiki_honbun/g101RG00002205.html.

Swearingen, Rodger, and Paul Fritz Langer. *Red Flag in Japan: International Communism in Action, 1919–1951*. Cambridge, MA: Harvard Universiry Press, 1952.

Takakuwa, Suehide, Joji Ogura, and Etsuji Sumiya. *Nihon gakusei shakai undō-shi: kyōto o chūshin ni*. Kyoto: Dōshishadaigaku shuppan-bu, 1953.

Takazawa, Kōji. *Rekishi toshite no shinsayoku*. Tokyo: Shinsen-sha, 1996.

Tanaka, Kōtarō. "Hōtei chitsujo iji no shomondai". *Hōsō Jihō* 5, no. 1 (January 1953): 1–30.

Tanaka, Kotaro. "Peace and Justice: Japan's Place in the Family of Nations". *American Bar Association Journal* 38, no. 8 (1952): 663.

Tatsuji, Fuse. "Mēdē kōhan no hōtei konran ni kansuru iken-sho o yonde". *Jiyū to Seigi* 4, no. 5 (May 1953): 44–47.

"The Constitution of Japan", 3 November 1946. https://japan.kantei.go.jp/constitution_and_government_of_japan/constitution_e.html.

Urabe, Noriho. "Rule of Law and Due Process: A Comparative View of the United States and Japan". *Law and Contemporary Problems* 53, no. 1 (1990): 61.

Villa, B L. "The US Army, Unconditional Surrender, and the Potsdam Proclamation". *The Journal of American History* 63, no. 1 (1976): 66.

Wada, Hideo. "The Administrative Court Under the Meiji Constitution". *Law Japan*, 1977.

Ward, Max M. *Thought Crime: Ideology and State Power in Interwar Japan*. Durham: Duke University Press, 2019.

Wesley, Sasaki-Uemura. *Organizing the Spontaneous: Citizen Protest in Postwar Japan*. Honolulu: University of Hawaii Press, 2001.
Yamanaka, Akira. *Sengo gakusei undō-shi*. Tokyo: Aoki shinsho, 1969.
Yomiuri Shimbun. "Shasetsu: hotei chitsujo iji no tame ni". 26 September 1952.

CHAPTER 3

The Bright Society, Public Security, and the Tokyo University Struggle

In the words of an early history of the Japanese student movement, the early to mid-1960s were a period of 'confusion and frustration.'[1] The 1960 Anpo failure, and resultant collapse of the Bund, left students depleted of energy and lacking a unifying cause. The spectacle of violent protest outside the Diet building and at the Prime Minister's residence, which resulted in the death of Kanba Michiko had, for many Japanese, felt like the collapse of the postwar democratic system itself. Kishi's successor, Ikeda Hayato, who assumed office on 19 July 1960 correctly identifying the Anpo protests as having turned the majority of Japanese away from divisive questioning of the foundations of Japanese democracy, made his central electoral platform a combination of pragmatic economism and welfare reform.[2] On election he set out a vision of Japanese national income doubling within the decade, and for those unable to reap the benefits of that growth, a social safety net. Income doubling was a great success: by the mid-1960s over 90% of Japanese self-identified as middle-class,[3] and by 1968 Japan had surpassed West Germany to become the second most productive nation after the US. The welfare state promised, however, was never fully realised: soon after election Ikeda stated in a speech that it was 'more important to encourage people to stand on their own two feet than to give them money with thoughts of salvation for the poor'.[4] Instead funds were channelled to Japan's large conglomerates to

C. Perkins, *The Tokyo University Trial and the Struggle Against Order in Postwar Japan*, New Directions in East Asian History,
https://doi.org/10.1007/978-981-99-7043-8_3

drive forward economic growth and infrastructure projects were used to provided functional equivalents for welfare in rural areas from which the LDP drew its voter base.[5] Yet with consumer electronics making their way into more and more households, general standards of living on the rise, and the spectacle of the 1964 Olympics marking Japan's triumphant re-entry onto the world stage, the established socialist parties found it increasingly difficult to articulate a compelling vision of an alternate future that could appeal to the masses.

By 1965, however, the student movement began a resurgence. Within the context of the dramatic escalation of the US war in Vietnam that year, student organisations once again challenged the JCP's hegemony over student politics, and in so doing formed new organisational sects that were assembled into anti-JCP student coalitions. As these coalitions engaged in increasingly violent confrontation with state authorities at sites associated with Japan's support of the war in Vietnam, Japan's security apparatus came to see non-JCP aligned student radicalism as a major threat to public order. And as the revolutionary writings of Che Guevara and Herbert Marcuse circulated amongst students in Japan, security officials argued that the unrest seen in Paris in May 1968—an attempted 'third revolution'—could very well be replicated in Tokyo with the renewal of Anpo in 1970.[6] Policing of these organisations was in the eyes of conservative elites, however, lacking in adequate vigour. While after the 1967 Sasebo incident plans were drawn up and efforts were made to prosecute more students under harsher laws, when indictments failed to translate into successful prosecutions, especially after the Shinjuku Riot Incidents in October 1968, criticism fell heavily on the courts for not adequately cooperating with prosecutors in bringing student radicals to heel.

This was the political context in which the Tokyo University struggle in 1968/69 played out. The occupation of Tokyo University started as a response to mistreatment of medical students, but as the occupation of the university continued, students broadened their struggle through the new All-Campus Joint Struggle Committee (*Zengaku kyōtō kaigi*, Zenkyōtō), whose goal was to foster an environment in which students could challenge Japan's bourgeois order and question their own complicity in the maintenance of that order. Bitter mass negotiations between Zenkyōtō and university authorities over the future of the university continued through 1968, while simultaneously students belonging to the JCP affiliated student organisation Minsei (*Nihon minshu seinen dōmei*) carried out sustained attacks on Zenkyōtō in an effort to raise the occupation. By 1969, with a symbolic cancelation of the university entrance exam all but certain, Japanese government officials made it clear they would no longer tolerate the occupation. After gaining cooperation from the university, between 18 and 19th of January 1969 state authorities flooded the campus with thousands of riot police in an effort to dislodge the 600 remaining student occupiers.

Public Security Post-Anpo and the Road to 1968

While the 1960 Anpo crisis had been averted, and Ikeda had adopted what would be dubbed by Japanese newspapers as his 'low posture' with regards politically sensitive issues, public security was still a major component of the early Ikeda agenda. Indeed, the follow-up slogan to 'income doubling in 10 years' was 'halving violent crime in 5 years.'[7] The sheer scale of the Anpo protests, the images of pitched battles between protesters and armed police, and the death of Kanba Michiko all presaged such a focus. But so too did a slew of right-wing incidents, the most spectacular of which being the murder on live television of Socialist Party Chairman Asanuma Inejirō by far-right student Yamaguchi Otoya in 1960.[8] The LDP response was to call for a strengthening of law and order, with a particular focus on violent crime. In 1961, Hayakawa Takashi, chairman of the Public Security Commission, wrote in the LDP publication *Saiken* that due to the rise in violent crime in Japan, especially violent crime committed by young people, 'the citizens of Japan were unable to live their lives in peace and safety'.[9] In response, Hayakawa set out a comprehensive plan to ensure a 'bright and peaceful society' for ordinary Japanese citizens. The founding principle of this plan was the need to stress the importance of order in community life (*kyōdōseikatsu no chitsujo*) and respect for the law.[10] To achieve this respect, he reasoned, the people must be educated about the role, responsibilities, and sacrifices of the police in protecting the public. The dignity of the courts, which the plan argued had been undermined by negative portrayals in the press and media, also needed to be upheld:

> In particular, reporting on cases in progress, depending on how it is handled, may give the public a distorted impression of trials and may also serve to divert the course of a trial, which would be tantamount to negating the trial system itself. Therefore, appropriate measures should be

> taken to ensure that the public has a correct understanding of trials and to control unjustified criticism of trials and collective pressure from outside.[11]

As in 1949 with the *Associations Control Ordinance*, while it was nominally right-wing terror in the spotlight, it was clear that left-wing social movements would also be subject to the new zero-tolerance to violence. 'Any debate that argues that left-wing group violence is acceptable while right-wing terror should be dealt with in the harshest possible terms is mistaken' argued Hayakawa in May 1961. He continued:

> For it is a fact that it is not legal demonstrations that most of the public are concerned about, but mass attacks that disregard human rights and mass violence that disregards the law, and that this is partly responsible for the triggering of right-wing terrorism. In view of the fact that at present some 180,000 civilians are killed, maimed, assaulted, terrorised, and made victims of violence in a single year, no humanist can afford to neglect these measures, let alone the fact that the general climate of violence and disregard for human life is a major cause of political violence.[12]

Within the context of this 'left–right theory of violence' (*sayū bōryokuron*), whereby left-wing excess was viewed as triggering right-wing terror, the LDP submitted to the Diet the Prevention of Political Violence Bill (*Seijiteki bōkōi nado bōshihōan*, Seibōhō) for consideration in May 1961. In effect, the bill would have expanded and strengthened provisions already contained in the 1952 Habōhō and aimed to give the authorities greater powers to intervene in, and ultimately disband, organisations deemed to be engaged in political violence. Commentators on the left were quick to claim that the law would be useless against right-wing terrorism, which they argued tended to be carried out by radicalised individuals, and as such could only be interpreted as a measure against organisations involved in organising social movements: i.e., the left. This evaluation off the mark, as the December 1961 Sanyu incident—an elaborate plot by right-wing ultranationalists belonging to the Kokushi-kai (National History Society) to assassinate the entire Ikeda Cabinet, a long list of labour union leaders, and eventually seize the National Diet—demonstrated.[13] Yet there were real concerns for the left. Under the proposed law, organisations designated as involved in political violence would be subject to strict control measures under the supervision of the Public Security Intelligence Agency (PSIA), which would be given powers to monitor and collect information about the organisation. Even the beleaguered Zengakuren rose from their internecine struggles to voice their concern over the Bill, arguing that 'for the LDP and the Ikeda cabinet, the Seibōhō was part of a longer-term policy of strengthening the imperialist system while defeating opposition forces.'[14]

The bill was eventually withdrawn in 1962 due to strong opposition both in the Diet and on the streets (including Zengakuren students of whom eight were arrested during protests), but the bill itself was an indication that despite the 'low posture' of the Ikeda cabinet, the policing of left-wing social movements was still a major priority.[15] After the failure of the Seibōhō police began to make increasing use of already existing laws to close down spaces for demonstration and manage demonstrators themselves, a practice known as *un'yo*. As Nick Kapur puts it, this involved 'making use of traffic laws, various laws against loitering or littering, noise control ordinances, curfew laws, building code violations, or any other existing laws available, selectively enforcing them to harass, hinder, or otherwise prevent protest activity.'[16] Protests near the National Diet compound were effectively banned under the existing control ordinances and any demonstration that appeared to violate the preconditions on which it was granted permission would be vigorously policed.[17]

Another important moment for the legal system came in the first half of the 1960s, this time for Japan's lawyers. In 1962 a report was commissioned on the feasibility of introducing a unified legal profession (*hoso ichigensei*) in Japan, whereby judges could be appointed from any qualified legal profession, and on the systems of appointment and remuneration of judges and prosecutors more generally. The impetus for the inquiry had been both practical and ideological. On the practical side, a shortage of judges coming through the current system, coupled with increasing delays in the delivery of judgements, suggested a need to widen the pool of potential judges. A unified system would do so by enabling any practicing lawyer to become a judge. The Federation of Japanese Bar Associations, which had long campaigned for an end to the system of career judges, also argued that the current system had created a widening gap between the bureaucratic judiciary and the people. The introduction of a unified system, they argued, was a step towards bridging this gap and helping to democratise the Japanese legal system. A commission made up members of both houses of parliament (7), judges (3), public prosecutors (3), practising lawyers (3) and persons with 'academic expertise' (3) began its investigation the following year, eventually meeting on 32 occasions over a 16-month period.[18] The commission submitted its final report (*Rinji shihō seido chōsakai ikensho*, from now *chōsakai ikensho*) to the Diet on 28th August 1964.

The outcome of the report was a great disappointment to Japan's community of lawyers. While the commission acknowledged that the *ichigen* system, if smoothly implemented, was one 'desirable' direction for the Japanese legal system, it concluded that the foundations for such a system were not in place. In addition to concerns over the feasibility of recruiting more lawyers and the issue of the concentration of lawyers in cities, the report concluded that the *ichigen* system would require 'improvement of the quality of lawyers' (*bengoshi no shitsu no kōjō*) 'and a strengthening of the trust and affinity between lawyers and the Japanese people.' Until these fundamentals were achieved, the report concluded, it would be wrong to proceed with revision. Rather, energy and resources would be better spent on strengthening the current system.[19] Just what 'improvement of the quality of lawyers' implied was bound up with a view of legal ethics and the role of lawyers vis-à-vis prosecutors and judges. As the Japan Federation of Bar Associations argued in their critique of the report:

> In the discussions of the Chōsakai on 'lawyers' ethics', there were comments such as: 'lawyers are too inclined to defend the interests of the parties and lack restraint from an official standpoint towards their clients'; 'lawyers are too urgent to protect the interests of their clients only and lack respect for the public interest or the legal order'; 'lawyers lack cooperation in reducing the burden on the courts for the proper administration of justice'; and so on. Such statements are made from a position that lacks any recognition of the fact that lawyers are supposed to maintain their independence, defend human rights against the unjust exercise of power, and realise social justice against injustice and unfairness. It is not in the public interest or inconsistent with law and order for lawyers to defend the human rights of parties as part of their professional responsibility. It should be noted deeply that such opinions can easily be used in a dangerous way, especially in the traditional atmosphere of our country, where the assertion of individual interests and rights is often considered as if it were inconsistent with the public interest. In other words, the emphasis on 'restraint from an official standpoint' - 'respect for the public interest and law and order' - as opposed to 'protection of the interests of the parties' - 'protection of the human life of the client' is a demand for authoritarian legal ethics, which is based on obedience to authority, and cannot be regarded as a correct understanding of legal ethics.[20]

In effect the proposal was shelved until such a time as the state deemed the legal profession had aligned their ethical orientation away from the rights of individual and towards the 'public interest', which was defined in terms of adherence to the current socio-political order. As will be discussed later, the question of the ethical obligations of the lawyer, and the balance between responsibilities to their clients and to the court would later become a central point of contention in the Tokyo University trial.

Meanwhile, the massification and increasing management of Japanese society provided the backdrop for a resurgence in student activism in the latter half of the 1960s. Despite the rising standards of living contradictions were piling up. As the conflict in Vietnam escalated dramatically from 1965 onwards it was increasingly difficult to reconcile Japan's Constitution, which renounced the right to wage war, with the Anpo that granted the US a base of operations on Japanese soil, the fact that the Japanese economy was benefiting greatly from US military special procurements from Japan, and the Ikeda (and from 1964 Satō Eisaku) cabinet's strategy of smoothing and deepening ties with the US.[21] Educational ideals of friendship, peace, and democracy butted awkwardly against Japan's intensely competitive, exam-centric mass education system. Meritocracy rang hollow for students and their families who knew that expensive cram schools were the only guarantee of successful entry into the elite national universities. Private universities expanded to cater for demand knowing full well they did not have the resources to deliver quality education at volume. The cities were becoming more polluted, congested, and alienating. By its peak in 1970 traffic accidents were causing 16,000 deaths per year.[22] And, although dating back to the 1950s, serious concerns over industrial pollution were seeping into the public consciousness. In 1967 researchers published a report demonstrating that industrial pollution at Minamata was causing villagers in the surrounding area to suffer horrifying illnesses. More pollution cases soon gained public recognition as citizens groups and their lawyers began to file high profile lawsuits.[23]

In this context, non-JCP student sects began to form alliances within Zengakuren to challenge the dominance of the JCP once again and push for direct action. In late 1964, non-JCP student sects clashed with riot police while protesting against the Ikeda government's decision to allow American Polaris nuclear submarines to dock in Japan and participated in mass protests against the normalisation of relations between Japan and South Korea in 1965. Unrest also began to erupt on university campuses across Japan, as non-JCP student groups protested against changes to student self-government in university dormitories. In 1966, in response to tuition fee increases proposed at Waseda University the previous year, students at Waseda went on a protracted strike that was only broken after riot police entered the campus and arrested 203 students.[24] Then in 1967 an alliance of three student sects within Zengakuren banded together to challenge the majority JCP youth organisation Minsei, who were once again criticised for their passivity. Like the Bund before them, this Sanpa (three faction) Zengakuren alliance argued for direct action in protest of Japan's complicity with the US war, and declared the struggle against the renewal of Anpo in 1970 had begun.[25]

In October 1967 Sanpa occupied Haneda airport to prevent Ikeda's successor Prime Minister Satō Eisaku from traveling to Saigon; during battles with police on the bridges that provide access to the airport a Kyoto University student, Yamazaki Hiroaki, was killed. A second Haneda Incident occurred the following month, during which thousands of riot police beat back the Sanpa students. In January 1968, a planned visit of the aircraft carrier *USS Enterprise*, which was suspected of carrying nuclear weapons, to the Sasebo naval base gave the Sanpa students a further focal point for their direct action. In mid-January, a range of activists, including JCP and Minsei, had converged on Sasebo, as had the amassed national media intent on capturing the promised scene of Sanpa-riot police conflict. The gathered press was not disappointed, as wooden stave wielding Sanpa students charged the police, and police, armed with water hoses, concussion grenades, and teargas cannisters, fought back. But as the violence continued the press got a little more than they bargained for as they too fell foul of indiscriminate police batons. Citizen by-standers, at first enthralled by the battle, began to admonish the police and support the students. Accounts of the violence meted out by the riot police made their way into the national papers. In these narratives, students were framed as underdog heroes fighting overwhelming state power. Citizens, including the journalists, became their outraged supporters. The space for action that had closed with Anpo had been reopened.[26]

While some commentators still saw behind the student violence the work of JCP puppet masters, Japan's public security apparatus quickly came to see the rise of Sanpa Zengakuren as a new type of threat to domestic security.[27] A report prepared by the PSIA and published in the National Police Academy journal *Keisatsugaku ronshū* argued that while the student movement had not fully recovered from their defeat in 1959/60 Sanpa was evidence that student factions within Zengakuren were once again coming together in common cause as the 'true militant mainstream which has carried the tradition of the [1959/60] Anpo Zengakuren.'[28] Sanpa's goal now was to unify the student movement, the report argued, to fully realise its self-appointed role in the inevitable protests against renewal of Anpo in 1970:

> ...there is a strong possibility that in the coming 1970s the Sanpa Zengakuren will stand in the forefront and play the role of "pioneer" in breaking through the barriers in the same way as "the unfortunate protagonists of the [1960] Anpo struggle".[29]

The report concluded with a warning to policy makers. The '1970 problem' the report argued was the biggest political issue now facing Japan, and student activists were busily rebuilding their movement in response. Anpo was not simply an issue of US-Japan relations for Sanpa Zengakuren: it was emblematic of a whole host of issues they associated with the 'strengthening of the ruling system of reactionary forces.' Sanpa was already recruiting first year students in preparation, the report concluded: 'The 1970 [Anpo] struggle on the student front has already begun.'[30]

In this heightened atmosphere, pressure began to mount on prosecutors and the judiciary for a more assertive approach to student unrest. This wave of criticism, which targeted supposed left-wing bias in the legal system, became known on the left as the legal backlash (*shihō handōka*). Previously, prosecutors had settled on a the approach that prosecution of students was counterproductive for managing public security as they took the view that in the courtroom battle that would inevitably ensue, student affiliation to their organisations would strengthen and any chance of student rehabilitation would dwindle.[31] But after the violent clashes and mass arrests at Haneda Airport, Sasebo, and at the US Army Field Hospital in Oji, Tokyo, and with renewal of the Anpo looming in 1970, the efficacy of this light-touch approach to managing public security came under sustained criticism from politicians and the media. Responding directly to the struggle at Oji, Minister of Justice Akama Bunzō stated at a press conference on 2nd April 1968 that:

> To suppress the activities of Sanpa Zengakuren and considering how those activities may develop in the future, I want to consider the utilization of the Anti-Subversive Activities Act (*Habōhō*) and laws governing rioting (*Sōranzai*). I would also like to find a solution to current problems preventing application of Anti-Subversive Activities Act by the end of April.[32]

In response the Supreme Public Prosecutor's Office (*Saikōken*) began preparations for an all-out assault on student activism. Building on the PSIA prediction of increased student unrest towards 1970, on 17th April the Supreme Public Prosecutor assembled all eight High Public Prosecutors and the heads of the 10 District Prosecutors into a *Public Security Labour Relations Liaison Committee* (*Kōan rōdō kankei renraku kyōgikai*) tasked with developing new policy towards student activism. Predicting an increase in student unrest, the committee discussed new approaches to prosecution including the potential and practical application of laws on rioting (*sōjōzai*) to left-wing activism, and contingency planning for scenarios which included the mobilisation of 400 prosecutors nationwide should it be required that the state prosecute upwards of 2000 students.[33] Writing in the journal of the Japan Criminal Policy Society, Tokyo High Public Prosecutors Office Chief Prosecutor Takeuchi Juhei called for a new approach to 'violent students' based in the science of criminal policy studies. The challenge for managing violent students, he argued, was in recognising two conflicting sides to the student activists. On the one hand when indicted the students presented as cold-hearted criminals of conviction (*kakushinhan*), who would not cooperate in any way with police and prosecutor investigations. But when charges were dropped, argued Takeuchi, amongst the students were those 'whose bloodshot eyes filled with tears, who told us their names and addresses, who allowed their worried parents to visit them.' Much as with medical treatment, mused Takeuchi in a telling metaphor, the approach to student unrest should be based on a combination of the hard science of Criminal Policy and the warmth of human compassion.[34]

Events in and around Shinjuku station in October became a watershed moment for experiments in more muscular policing of student unrest. On October 8 between 6000 and 8000 students descended on Shinjuku station in an attempt at preventing shipments of jet-fuel they believed destined for American use in the Vietnam War.[35] While the students were successfully beaten back by the police, there was still a sense among state officials that the crackdown had not gone far enough. A cabinet meeting on 10 October declared that 'approaches to student policing are still lax', and Chief Cabinet Secretary Kimura Toshio ordered the Ministry of Justice and the National Police Agency to further investigate the use of rioting laws for subsequent demonstrations. Of particular concern to the state was the upcoming Anti-War Day on 21 October, in relation to which the Ministry of Justice, the Supreme Public Prosecutor's Office and the National Police Agency concluded that if the same level of chaos were to be witnessed in and around Shinjuku Station, students would be arrested for rioting.[36]

In the event, the state got its chance. In what became known as the Shinjuku Riot Incident of 21 October (*Shinjuku sōranjiken*), between 3,000 and 7,000 students belonging to anti-JCP student organisations clashed with 10,000 police officers. As prosecutors and a delegation of 20 LDP politicians looked on in horror, over 700 students and bystanders were arrested, of whom 80% were anti-JCP students. Damages were estimated at 200, 000, 000 yen. Authorities also noted that 15% of those arrested were onlookers (*yajiuma*), of whom 90% had criminal records: a worrying development of mass participation in student unrest that would need new policing strategies.[37] A Cabinet Office report, from which the above statistics were taken, argued that while it was doubtful there would be another incident of the scale of Shinjuku in 1968, such incidents would more than likely occur again in 1969 and those incidents would likely take place on a greater scale. In its concluding statement, however, the report struck a cautious note with regards to policing students:

> In short, if they [student factions] are of a spirit that will not yield to any kind of hardship or oppression, stricter measures taken by the authorities will, in turn, drive them into the path of the heretics of society, the "enemies of peace", a vicious and ruthless group of criminals who are dedicated to the destruction and murder of others. It also means that international plotting forces and domestic plotting elements will increasingly seek to extend support to them and to graft behind their backs, in order to exploit them for their own ideological purposes and political gain. This is a point that the government and security authorities must consider carefully.

Once the dust had settled it became clear that while the mass-arrest approach to the Shinjuku Incident had netted an impressive number of bodies, the majority of prosecutors' detention requests were still being rejected by the courts, and only 21 activists were eventually prosecuted for rioting.[38] In fact, despite the massive number of arrests, detention and indictment ratios were *lower* than those for the Haneda Incidents of October and November 1967. Conservative commentators identified two obstacles to more effective policing of students. First, the law on rioting was still difficult to apply in practice—both in terms of adequate substantiation and given that its use would likely lead to protracted courtroom battles. But furthermore, application of the law seemed too little too late. As an editorial reflecting on the Shinjuku incident in the Yomiuri put it, why were activists, who the authorities knew were armed with sticks and rocks, allowed to gather for an 'illegal' protest in the first place? 'If the security arrangements and methods had been proper,' the paper speculated pointedly, 'the illegal activities would not have escalated to the point that required policing as rioting'.[39] In response, authorities called for the writing into law of a new criminal offence that would aid in more proactive policing. As one Police official was quoted: 'We should make preparation for rioting [*sōdōyobi*] a crime, and punishment should be more severe and serious.'[40] Indeed, such a crime, which carried a maximum sentence of three years imprisonment, had already been formulated by Japan's Legislative Council (*Hōsei shingikai*), and for security minded commentors the scenes at Shinjuku station necessitated its speedy legislation.[41]

But political anger also turned towards the courts. Chairman of the National Public Safety Commission Akazawa Masamichi made his displeasure quite apparent, stating that 'it is problematic if they [students] are released as soon as they are arrested. I want the courts to support the police more.'[42] The pressure was sustained the following month in a special edition on student unrest in the right-leaning magazine *Keizai jidai*. For the editors of the feature, the Shinjuku incident had demonstrated the excess of students' 'chaotic' [*muchitsujo*] actions, and with the 1970 renewal of Anpo on the horizon, had 'deepened a sense of fear' in the nation. 'It is the irresponsibility to believe that destruction is the only way to create something new that is so dangerous,' the editorial concluded: 'How should we deal with these runaway student movements?'[43] In his article, subtitled 'More than anything from a foundation of order', Former LDP Speaker of the House of Representatives and Chairman of the LDP's Security Treaty Investigative Committee (*Anpo chōsa kai*) Funada Naka provided an answer to this question. 'We must crack down hard on illegal student activities,' he stated, 'cheap compassionate arguments such as 'because they are young' or 'because they are fighting Americans (as in the case of the US military bases)' should not be tolerated.' A far more assertive approach was required to secure order:

> While prosecution is only one form of suppressing violence, it is particularly necessary to establish a system for prosecuting leaders and activists, and to handle actions swiftly and properly at every stage, from detention to post-trial. In view of the recent situation of arrests, prosecutions, bail, and bail for riots for Sanpa Zengakuren, a major decisive factor in reducing the fighting strength of Zengakuren is to arrest a large number of leaders and activists and to do everything possible to secure measures to keep them in detention as long as possible.[44]

Likewise, in the same special edition, newly appointed Head of the Ministry of Education, Science, Sports and Culture (Monbushō) Sakada Michita argued that the students' actions were a clear threat to 'public order' (*kōan chitsujo*) that could no longer be considered protected by the Constitution as freedom of expression. It was obvious to Sakada that student activists should be charged for rioting (*sōranzai*). But Sakada went even further than Funada in his criticism of current legal arrangements. By wearing helmets to 'submerge themselves in the movement and commit irresponsible behaviour repeatedly', he argued, students were taking advantage of the concept of the individual at the heart of postwar Japan's Code of Criminal Procedure:

> Even if they are arrested, [students] must be released from prison within 48 hours, and because they exercise their right to silence, it is very difficult to gather any evidence [against them]. Blind spots in the Code of Criminal Procedure have allowed recent student movements and acts of mass violence to be passed off as political movements, despite the obvious fact that they should be punished. This is a big problem for the future.[45]

The most strident condemnation, however, came from Kokugakuin University Professor of Economics Kitaoka Juitsu. For him the radical student organisations were part of a 'treasonous' (*baikokuteki*) plot to destroy Japan's national defences and enable the JCP (as an extension of international communism) to take control of Japan. As treasonous organisations, he advocated that the 1952 Subversive Activities Prevention Act be revised and used to make student factions illegal. Kitaoka's final words were used to evoke an image from the past. The Japanese had historically demonstrated a lack of moral courage, he argued, and after the Manchurian Incident, and despite having the power to do so, parliament had not stood up to a small number of right-wing activists. 'The fact that we succumbed to such a small number of terrorist attacks, and were thus unwillingly drawn into the war in East Asia, is a matter of great regret for all Japanese,' argued Kitaoka. 'I hope this can be prevented from happening again through legal provision and police power.'[46]

The Tokyo University Struggle

The events that took place between 1968 and 1969 at Tokyo University were part of the general surge of student activism that had begun in 1965. It is, however, important not to conflate the student action at Tokyo University with the various student faction led incidents discussed above. While the student factions or sects were an important part of the story of the Tokyo University struggle, they were one part of a complex picture of various student organisations working within, or in the case of JCP-aligned students against, a new organisation framework for student action that emerged halfway through 1968: the All-Student Joint Struggle Committee (*Zengaku kyōtō kaigi*, from now Zenkyōtō). Rather than a discrete political organisation, however, Zenkyōtō was a shared framework for praxis structured around anti-authoritarian principles whose goal was not the furtherance of the organisation or anyone political cause, but the facilitation of the students' self-development through struggle.[47] While outrage at the Vietnam war and concern regarding university autonomy were shared by all those operating under the Zenkyōtō umbrella, there where tensions between non-aligned radical students, whose goals were mostly related to the questions concerning the university and the place of students within it, and political student sects (*tōha*) who wished to articulate the Tokyo University struggle within the wider political mobilisation against the 1970 Anpo. And while the ideal of Zenkyōtō was of a new anti-hierarchical movement, its principles were at odds with the political student factions, who worked within the Zenkyōtō framework but were more wedded to their own specific (if complex and evolving) ideological perspectives within the context of their declared struggle against the Japanese state.[48] The tensions that manifested within the student support groups as the Tokyo University trial continued can be traced back to the different world views of the political factions and the non-aligned radical students in this period.

Since March 1965, medical students at Tokyo University had been agitating for revision of the one-year unpaid internship which was a mandatory element of their degrees, but which they saw as exploitative of their labour and potentially dangerous for patients. Their efforts were ignored by university authorities and by January 1968 medical students had had enough. Arguing that their exploitation was part and parcel of the commercialisation and rationalisation of the Japanese medical industry, which was itself a microcosm of the values of the nation, the young medics, now organised as the Young Medics Association (*Sei'i ren*), moved at their general conference on 27th January to go on indefinite strike.[49] Two days later on 29 January, 200 students picketed the Medical School final exams. The response from the faculty was a blunt appeal to moral expectations in order to rearticulate the students within both the university and national communities. Students were not only betraying their education, they argued, they were also doing great damage to the society they should be serving. Exams would be rescheduled. If students did not take the opportunity, they would be refused another.[50]

Then, a scuffle between medical school staff and protesting students around and inside the medical school on the night of 19 February, which became known as the Harumi incident, gave the necessary pretext for the authorities to toughen their posture by issuing punishments, including expulsions and suspensions, to 17 students.[51] The students protested that they had not been given the chance to tell their side of the story. Indeed, one of the accused had been 700 miles away in Kyushu at the time of the incident. The whole episode had the air of a stitch-up.[52] Nevertheless student voices fell on deaf ears. On 11 March proposals to carryout disciplinary action were submitted to the University Council (*hyōgikai*) and were ratified by university President Ōkōchi Kazuo. Students across the university reacted with fury to this 'unjust punishment' (*futō shobun*), while Sei'i ren occupied the medical school library and disrupted the 28 March graduation ceremony. These actions, however, did little to change the minds of the university administration, who remained steadfast in their no-negotiation stance. In the face of this intransigence, the medical student strike committee decided to occupy the symbolic heart of the Tokyo University, Yasuda Auditorium.

They carried out their plan on 15 June. There was, however, a mix of feelings towards the occupation at this time, and it would be wrong to portray action as spontaneous and unified as in some accounts.[53] This was due to the organisational structure of students within the medical school student government committee. Broadly speaking there were three different bodies of students: old-left JCP aligned students (*Minsei*), New Left activists that were associated with political factions (*tōha*), and politically non-aligned radicals (*nonsekuto rajikaru*). While all students were united against the punishments of their peers, they did not agree on the best way to act. In general, the non-aligned students, and at least initially Minsei, were against the occupation. However, faction students, who were the most politically active in the student movement, were in leadership positions within the class committees and made it clear that they were intent on occupying Yasuda even if committee decisions went against them. For many medical students then, the occupation was something they did out of obligation and a sense of inevitability.[54] It was the university administration's reaction to the occupation that brought the three bodies of student together. On 17 June President Ōkōchi ushered onto campus 1200 Riot Police to expel the students and normalise the campus (*gakuen no seijiōka*). In fact, this is what the faction leadership of Sei'i ren had been banking on: they were convinced that the occupation would be met with force, and that force would galvanise the student body.[55] Their prediction turned out correct. On hearing of the police intervention on campus, 300 students gathered outside Yasuda Auditorium and by the end of the day graduate students had formed the All-University Struggle Alliance (*Zengaku tōsō rengō*, Zentōren).[56]

Zentōren's platform can be usefully read in the context of the outcome of the Poporo incident trials. As discussed in the previous chapter the precedent set by in the Poporo incident was in effect a solidification of the state's attempts in the 1950s to position students outside the realm of responsible political actors. The 1963 Supreme Court ruling had recognised the importance of university self-governance for the purposes of conducting and disseminating research and located the authority for self-governance with the university professoriate. Freedom and autonomy were essential for scholarship but special consideration did not extend to activities outwith academic pursuits. Within this context, students were classified as users of the university facilities for educational reasons and subject to the authority of the university governing. Students' right to academic freedom within this context extended only to the right to learn from their tutors without interference, and again discounted any other form of activity on campus as falling beyond the bounds protected by academic freedom. In this context, Zentōren argued the treatment of medical students was symptomatic of a greater problem plaguing the university. Using riot police to normalise the campus showed that the university authorities' understanding of self-governance meant 'self-governance by the professoriate'. Attempts by department heads to designate the problem as confined to the medical school rendered those professors complicit. It was time for students across the university to unite in taking indefinite strike action.[57]

One by one departmental student associations responded to this call. The medical faculty remained unmoved: when the Literature department voted to join the strikes Head of the Medical School Toyokawa Kōhei stated directly that he had 'no intention of repealing the punishments or meeting with students from other departments.'[58] Nevertheless, President Ōkōchi, who even though in his heart of hearts did not believe in negotiating with the masses, reluctantly agreed to meet with representatives of the protesting student associations. The outcome was disastrous. On 28 June, with the 3000 seat Yasuda Auditorium packed to the rafters with both Zentōren and as yet non-aligned students (who were generally receptive to the President), Ōkōchi stood up and explained to the crowd how he had simply requested the help of the riot police to resolve the crisis and maintain the respect and dignity of university staff. As can be expected, this lack of contrition and apparent avoidance of responsibility provoked an angry reaction from the audience. After repeatedly calling for quiet, Ōkōchi was whisked away from the hall for medical reasons and the meeting fell apart.[59]

This performance only served to inflame and spread student outrage: even those non-aligned students who had been keen to hear Ōkōchi's side of the story walked away from the meeting feeling deeply troubled.[60] Here was a university that treated its students with contempt, which spoke the language of autonomy and self-governance only when that language suited their needs and had very little interest in entering real negotiations. For Zentōren, it was clear that the university was not interested in making decisions at discussions with students and that the university saw the punishment of medical students (excluding the one unfortunate procedural mistake) as legitimate. Resolve to escalate the strike hardened and on 2 July students occupied Yasuda Auditorium for the second time.[61] Simultaneously, science and engineering graduate students set up a 'tent village' around Yasuda clock tower from which to reach out further to non-political (*nonpori*) students. Three days later, on 5 July

1968, 4,000 students held a conference in the Yasuda 'liberated auditorium' (*kaihō kōdō*) at which the University of Tokyo All-Student Joint Struggle Committee (*Tōdai zengaku kyōtō kaigi*, Zenkyōtō) was formally established.

Zenkyōtō, which subsumed the graduate organisation Zentōren and the organisation of assistant professors (*Zengaku joshu kyōtō kaigi*), then issued seven demands to the university. This document started with the original demand that the punishments given to medical school students be repealed and the decision to allow riot police onto campus be condemned. But it went further to demand amnesty for all students involved in the struggles to date, and that 'those with responsibility, take that responsibility and resign'.[62] On 10 August, the university gave its final response in the form of a 'public notice' (*kokuji*) mailed to individual students over the summer break. In the letter the university promised to roll back the sanctions on medical school students and convene a new investigation into the circumstances that led to the punishments. The letter also demonstrated, in a roundabout way that seemed more concerned with student reaction than the action of itself, remorse for use of riot police on campus and pledged to avoid at all costs doing so again. Alongside the letter, Head of the Medical School Toyokawa Kōhei and Head of the University Hospital Ueda Hideo, who were blamed for the punishments, were removed from their positions. On first reading this looked like a student victory. Yet the final paragraphs of the letter were reserved for a criticism of the students. No matter the reason, the letter stated, 'group action that uses illegal force to interrupt the functioning of the university was anti-intellectual [*hichiseiteki*] activity that had no place on a university campus.' Therefore, over and above all else, if the university were to avoid calling upon the riot police again, students would have to 'bravely and with solemn conviction strive to end all violent action (*bōryokuteki kōi*) on campus.'[63] Matters were made worse when the Yomiuri Newspaper reported that President Ōkōchi had edited out from the final letter a statement that the use of riot police was a matter of 'deep self-examination for the university' (*daigaku toshite fukaku jisei surumono de aru*).[64]

Zenkyōtō responded to the 10.8 Notice with disapproval. This was because students were now not negotiating simply for outcomes within the current structure of governance but were arguing for a re-evaluation of students' position and identity within the university and as such for a fundamental change in university values.[65] The notice had only reinforced the sense that students were merely there to be acted upon by the administration. First by sending the notice to students' homes, the university had ignored their calls for mass negotiation thereby refusing what the students saw as their right to speak and be heard: student responses repeatedly decried the unidirectional (*ippen*) nature of the notice as closing any space for dialogue. Second, by reducing the Harumi incident to a matter of process with the medical school which the university continued to hold sole power over, authorities had downplayed the significance of the incident for the rest of the student body. Third, by laying at the students' feet the blame for using the riot police, the university had legitimised its violence while making illegitimate students' right to collective action. In other words, the notice pushed upon student activists the simple identity of violent groups whose values contradicted the 'common sense' values of the university as a moral community. Finally, Zenkyōtō decried the notice for saying nothing in response to fundamental questions the conflict was raising about university governance, or indeed the nature of the university that the authorities were so keen to protect. As Zenkyōtō argued:

> Today, what goes by the moniker of university self-governance is nothing more than governance by the association of department professors. This association has, on the one hand, organised the system of academic education and research at the behest of capital, and at the same time, as an agent of state power, has acted to suppress the autonomous activities of students. This has been made clear in the recent struggle at the Tokyo University.[66]

Zenkyōtō aligned junior professors, asked similar questions. In their critique issued on 25 August they challenged the easy distinction made by the university between violence (*bōryoku*) and reason (*risei*) that enabled disqualification of students who used violence from the moral community of the university. In a response to this tactic the junior professors did not deny the violence of student action. Instead, they argued that the distinction between violence and reason was itself false: 'violence is the last form of reason' they argued, and 'condemnation of violence without asking "why" was an age-old method used by those in power to supress the dissent of the oppressed'.[67] On the university itself the junior professors argued there was a central contradiction at its heart. Within the Japanese political structure, universities had always been viewed as a method of developing bureaucratic and technical human capital. Universities provided resources for the state. But within the academy, professors believed they were safe within their ivory towers to engage in the pursuit of pure knowledge. To maintain that illusion, however, the professors made ever more concessions to the state power structure, until finally the governing class of the university took on the role of supporting state goals as a means of maintaining their own privilege.[68]

Over the summer the back and forth continued between students and the university administration. Within the medical school the new head of department Kobayashi Shin wrote to students individually with varying proposals for ending the strikes, including a plan to hold an extraordinary graduation ceremony to allow fourth year students to complete their education. Although there was some support for these proposals within the medical school student body (on 22 August 118 students came out in favour of ending the strikes), the Zenkyōtō affiliated students had been cut out of the negotiations and demanded public consultation. When this was refused 300 medical students occupied the medical school building.[69]

On 29th August an article about the activities of Zenkyōtō students appeared on the Yomiuri Shimbun. The article described the five-hour detention by medical school students of the Head of the Department of Medicine Kobayashi. According to the journalist, Kobayashi had planned to meet with students that day but on witnessing student 'zigzag' demonstrations outside the building had feared for his safety and decided against it. This had apparently angered the students who, armed with wooden staves (*gebabō*) flooded into a room on campus where Kobayashi was giving a press conference, and bundled him off. There it was stated Kobayashi was subject to five hours of 'collective bargaining' (*dankō*) with the students over the status of graduations. The article carried a photograph of Kobayashi clutching a wet towel to his forehead, surrounded by students wearing face coverings.[70] Zenkyōtō responded with condemnation of the article, which they viewed as an attempt to discredit the movement in the public eye as little more than violent mob rule. The war of words between students and the newspaper took on a more significant dimension when the journalist who wrote the article claimed that, when he entered the building occupied by the medical students he had been attacked and sustained significant injuries that required hospitalisation. The students did not deny that the journalist had entered the occupied building, and on doing so was subject to critique by those students present as to the nature of the August 29th article. But they categorically denied any violence against the journalist, instead claiming he had feigned injury as another reporter was passing by in order to escape the students' questioning.[71] No matter which account was true, the August 30th edition of the Yomiuri condemned the medical students for their 'yakuza like' actions and called for a thorough police investigation. 'Crimes such as assault that might occur in the future could go unnoticed,' cautioned the paper, 'and the law may no-longer extend to universities.'[72] After an investigation on 14th October, plainclothes police officers entered Tokyo University campus and arrested third year medical student Miyoshi Jō.[73]

This incident provoked former Monbushō Minister Nadao Hirokichi to issue a scathing rebuke of the Tokyo students. In an article that appeared on the same page as the Yomiuri's condemnation, Nadao expressed his dismay at students who through their actions had disturbed the values of the university community, freedom of research, and in barricading medical buildings, put lives at risk. Nadao questioned whether indeed students involved in perpetrating these acts should be treated as students at all. Nadao's evaluation, however, was not limited to the moral community of the university. 'The actions of students who do not choose the [correct] method to achieve their aims,' he argued, 'would not be allowed by the people (*kokumin*). It is fine to reason with the students. But to leave the situation as it stands would be problematic.' Nadao's position was that, should the unrest on campus continue it would only be right and proper to prepare to expel a section of the student body (*ichibu gakusei*). In a clear indication that the state was watching events closely, Nadao noted that 'patience was coming to an end', and if the situation was not resolved soon, 'there would be no option other than to take measures.'[74]

Meanwhile another force was building that help define the boundaries of Zenkyōtō as a community: the JCP and their student wing Minsei. As noted above Zenkyōtō was a union of non-aligned and political faction students and these two groups of students had varying outlooks on the movement. In general, non-sect students were motivated by injustices at the university: namely the treatment of medical school students, use of riot police on campus, and the high-handed manner in which the university administration conducted themselves. Students belonging to political sects, however, were more likely to place the university struggles within the context of broader political issues such as the Vietnam War and the 1970 renewal of the Anpo security alliance with the United States. What united them was their opposition to the Japanese Communist Party and their student organisation Minsei. While up until this point, Minsei had gone along with Zenkyōtō, the JCP were beginning to view the action on campus as dangerously destabilising of their hegemony.[75] In late August/early September the JCP decided to move to the end game of this battle. The party began by issuing decrees in the national press and their own publication Akahata denouncing the violence on campus and calling of its immediate cessation. A few days later the JCP dispatched a group of trained activists whose job was to disrupt Zenkyōtō occupation of buildings and bring the activism to an end.[76] The violence soon ramped up as Minsei and students belonging to the various political sects clashed in pitched battles and took hostages on both sides.[77] By 12 October the entire campus was on indefinite strike.

On 1 November President Ōkōchi finally bowed under the pressure and resigned. In a letter addressed to students Ōkōchi admitted that the punishment of students over the Harumi Incident, had been a mistake that, despite intentions to the contrary, had exacerbated tensions between students and faculty.[78] Ōkōchi was frank in his criticism of his medical school colleagues. By not following due process, including the failure to seek out the students' side of events before issuing the punishments, the medical school faculty had contributed to the erosion of trust and escalation of the strikes. Therefore, the punishments would be rescinded. He was also contrite about his decision to call the riot police onto campus, lamenting both a lack of foresight as to the impact of the decision on student sentiment, and his lack of engagement with the wider university community before taking the fateful decision. Yet, much like the 10.8 notice, Ōkōchi returned to the question of student violence, calling for students to look deep within themselves and question whether their actions were merited. Ōkōchi finished with a vision of a new university in which students' opinions of the future of the university were listened to, especially with regards to the disciplinary system. Yet as the Asahi Newspaper noted astutely in an editorial two days after the resignation, Ōkōchi's final overture missed the point of the conflict, which was now well past the question of the university's disciplinary procedures. Instead, the problem was rooted in a shift in the position of the university, brought about by the massification of higher education, within Japanese society. For student activists the university was a microcosm of a social system that was fundamentally unjust, and destruction of that system was proof of liberation from it. Massification of education had made students the centre of the university, but the old structures of governance placed their education low down on the list of university priorities.[79]

In November Ōkōchi and the previous administration was replaced by acting Principal Katō Ichirō and a new senior leadership team. Katō, a comparatively younger and more energetic man, quickly reached out to students to start negotiations to end the strife on campus.[80] His strategy was to view past issues as resolved with the resignation of Ōkōchi and his team and reframe the current issue as how best to bring the current struggle to an end. In doing so Katō placed upon students responsibility for organising democratic representation at mass meetings. Should students fail at arranging such representation that was for Katō a problem of their organisations and not the university administration.[81] Katō wasn't there to appease or prevaricate: the point now was to negotiate and get on with the job of running the university.[82] This message was addressed to the entire student body, not just Zenkyōtō. Indeed, at this point three distinct groups of students were all vying for hegemony in these negotiations. Alongside Zenkyōtō and Minsei, who were variously engaging and disengaging with negotiations, another group of students were beginning to question the rationale and direction of the movement. These students, who came together as an anti-strike organisation, differed from the more militant students in how the Tokyo University struggle was articulated with wider politics. The anti-strike students (mostly 4th year students worried about their future) were keen to limit the scope of the issue to the events at the university itself, which for them had been deplorable but were now on the way towards resolution.[83] After the JCP intervention into affairs on campus, this new anti-strike group of students became uneasy bedfellows with Minsei, and together they engaged with the new line from the administration. Indeed, when on 2 December Katō issued a long statement to students detailing his administration's negotiating position for ending the strikes this partnership strengthened and gathered momentum.[84]

Naturally Zenkyōtō saw these developments as a threat. In their eyes Katō's overtures still did not satisfy the 'seven demands', especially in terms of taking responsibility for the breakdown on campus. What's more, the resignation of the Ōkōchi administration appeared evidence of Zenkyōtō's capacity to enact change. And Minsei was playing a double game of appealing to rationality and negotiation with the administration and non-political students, while engaging violently with Zenkyōtō as a highly organised force. In a sense Zenkyōtō could now only double down on their strategy by calling for the complete occupation of the campus. This was the start of a number of clashes between Zenkyōtō students and Minsei students and activists, many of whom were shipped in by the JCP to bolster numbers as part of the JCP's concerted effort to end the struggles and regain their hold on student politics.[85] Violence that had been mainly symbolic was now characterised in terms of 'war' (*sensō*), with clearly defined enemies and the goal of causing harm on both sides.[86] As talks continued to break down Katō made a final overture to students via a handwritten message. This overture, however, was ultimately rejected by Zenkyōtō on 23 December. Zenkyōtō did not see in the administration the sense of responsibility they demanded; and the New Left sects at the heart of Zenkyōtō did not wish to give up the opportunity granted by the struggle to further their own political aims.[87]

At the end of December, a new deadline began to loom: the date of the university entrance exams. In no uncertain terms, the Monbushō made good on its promise to intervene in the dispute by declaring that, should the struggle remain unresolved by around 15th January, the university entrance exams would be cancelled.[88] Such a cancellation would be a major blow to the institution and came to represent a line in the sand the administration would not cross. It was also a decision that arguably impinged on university autonomy and as such broke the law. As observers at the time noted, in discussions between the Monbushō and the Tokyo University administration the Monbushō had repeatedly stated that the decision to hold the exams was not solely up to the University, although legally the Monbushō had no formal power to order the cancelation. Indeed, the Tokyo University council criticised this proclamation by the Monbushō as transgressing the principle of university autonomy, to which the Monbushō argued back that given the situation the professoriate had lost their qualifications to speak on the matter.[89] Yet the university administration was beginning to resort once again to calling in the police to intervene in the battles that were occurring between Zenkyōtō and Minsei students. On 9th January, the two groups clashed over the occupation of the Department of Economics, which resulted in over one hundred casualties across both sides. In response Katō called upon the police to remove 'students in revolt' (*hanran gakusei*) from campus. The Monbushō viewed this intervention with approval stating that calling on police should be considered a natural option (*tōzen no socchi*) for the university administration.[90]

All eyes were now on a final meeting between faculty and students at Chichibunomiya Rugby Stadium on 10 January 1969. Four members of the administration including Katō met with roughly 50 elected representatives of the student body, while in the stands sat roughly 1,500 academic members of staff and 7,500 students. Zenkyōtō affiliated students, who saw the meeting as a method of channelling and thereby repressing the movement, however, had no interest in the event. Those who tried to enter to disrupt proceedings were either arrested by the large riot police presence or chased away by students who wanted the meeting to be a success.[91] Much to Zenkyōtō's chagrin the outcome of the meeting was a new set of terms of engagement ('10 demands' (*10-kōmoku*)) that was decided and returned to class and departmental groups for discussion. From the perspective of Zenkyōtō students the university, riot police, Minsei, and the anti-strike student body were now all aligned against them. Indeed, in the wake of Chichibunomiya Rugby Stadium meeting department after department voted to end the strike, while Minsei students continued their assault on barricaded buildings.[92]

On 12 January Zenkyōtō declared publicly their resolve to ignore the '10 demands' and departmental resolutions to end the strikes. Over the next few days barricades were strengthened, food stockpiled and tools for repelling the riot police/Minsei, who had in Zenkyōtō's estimation become one entity, was prepared. Students from all over Japan also heeded the call from the political sects to bolster numbers. On 15 January Zenkyōtō held a last general meeting in the Yasuda Auditorium. Over 6,000 riot police and 500 plainclothes police were now massing outside the university campus and had been instructed to search and arrest any students entering the university on the basis of a declaration by Katō that from the 15th no entry onto campus would be permitted.[93] On the evening of the 17th students in Yasuda Auditorium received a phone call from Katō. Stating that the students were in possession of dangerous materials, he warned that should the students not leave the occupied buildings he would be forced to call in the riot police.[94] In fact, Katō had already made formal overtures to the police, but the authorities were still holding out on committing. The reason for this was that the state wanted formal approval by the university of any action on campus so as to avoid any charge of breaching the norm of university autonomy. On the same day as Katō made his phone call to Zenkyōtō, the government had made an announcement to the press stating that while they were preparing to investigate the students, they were waiting for the university to make a formal written request for police intervention in which the university granted the police a free hand in normalising the campus and promised to cooperate with the police in any subsequent investigations. That night the university leadership agreed to these terms, committed to seeing the normalisation of the campus through, and agreed that other than academics and the police no one else would be allowed access to the campus.[95]

With these agreements in place the riot police began their assault on the morning of the January 18th. Simultaneously the Chairman of the National Security Commission Araki Masuo made a public statement reinforcing their unity with the university administration. 'The police have been cautiously deliberating [the use of riot police], but ultimately decided to deploy under the assurance of complete support from the University of Tokyo administration' said Araki to assembled journalists. 'The police force intend to exert their full efforts while prudently focusing on preventing any risk to human lives.'[96] Using riot shields, batons, tear gas, high-pressure hoses used to spray students with cold water laced with tear gas liquid, and for one fleeting moment a helicopter, the riot police systematically broke through the barricades and arrested students. Zenkyōtō responded with rocks and Molotov cocktails. The battle was fierce, but the students, who had limited food and little to no sleep, could only last so long. By 5:15pm on the 19th the occupations were over.

The Politics and Thought of Zenkyōtō

Before moving on to an investigation of the first stages of the Tokyo University trial, it is important to set out in greater detail the thought that animated Zenkyōtō and the sort of politics they were engaged in. One persistent view of'68 in Japan is that what politics there was quickly devolved into nihilism, violence, or at best simply a search for the self.[97] On this view, once Zenkyōtō refused to negotiate with the University authorities they stopped engaging in politics. This view, however, takes an overly narrow view of the realm of political action, and misinterprets what social movements such as Zenkyōtō do. As Nagasaki Hiroshi has recently argued '[t]o stipulate that a political movement means demanding rights solely through legal forms is to remain trapped within a preliminary ideal; we must not overlook the fact that a political movement could simultaneously be a mutual ethical elevation between subjects:'68 changed the *style* of politics'.[98] But even more than this, as Kosugi Ryōko has noted, it is perhaps most productive to view Zenkyōtō as a shared cognitive framework for social praxis, as a 'process in formation' producing new forms of social meaning and social spaces in which that meaning could be taken in further directions.[99]

The intellectual seeds for this change in style had been sown in the wake of the 1959/60 Anpo struggle. For thinkers such as Yoshimoto Taka'aki and Tokoro Mitsuko, among others, the failure of the Anpo demonstrations pointed to a need to reject preestablished notions of political leadership, vanguardism, and the role of progressive elites and intellectuals in the business of political change.

Reflecting this stream of post-Anpo thought, Zenkyōtō defined themselves against organisations—such as the JCP and Minsei—who they viewed as only interested in level institutional politics. Instead, Tokyo Zenkyōtō targeted the fundamental order of the Japanese state, first in how it manifested in the university, and then more broadly in society at large. In doing so Zenkyōtō created through media, writings, debates, and activities, what Ando Takemasa terms 'discourse spaces' of shared understanding: counter hegemonic communities where students questioned the Japanese sociopolitical order and produced theoretical tools to guide their praxis.[100] Key to the structure of these discourse spaces were the closely related concepts of everydayness (*nichijōsei*) and self-negation (*jiko hitei*). If the object of the Zenkyōtō movement was the dismantling of Japan's postwar order, the concept of 'everydayness' referred to where and how that order manifested in common sense patterns and routines of thinking and doing which normalised structures of inequality and violence. As one student put it, everydayness was 'the dominant way of thinking—everything ranging from people's art of living better to the cognitive system academically discussed by intellectuals.'[101] In this sense, Zenkyōtō saw their project as discovering and dismantling structures of social control in a process of transforming their own political subjectivities. For Tokyo Zenkyōtō students in particular, this orientation to the everyday meant rigorously questioning their own positions as future elites who would benefit from and (without intervention) likely propagate the systems of inequality and violence they opposed.

This questioning manifested in the practice of 'self-negation' (*jiko hitei*), a concept drawn from the writing of philosopher Yoshimoto Taka'aki.[102] Yoshimoto was a harsh critique of both the postwar political and economic consensus and the establishment leftwing response (both JCP and progressive intellectual) which he held responsible for the Anpo failure. In place of the vanguardist approach to political revolution in Japan seen with Anpo, Yoshimoto held a nativist view that located the wellspring of revolution in the everyday lives of the masses.[103] The role of the intellectual was thus not one of leadership, but of developing positions that captured the actual lived experience of life—its tensions, contradictions, and struggles. Zenkyōtō adopted and extended this perspective, generalising self-denial as a method of achieving a universalism that would allow connection with the struggling masses. This process began in the research community of Tokyo University. As young researchers became more involved in rallies and off-campus activism, some began to reflect on the strangeness of returning from heated struggles in the streets and fields to the quiet security of their labs and offices. As Yamamoto Yoshitaka, the main representative of Zenkyōtō, put it, the correct response to this tension was not simply to give up on being a researcher. To do so would simply to flee from the contradiction of experience, rather than to approach it as a problem to be solved. Rather, the answer was to:

> ...examine one's own everyday existence on the basis of thorough critical principles and to strive to develop universal awareness. Then in accordance with this awareness so obtained, we must deny the self that is parasitic on society and hostile to the working class, and from there practise social revolution. I can only say this in abstract terms, but it is the only possible conclusion.[104]

As the Zenkyōtō movement took form, however, the praxis of self-negation spread beyond communities of researchers and was adopted by students more generally. The barricaded spaces of the university enabled students to experiment with new social roles, forms of governance, and forms of communication as an antidote to the normalised postwar they saw and experienced outside.[105] In this they were influenced by the writing of Tokoro Mitsuko, in particular her 1966 essay 'The organization to come'.[106] For Tokoro, traditional forms of institutional politics, including those of the major opposition parties and the JCP, did nothing to challenge the underlying capitalistic logic of rationalisation and quantification that was the root cause of alienation in postwar Japan. In contrast, the political organisation Tokoro envisaged as a vehicle for self-realisation was fluid, anti-hierarchical, and in a constant state of motion. Decisions were made collectively and those who did not agree could opt out of action without putting their membership of the community at risk. Self-negation was crucial for the functioning of these new communities, as only through the negation of the ego could space be created for others in the community to thrive.[107]

In a sense these principles of fluidity, negation and individual self-realisation are difficult to square with the fact that, as discussed earlier in this chapter, violent direct action, what the students termed gewalt (*gebaruto*), was not precluded from these discourse spaces. But as we have seen, any easy distinction between violence and reason was negated in Zenkyōtō thought through the recognition that rationality was less a universal value and more a historically contingent set of values that normalised social and political arrangements which themselves produced violent outcomes. And indeed, the mass use of riot police to suppress student action when that order became unstuck only served to demonstrate for Zenkyōtō the inseparability of state violence, the university, and postwar order. In this way Zenkyōtō characterised their gewalt as for emancipation and 'social justice' in contrast to state 'violence of oppression'.[108] It was a seeming lack of sensitivity among the professoriate to this contradiction that drew so much of Zenkyōtō students' anger. As such, acts of violence were to be seen as a contrast to the 'irresponsibility' and 'lack of thought' demonstrated by the professors. In the students' words: 'they [the professoriate] have to realise that, compared to the many hundreds, many thousands of pages they [the professors] write in academic papers, just one of the stones we throw has far more "weight."'[109] Indeed the stones, helmets and staves used by the students served a symbolic role as part of the juxtaposition of their action with the inaction of the bureaucracy of the university. Importantly gewalt was also seen by student activists as a method in the realisation of their self-negation. The riot police, Minsei, and right-wing students were for student activists a physical manifestation of the intangible sense of everyday order they were struggling against. Thus, confrontation with them was an externalisation of self-negation and a yardstick of progress.[110]

A final point to make is that, as a structure for thought and action, Zenkyōtō itself was not programmatic. Neither was it future oriented in the sense of building new institutional structures. As one non-aligned member of Zenkyōtō interviewed for an early study on the movement put it: 'We had no idea of what lay ahead or even a rough sketch of the immediate future, but we were certain that if we tied ourselves to any organizational pattern we would gradually become absorbed by it.'[111] Their politics, in contrast, hinged on the potential for transformation produced by spontaneous action in the present. Confrontation was productive in that it created breaches in the everyday order—be that external or internal—from which new possibilities were made possible. In other words, negation itself, with Zenkyōtō serving as a loose structural vehicle, was a politics of process without any discernible end. In this regard transformation was not at the level of the collective but the individual; as Nagasaki Hiroshi puts it the 'we' emphasised by previous Marxist approaches to political change was replaced with a multiple 'I's in a process of becoming through perpetual struggle.[112] Nevertheless it was the collective that facilitated the process of transformation, and it was this struggle to retain the collective that would be key to the trial.

Notes

1. Kurata Kazunari, *Shinsayoku undō zenshi* (Tokyo: Ryūdō shuppan, 1978), chap. 3.
2. David Chiavacci, "The Social Basis of Developmental Capitalism in Japan: From Post-War Mobilization to Current Stress Symptoms and Future Disintegration," *Asian Business & Management* 6, no. 1 (2007): 35–55.
3. David Chiavacci, "From Class Struggle to General Middle-Class Society to Divided Society: Societal Models of Inequality in Postwar Japan," *Social Science Japan Journal* 11, no. 1 (June 10, 2008): 5–27.
4. Yumiko Iida, *Rethinking Identity in Modern Japan, Nationalism as Aesthetics* (London: Routledge, 2005), 117.
5. Margarita Estevez-Abe, *Welfare and Capitalism in Postwar Japan* (Cambridge: Cambridge University Press, 2008).
6. Naikaku kanbō naikaku chōsa-shitsu, *1970-nen ni shōten o awaseta kokunai sōdō ni kansuru yosō to sho bunseki: bōdō toshigerira-sen no jissō* (Tokyo: Naikaku kanbō naikaku chōsa-shitsu, 1968), chap. Preface.
7. Hayakawa Takashi, "hanzai bōshi kihon taisaku yōkō," *Saiken* 15, no. 3 (March 1961): 23.
8. Other incidents include the attempted murders of Socialist Party Leader Kawakami Jōtarō on June 17 1960, former Prime Minister Kishi on July 15 of the same year. The Furyu mutan incident of 1 February 1961, in which a right-wing youth murdered the maid

and critically injured the wife of *Chūō Kōrōn* President Shimanaka Hoji, after the magazine published a short story that featured the beheading of the emperor, empress and the rest of the royal family. Shimanaka was the target but was not at home at the time of the attack. See Nick Kapur, *Japan at the Crossroads: Conflict and Compromise after Anpo* (Harvard University Press, 2018), 251–62,

9. Hayakawa Takashi, "hanzai bōshi no kihon taisaku," *Saiken* 15, no. 3 (March 1961): 20.
10. Hayakawa, "Hanzai bōshi kihon taisaku yōkō," 23.
11. Ibid., 24.
12. Hayakawa Takashi, "Ika ni shite bōryoku o tsuihō subeki ka," *Seisaku Geppō* 64, no. 99 (May 1961): 4–7.
13. Kapur, *Japan at the Crossroads: Conflict and Compromise after Anpo*, 255. Peter J. Katzenstein, *Cultural Norms and National Security: Police and Military in Postwar Japan*, Cornell Studies in Political Economy (Cornell University Press, 1996), 78–79.
14. Tōgakuren shoki-kyokku, "10 12, 10 18-to-gaku ren no kyōryokuna tatakai de sei bōhō no kokkai shingi o funsai sei yo! (tsūtatsu)," in *Shiryō: Sengo Gakusei Undō Shi 6*, ed. Mitanishobo henshu-bu (Tokyo: Mitanishobo, 1969), 97.
15. Miyauchi Hiroshi, "Anpo taisei to chian seisaku" (Tokyo: Rōdō junpō-sha, 1966), 148. See also Katzenstein, *Cultural Norms and National Security: Police and Military in Postwar Japan*, 78.
16. Kapur, *Japan at the Crossroads: Conflict and Compromise after Anpo*, 225. See also Katzenstein, *Cultural Norms and National Security: Police and Military in Postwar Japan*, 78–79.
17. Kapur, *Japan at the Crossroads: Conflict and Compromise after Anpo*, 224.
18. "Rinji shihō seido chōsa-kai setchi-ho," Pub. L. No. 122 (1962), https://hourei.ndl.go.jp/simple/detail?lawId=0000053917&current=-1., Article 4.
19. The full report was published in "Tokushū: rinji shihō seidō chōsa-kai iken-sho," *Jurisuto*, no. 307 (September 1964).
20. Nihon bengoshi rengōkai, *Rinji shihō seido chōsa-kai iken-sho hihan* (Tokyo: Nihon bengoshi rengōkai, 1967), 16. The Tokyo Bar Association made similar points in their earlier criticism of the report, see Tōkyō bengoshikai, *Rinji shihō seido chōsa-kai iken-sho hihan* (Tokyo: Tōkyō bengoshikai, 1965), 73–75. For a more

charitable interpretation see the discussions in "Tokushū: rinji shihō seido chōsa-kai iken-sho."

21. For the smoothing of relations between the US and Japan during the Ikeda years see Nick Kapur, "Mending the 'Broken Dialogue': U.S.-Japan Alliance Diplomacy in the Aftermath of the 1960 Security Treaty Crisis," *Diplomatic History* 41, no. 3 (January 31, 2017): 489 517.
22. Oguchi Takashi, "Achieving Safe Road Traffic—The Experience in Japan," *IATSS Research* 39, no. 2 (2016): 110–16.
23. Frank K. Upham, *Law and Social Change in Postwar Japan* (Cambridge, Mass.: Harvard University Press, 1987), 35.
24. Kurata, *Shinsayoku undō zenshi*, 138–72.
25. William Marotti, "AHR Forum Japan 1968: The Performance of Violence and the Theater of Protest," *The American Historical Review* 114, no. 1 (2009): 103.
26. Ibid., 129–30.
27. For example Murai Jun, a veteran of the prewar Home Ministry and the first chief of both the Security Division of the National Regional Headquarters (1948) and the Cabinet Research Office (1952), wrote that, along with youth crime and corruption, the revolutionary energy of student radicals was one of the three main threats to peace and security in late 1960s Japan, but the JCP could, like the student vanguard, turn to violent insurrectionism in their effort to destroy Japanese society at any moment. 'I believe that we must be courageous and responsible in decisively eliminating any and all movements that make the Japanese people miserable.' See Murai Jun, "Shin kyokumen o mukaeta chian taisaku," *Dōkō*, no. 1267 (January 1968): 65–73.
28. "1970-nen o mezasu gakusei undō (Kōanchōsachō Shiryō 'wagakuni No Kyōsan Shugi Undō No Sho Dōkō' Yori)," *Keisatsugaku Ronshū* 21, no. 1 (January 1968): 165.
29. Ibid., 178.
30. Ibid., 178–79.
31. Aoki Hisa, "Shihōkisha zadankai: tōdai saiban," *Hōgaku Seminā*, no. 163 (September 1969): 137.
32. "Sōjōzai tekiyō mo: sanpakei zengakuren ni Akama hōsōdan," *Yomiuri Shimbun*, April 2, 1968.
33. This change in prosecutorial policy towards student unrest is discussed in Aoki, "Shihōkisha zadankai: tōdai saiban," 137.

34. Takeuchi Juhei, "Keijiseisakuteki kōryo," *Tsumu to Batsu* 5, no. 4 (1968): 2–4.
35. Marotti, "AHR Forum Japan 1968: The Performance of Violence and the Theater of Protest," 133.
36. "Sōran-zai tekiyō no shinjuku demo," *Hōritsu Kōron* 185, no. 17 (December 1968): 72–76.
37. Naikaku kanbō naikaku chōsa-shitsu, *1970-nen ni shōten o awaseta kokunai sōdō ni kansuru yosō to sho bunseki: bōdō toshigerira-sen no jissō*.
38. "Shinjuku jiken de hatsu hanketsu tōkaidai-sei ni shikkō yūyo/ tōkyō chisai," *Yomiuri Shimbun*, March 14, 1969.
39. "Sōrantaisaku ni banzen wo kise," *Yomiuri Shimbun*, October 23, 1968.
40. "Seikai memo: daigaku mondaikon, kitai atsumete hassoku e," *Yomiuri Shimbun*, November 11, 1968.
41. "70nen no chian taisaku, shinkyokumen ni 'yobizai' rippo o," *Yomiuri Shimbun*, October 23, 1968. The draft legislation read: 'A person who, with the intent to commit the offence of rioting, conspires with two or more persons to assemble a large crowd or to prepare a weapon, shall be punished with imprisonment or imprisonment with hard labour for a term not exceeding three years.'
42. Nakata Naoto, "'Tōdai saiban' to shihō no handō-ka," *Zen'ei*, no. 302 (December 1969): 211–24.
43. "Tokushū bōsō suru gakusei undō to chian taisaku," *Keizai Jidai* 33, no. 12 (December 1968): 16.
44. Funada Naka, "Gakusei bōdō taisaku shian—naniyori mo hō chitsujo sonchō no tettei kara," *Keizai Jidai* 33, no. 12 (December 1968): 17–19.
45. Sakada Michita, "Kageki gakusei undō ni genjuna torishimari o," *Keizai Jidai* 33, no. 12 (December 1968): 22.
46. Kitaoka Juitsu, "Shinjuku gakusei sōran to sono haikei," *Keizai Jidai* 33, no. 12 (December 1968): 32–34.
47. Donald Frederick Wheeler, "The Japanese Student Movement: Value Politics, Student Politics and the Tokyo University Struggle" (1974).
48. Kosugi Ryōko, "Zenkyōtō to wa nandatta no ka: tōdaitōsō ni okeru sankasha no kaishaku to imizuke ni chakumoku shite," *Ōhara Shakaimondai Kenkyūjo Zasshi* 697 (2016): 33–48.

49. Sutoraiki jikkōsengen, Tōdaitōsō zengaku kyōtōkaigi, ed., *Toride no ue ni wareranosekai o: dokyumento tōdaitōsō* (Tokyo: Aki shobō, 1969), 25.
50. Igakka sotsugyōshiken ni kan suru tsūchi. Ibid., 26–27.
51. For an account of this 'Harumi incident' see *Harumi-jiken no keika* in document p. 29. Medical schools staff argued that students had entered the building and disrupted the peace of the hospital. Students on the other hand claimed that after approaching faculty they had been attacked. Harumi Kenichi an assistant tutor at the hospital, had been particularly vigorous in his 'defence' of the professors. Students claim they were eventually invited into the hospital for a discussion, but when they arrived at the designated room it was empty, and they were set upon once again by staff who accused the students of attacking professors.
52. Guy Thomas Yasko, "The Japanese Student Movement 1968–70: The Zenkyoto Uprising" (1997), 14.
53. For example, Shima Taizō, *Yasuda kōdō: 1968–1969* (Tokyo: Chūōkōronshinsha, 2005).
54. Ryōko Kosugi, *Tōdaitōsō no katari: shakai undō no yoji to senryaku* (Tokyo: Shin'yōsha, 2018), 147.
55. Ibid., 150.
56. Shima, *Yasuda kōdō: 1968–1969*, 52–53.
57. Tōdaitōsō zengaku kyōtōkaigi, *Toride no ue ni wareranosekai o: dokyumento tōdaitōsō*, 69–70.
58. Shima, *Yasuda kōdō: 1968–1969*, 56.
59. Oguma Eiji, *1968: Wakamono-tachi no hanran to sono haikei* (Tokyo: Shin'yōsha, 2009), 711–13.
60. Ibid., 712.
61. Zengaku tōsō rengō (daigakuin), "Yōkyū kantetsu made kōdōnai mukigen tōgishūkai wo!," in *Toride no ue ni wareranosekai o: dokyumento tōdaitōsō* (Tokyo: Aki shobō, 1969), 85.
62. Tōdaitōsō zengaku kyōtōkaigi, ed., "Kyōtō kaigi nyūsu no. 1," in *Toride no ue ni warera no sekai o: dokyumento tōdaitōsō* (Tokyo: Aki Shobō, 1969), 112.
63. Tōdaitōsō zengaku kyōtōkaigi, *Toride no ue ni wareranosekai o: dokyumento tōdaitōsō*, 125.
64. Oguma, *1968: Wakamono-tachi no hanran to sono haikei*, 753.
65. Ibid.

66. Tōdai tōsō zengaku kyōtō kaigi, "Daigaku tōkyoku no 'saishu hōshin' ni tai suru ware ware no taido," in *Toride no ue ni wareranosekai o: dokyumento tōdaitōsō*, ed. Tōdai tōsō zengaku kyōtō kaigi (Tokyo: Aki Shobo, 1969), 126–30.
67. Zengaku joshu kyōtō kaigi, 25 August 1968. *Gakusei fuzai no daigaku. 8.10 Kōkoku hihan.* In Tōdaitōsō zengaku kyōtōkaigi, *Toride no ue ni wareranosekai o: dokyumento tōdaitōsō*, 131–38.
68. Zengaku joshu kyōtō kaigi, "Gakusei fuzai no daigaku. 8.10 kōkoku hihan," ed. Tōdaitōsō zengaku (Tokyo: Aki shobo, 1969), 131–37.
69. Shima, *Yasuda kōdō: 1968–1969*, 86–87.
70. "Igakubu-chō kan-zume 5-jikan kakuzai-te ni 'taishūdankō' tōdai igakubu honkan mo fūsa," *Yomiuri Shimbun*, August 29, 1968.
71. Tōdaitōsō zengaku kyōtōkaigi, *Toride no ue ni wareranosekai o: dokyumento tōdaitōsō*, 153.
72. "Yomiuri Sunpyō," *Yomiuri Shinbun*, August 30, 1969.
73. "'Miyoshi' tōdai de taiho honsha kisha bōkō jiken shifuku keikan ne komi osou/ keishichō," *Yomiuri Shinbun*, October 14, 1968.
74. "Gakusei shidō o tsuyomeru monbushō no daigaku taisaku," *Asahi Shimbun*, August 30, 1968.
75. Kosugi, *Tōdaitōsō no katari: shakai undō no yoji to senryaku*, 157.
76. Shima, *Yasuda kōdō: 1968–1969*, 89–92.
77. Kosugi, "Zenkyōtō towa nandatta no ka: tōdaitōsō ni okeru sankasha no kaishaku to imizuke ni chakumoku shite," 42. p. 42.
78. "Ōkōchi sōchō no 'hansei to shokai' zen'yō kiroku 'gakusei shokun e'," *Asahi Shimbun*, November 2, 1969.
79. "Shasetsu: ōkōchi sōchō no jinin to daigaku funsō," *Asahi Shimbun*, November 3, 1969.
80. Tōdaitōsō zengaku kyōtōkaigi, *Toride no ue ni wareranosekai o: dokyumento tōdaitōsō*, 248.
81. Shima, *Yasuda Kōdō: 1968–1969*, 129–30.
82. Hiroshi Nagasaki, "On the Japanese'68," in *The Red Years: Theory, Politics, and Aesthetics in the Japanese'68*, ed. Gavin Walker (London: Verso, 2020), 18.
83. Kosugi, *Tōdaitōsō No Katari: Shakai Undō No Yoji to Senryaku*, 231–33.
84. Ibid., 238.

85. These groups were known to Zenkyōtō as 'outsider forces' (*gaijin butai*) were directed by the JCP, who had set up a command post in an inn just outside the main entrance to the campus. Ibid., 242.
86. Ibid., 245–50.
87. Ibid., 255.
88. Asahi Shimbun 1969, "Monbushō to tōdai yūgata hanashiai byushi nado: tōdai funsō," *Asahi Shimbun*, January 14, 1969.
89. Arikura Ryōkichi, *Kenpōchitsujo no hoshō* (Tokyo: Nihonhyōron-sha, 1969).
90. "Kyō no shūkai hiraku: katōdaikō ga seimei," *Asahi Shimbun*, January 10, 1969.
91. Kosugi, *Tōdaitōsō no katari: shakai undō no yoji to senryaku*, 267.
92. Tōdaitōsō zengaku kyōtōkaigi, *Toride no ue ni wareranosekai o: dokyumento tōdaitōsō*, 496.
93. *Tōdai* tōdaitōsō bengodan, *1. 18, 19 Tōsō saiban bōtō chinjutsu-sho* (Tokyo: Jiritsu-sha, 1970), 161.
94. Shima, *Yasuda kōdō: 1968–1969*, 221–23.
95. *Tōdai* bengodan *1. 18, 19 Tōsō saiban bōtō chinjutsu-sho*, 163.
96. Ibid., 164.
97. Nick Kapur, *Japan at the Crossroads, Conflict and Compromise after Anpo* (Cambridge, Mass.: Harvard University Press, 2018), op. 153. According to Oguma Eiji between the occupation of Yasuda Auditorium in July 1968 and the declaration of complete occupation of the university that autumn, the movement became about 'self-expression and self-negation'. Oguma makes clear the differentiation with what he sees as politics proper: 'The desperate defence of Yasuda Auditorium, even if political suicide, became a method of self-expression'. Oguma, *1968: wakamono-tachi no hanran to sono haikei*, 909.
98. Nagasaki, "On the Japanese'68."
99. Kosugi, "Zenkyōtō to wa nandatta no ka: tōdaitōsō ni okeru sankasha no kaishaku to imizuke ni chakumoku shite," 46. Kosugi draws on the work of Ron Eyerman and Andrew Jamison. See: Ron Eyerman and Andrew Jamison, *Social Movements: A Cognitive Approach* (Pennsylvania: The Pennsylvania State University Press, 1991).
100. Ando Takemasa, *Japan's New Left Movements: Legacies for Civil Society* (Abingdon: Routledge, 2014).
101. Ibid., 73.

102. For Yoshimoto Taka'aki see: Lawrence Olson, "Intellectuals and 'The People'; On Yoshimoto Takaaki," *Journal of Japanese Studies* 4, no. 2 (July 1, 1978): 327–57.
103. Guy Thomas Yasko, *The Japanese Student Movement 1968–70*, 1997, 78–79.
104. Cited in Kurata, *Shinsayoku undō zenshi*, 205. Also in Takazawa Kōji, *Rekishi toshite no shinsayoku* (Tokyo: Shinsen-sha, 1996), 37.
105. Chelsea Szendi Schieder, "Human Liberation of 'Male Romance'? The Gendered Everyday of the Student New Left," in *The Red Years: Theory, Politics, an Aesthetics in the Japanese'68*, ed. Gavin Walker (London: Verso, 2020), 143–59. As Schieder and Shigematsu both argue, however, these new roles were still governed by hegemonic gender norms. Setsu Shigematsu, *Scream from the Shadows: The Women's Liberation Movement in Japan* (University of Minnesota Press, 2012).
106. This essay is reproduced in Tokoro Mitsuko, *Waga ai to haran* (Tokyo: Zen'ei-sha, 1969).
107. Ferran de Vargas, "Japanese New Left's Political Theories of Subjectivity and Ōshima Nagisa's Practice of Cinema," *Positions: Asia Critique* 30, no. 4 (2022): 686–87.
108. Ando, *Japan's New Left Movements: Legacies for Civil Society*, 74.
109. Tōdai zenkyōtō and Komaba kyōtō kaigi, eds., *Kutsujoku no maisō* (Tokyo: Aki shobō, 1970), 269. One of the most infamous examples of student disdain for postwar liberal intellectuals was their treatment of perhaps the most representative of that generation: Maruyama Masao. See Rikki Kersten, "The Intellectual Culture of Postwar Japan and the 1968–1969 University of Tokyo Struggles: Repositioning the Self in Postwar Thought," *Social Science Japan Journal* 12, no. 2 (November 18, 2009): 227–45.
110. Ando, *Japan's New Left Movements: Legacies for Civil Society*, 75–76. It is important to note that this commitment to gewalt formed an important part the criticism levelled at the New Left by the feminist activists who would go on to form ūman ribu. These thinkers saw commitment to violent action as an expression of a 'masculine logic of productivity' which simply reproduced the gendered norms of postwar Japanese society in a different form. See Shigematsu, *Scream from the Shadows: The Women's Liberation Movement in Japan*.

111. Cited in Wheeler, "The Japanese Student Movement: Value Politics, Student Politics and the Tokyo University Struggle," 368. See also Ferran De Vargas, "Throwing Ideology Away: Yoshimoto Takaaki's Theory of Taishū and Terayama Shūji's Film Parody of the People," *Japan Forum*, 2023, 1–20.
112. Nagasaki, "On the Japanese'68," 31.

References

"1970-nen o mezasu gakusei undō (kōanchōsachō shiryō 'wagakuni no kyōsan shugi undō no sho dōkō' yori)." *Keisatsugaku Ronshū* 21, no. 1 (January 1968): 157–79.

Ando, Takemasa. *Japan's New Left Movements: Legacies for Civil Society*. Abingdon: Routledge, 2014.

Aoki, Hisa. "Shihōkisha zadankai: tōdai saiban." *Hōgaku Seminā*, no. 163 (September 1969): 136–51.

Arikura, Ryōkichi. *Kenpōchitsujo no hoshō*. Tokyo: Nihonhyōron-sha, 1969.

Asahi Shimbun. "Gakusei shidō o tsuyomeru monbushō no daigaku taisaku." August 30, 1968.

Asahi Shimbun. "Kyō no shūkai hiraku: katōdaikō ga seimei." January 10, 1969.

Asahi Shimbun. "Monbushō to todai yugata hanashiai byushi nado: todai funso." January 14, 1969.

Asahi Shimbun. "Ōkouchi sōchō no 'hansei to shokai' zen'yō kiroku 'gakusei shokun e'." November 2, 1969.

Asahi Shimbun. "Shasetsu: ōkōchi sōchō no jinin to daigaku funsō." November 3, 1969.

Tōdaitōsō bengodan. *Tōdai 1. 18, 19 tōsō saiban bōtō chinjutsu-sho*. Tokyo: Jiritsu-sha, 1970.

Tōkyō bengoshikai. *Rinji shihō seido chōsa-kai iken-sho hihan*. Tokyo: Tōkyō bengoshikai, 1965.

Chiavacci, David. "From Class Struggle to General Middle-Class Society to Divided Society: Societal Models of Inequality in Postwar Japan." *Social Science Japan Journal* 11, no. 1 (June 10, 2008): 5–27.

———. "The Social Basis of Developmental Capitalism in Japan: From Post-War Mobilization to Current Stress Symptoms and Future Disintegration." *Asian Business & Management* 6, no. 1 (2007): 35–55.

Estevez-Abe, Margarita. *Welfare and Capitalism in Postwar Japan*. Cambridge: Cambridge University Press, 2008.

Eyerman, Ron, and Andrew Jamison. *Social Movements: A Cognitive Approach*. Pennsylvania: The Pennsylvania State University Press, 1991.

Funada, Naka. "Gakusei bōdō taisaku shian—naniyori mo hō chitsujo sonchō no tettei kara." *Keizai Jidai* 33, no. 12 (December 1968): 17–19.
Hayakawa, Takashi. "Hanzai bōshi kihon taisaku yōkō." *Saiken* 15, no. 3 (March 1961): 23–26.
———. "Hanzai bōshi no kihon taisaku." *Saiken* 15, no. 3 (March 1961): 20–22.
———. "Ika ni shite bōryoku o tsuihō subeki ka." *Seisaku Geppō* 64, no. 99 (May 1961): 4–7.
Iida, Yumiko. *Rethinking Identity in Modern Japan, Nationalism as Aesthetics.* London: Routledge, 2005.
Juhei, Takeuchi. "Keijiseisakuteki kōryo." *Tsumu to Batsu* 5, no. 4 (1968).
Tōdai tōsō zengaku kyōtō kaigi. "Daigaku tōkyoku no 'saishu hōshin' ni tai suru ware ware no taido." In *Toride no ue ni wareranosekai o: dokyumento tōdaitōsō*, edited by Tōdai tōsō zengaku kyōtō kaigi, 126–30. Tokyo: Aki Shobo, 1969.
Zengaku joshu kyōtō kaigi. "Gakusei fuzai no daigaku. 8.10 kōkoku hihan." In Toride no ue ni wareranosekai o: dokyumento tōdaitōsō, edited by Tōdai tōsō zengaku kyōtō kaigi, 131–137 Tokyo: Aki Shobo, 1969.
Kapur, Nick. *Japan at the Crossroads: Conflict and Compromise after Anpo.* Harvard University Press, 2018.
———. *Japan at the Crossroads, Conflict and Compromise after Anpo.* Cambridge, Mass.: Harvard University Press, 2018.
———. "Mending the 'Broken Dialogue': U.S.-Japan Alliance Diplomacy in the Aftermath of the 1960 Security Treaty Crisis." *Diplomatic History* 41, no. 3 (January 31, 2017): 489 517.
Katzenstein, Peter J. *Cultural Norms and National Security: Police and Military in Postwar Japan.* Cornell Studies in Political Economy. Cornell University Press, 1996.
Kersten, Rikki. "The Intellectual Culture of Postwar Japan and the 1968–1969 University of Tokyo Struggles: Repositioning the Self in Postwar Thought." *Social Science Japan Journal* 12, no. 2 (November 18, 2009): 227–45.
Kitaoka, Juitsu. "Shinjuku Gakusei Sōran to Sono Haikei." *Keizai Jidai* 33, no. 12 (December 1968): 32–34.
Kosugi, Ryōko. *Tōdaitōsō no katari: shakai undō no yoji to senryaku.* Tokyo: Shin'yōsha, 2018.
———. "Zenkyōtō to wa nandatta no ka: tōdaitōsō ni okeru sankasha no kaishaku to imizuke ni chakumoku shite." *Ōhara shakaimondai kenkyūjo zasshi* 697 (2016): 33–48.
Kurata, Kazunari. *Shinsayoku undō zenshi.* Tokyo: Ryūdō shuppan, 1978.
Togakuren shoki-kyokku. "10 12, 10 18-to-gakuren no kyōryoku na tatakai de seibōhō no kokkai shingi o funsai sei yo! (Tsūtatsu)." In *Shiryō: Sengo Gakusei Undō Shi 6*, edited by Mitanishobo henshu-bu. Tokyo: Mitanishobo, 1969.

Marotti, William. "AHR Forum Japan 1968: The Performance of Violence and the Theater of Protest." *The American Historical Review* 114, no. 1 (2009): 97 135.

Mitsuko, Tokoro. *Waga ai to haran*. Tokyo: Zen'ei-sha, 1969.

Miyauchi, Hiroshi. "Anpo taisei to chian seisaku." Tokyo: Rōdō junpō-sha, 1966.

Murai, Jun. "Shin kyokumen o mukaeta chian taisaku." *Dōkō*, no. 1267 (January 1968): 65–73.

Nagasaki, Hiroshi. "On the Japanese '68." In *The Red Years: Theory, Politics, and Aesthetics in the Japanese '68*, edited by Gavin Walker, 12–37. London: Verso, 2020.

Nakata, Naoto. "'Tōdai saiban' to shihō no handō-ka." *Zen'ei*, no. 302 (December 1969): 211–24.

Oguchi, Takashi. "Achieving Safe Road Traffic—The Experience in Japan." *IATSS Research* 39, no. 2 (2016): 110–16.

Oguma, Eiji. *1968: Wakamono-tachi no hanran to sono haikei*. Tokyo: Shin'yōsha, 2009.

Olson, Lawrence. "Intellectuals and 'The People'; On Yoshimoto Takaaki." *Journal of Japanese Studies* 4, no. 2 (July 1, 1978): 327–57.

Nihon bengoshi rengōkai. *Rinji shihō seido chōsa-kai iken-sho hihan*. Tokyo: Nihon bengoshi rengōkai, 1967.

Rinji shihō seido chōsa-kai setchi-hō, Pub. L. No. 122 (1962). https://hourei.ndl.go.jp/simple/detail?lawId=0000053917&;current=-1.

Sakada, Michita. "Kageki gakusei undō ni genjūna torishimari o." *Keizai Jidai* 33, no. 12 (December 1968): 22–23.

Schieder, Chelsea Szendi. "Human Liberation of 'Male Romance'? The Gendered Everyday of the Student New Left." In *The Red Years: Theory, Politics, an Aesthetics in the Japanese '68*, edited by Gavin Walker, 143–59. London: Verso, 2020.

Shigematsu, Setsu. *Scream from the Shadows: The Women's Liberation Movement in Japan*. University of Minnesota Press, 2012.

Shima, Taizō. *Yasuda kōdō: 1968 - 1969*. Tokyo: Chūōkōronshinsha, 2005.

Naikaku kanbō naikaku chōsa-shitsu. *1970-nen ni shōten o awaseta kokunai sōdō ni kansuru yosō to sho bunseki: bōdō toshigerira-sen no jissō*. Tokyo: Naikaku kanbō naikaku chōsa-shitsu, 1968.

"Sōran-zai tekiyō no shinjuku demo." *Hōritsu Kōron* 185, no. 17 (December 1968): 72–76.

Takazawa, Kōji . *Rekishi toshite no shinsayoku*. Tokyo: Shinsen-sha, 1996.

Tōdaitōsō zengaku kyōtōkaigi, ed. "Kyōtō kaigi nyūsu no. 1." In *Toride no ue ni warera no sekai o: dokyumento tōdaitōsō*, 112. Tokyo: Aki Shobō, 1969.

———, ed. *Toride no ue ni wareranosekai o: dokyumento tōdaitōsō*. Tokyo: Aki shobō, 1969.

"Tokushū bōsō suru gakusei undō to chian taisaku." *Keizai Jidai* 33, no. 12 (December 1968): 16.
"Tokushū: rinji shihō seido chōsa-kai iken-sho." *Jurisuto*, no. 307 (September 1964).
Upham, Frank K. *Law and Social Change in Postwar Japan*. Cambridge, Mass.: Harvard University Press, 1987.
Vargas, Ferran de. "Japanese New Left's Political Theories of Subjectivity and Ōshima Nagisa's Practice of Cinema." *Positions: Asia Critique* 30, no. 4 (2022): 679–703.
———. "Throwing Ideology Away: Yoshimoto Takaaki's Theory of Taishū and Terayama Shūji's Film Parody of the People." *Japan Forum*, 2023, 1–20.
Wheeler, Donald Frederick. "The Japanese Student Movement: Value Politics, Student Politics and the Tokyo University Struggle," 1974.
Yasko, Guy Thomas. *The Japanese Student Movement 1968–70*, 1997.
———. "The Japanese Student Movement 1968–70: The Zenkyoto Uprising," 1997.
Yomiuri Shimbun. "70-nen no chian taisaku, shinkyokumen ni 'yobizai' rippo wo." October 23, 1968.
Yomiuri Shimbun. "Igakubu-chō kan-zume 5-jikan kakuzai-te ni 'taishūdankō' tōdai igakubu honkan mo fūsa." August 29, 1968.
Yomiuri Shimbun. "Seikai memo: daigaku mondaikon, kitai atsumete hassoku e." November 11, 1968.
Yomiuri Shimbun. "Shinjuku jiken de hatsu hanketsu tōkaidai-sei ni shikkō yūyo/ tōkyō chisai." March 14, 1969.
Yomiuri Shimbun. "Sōjōzai tekiyō mo: sanpakei zengakuren ni akama hōsōdan." April 2, 1968.
Yomiuri Shimbun. "Sōrantaisaku ni banzen wo kise." October 23, 1968.
Yomiuri Shinbun. "'Miyoshi' tōdai de taiho honsha kisha bōkō jiken shifuku keikan ne komi osou/ keishichō." October 14, 1968.
Yomiuri Shinbun. "Yomiuri sunpyō." August 30, 1969.
Zengaku tōsō rengō (daigakuin). "Yōkyū kantetsu made kōdōnai mukigen tōgishūkai wo!" In *Toride No Ue Ni Wareranosekai o: dokyumento tōdaitōsō*, 85. Tokyo: Aki shobō, 1969.
Tōdai Zenkyōtō and Komaba kyōtō kaigi, eds. *Kutsujoku no maisō*. Tokyo: Aki shobō, 1970.

CHAPTER 4

Mass Arrest, Mass Prosecution, Mass Detention

This chapter examines the immediate aftermath of the Tokyo University struggle. Progressing broadly chronologically, the chapter first documents the initial strategies of police and prosecutors in the detention and interrogation of students, and how the students' support groups, which included a group of roughly 50 young lawyers, attempted to document, contest, and offer support to those detainees. Very early on it became clear that with this incident came a sea-change in prosecutorial and judicial approaches to student unrest, leading to not only the biggest indictment for a single incident in Japanese history, but also a significant change in the court's attitudes towards detention and bail requirements for students. Students who complied with prosecutors in confessing their crimes and appearing before a judge under state appointed representation—students who became known as the *hansei gumi*, or repentant group—were processed quickly and received suspended sentences in demonstrations of 'benevolent paternalism' on behalf of the judiciary.[1] Those who resisted the process, however, found their applications for bail repeatedly denied under the aegis of the court's 'governance'—a term that seemed to signal the courts' new active role in managing the students as a problematic moral community. As the trials of the repentant group began, the students' legal team challenged the legitimacy of the courts by arguing they were now an extension of Japan' security apparatus.

C. Perkins, *The Tokyo University Trial and the Struggle Against Order in Postwar Japan*, New Directions in East Asian History,
https://doi.org/10.1007/978-981-99-7043-8_4

Surveying the Aftermath

Since the riot police had been used to break a six-month students strike at Sophia (Jōchi) University in December 1968 and with Katō Ichirō taking a firmer stance in negotiations, Zenkyōtō had envisaged the need for a support group for what now seemed like an inevitable wave of arrests. After numerous discussions Zenkyōtō resolved to establish a relief organisation (Zenkyōtō kyūtai-bu), whose role would be to prevent the arrests of students; minimise the impact of detention on those students who were arrested; develop legal strategy for courtroom battles; and gain knowledge about conditions in prison. This organisation originally comprised of students belonging to the Law Department Zenkyōtō Council and was established to supersede and absorb already existing support groups established in the wake of the Yomiuri Journalist Incident. The new relief organisation began activities in earnest after the arrest of 142 Zenkyōtō students at the Seven Department Rally (*nana gakubu shūkai*) at Chichubunomiya rugby ground on 10 January 1969. Soon the Zenkyōtō kyūtai organisation moved under the umbrella of the newly established Tokyo University Struggle Unified Relief Headquarters (Tōdaitōsō tōitsu kyūtai honbu, Tōitsu kyūtai), which had been set up to reach beyond Zenkyōtō to all organisations and private citizens with a connection to the incident and which, along with non-sect radicals, was comprised of the various faction support groups.[2] Tōitsu kyūtai split their work into six areas: medical relief, legal support, financial support, information dissemination, external relations, and record taking.

As with its support infrastructure, Zenkyōtō had also been developing a relationship with a group of around 50 mostly young lawyers, who Zenkyōtō had been inviting for campus visits since November of 1968. On the night of January 18th as the battle between Zenkyōtō students and riot police raged the lawyers, referred to as the Bengodan, called an emergency meeting. It was decided that night that the lawyers would begin the job of defending the students on campus the following morning. When the Bengodan attempted to gain access to the campus to document events and begin the work of talking to their clients on the 19th, however, they were met with resistance by the university authorities. They were first greeted by an assistant to Acting President Katō, Professor Sakamoto Yoshikazu, who urged the team to 'act as a link between the university and the students to persuade them not to act in vain'.[3] After refusing to do any such thing the Bengodan set up shop at an inn close to campus where they received a phone call from Professor Hirano Ryūichi, an expert in criminal law who would later succeed Professor Katō as Dean of the Faculty of Law.[4] After some negotiation, the lawyers were invited to a meeting with Professor Hirano, who from 1 p.m. pursued doggedly the question of whether the legal team were in fact the students' lawyers and if so whether there was any documentary evidence to prove the students had requested their presence. By 4.30 p.m. the lawyers convinced Professor Hirano that their presence was legitimate and were allowed to enter the campus via its famous Red Gate.[5] By that time, however, the Tokyo University struggle was over. Students were either being detained by the police or, in cases of injury, transported to the university hospital where they received treatment before being moved to police medical centres or holding cells.

By the January 18th and 19th showdown with the riot police, Tōitsu kyūtai had already started fundraising efforts (known as *kanpa,* a Japanese transliteration and contraction of the Russian word kampaniya, or campaign).[6] An account of fundraising outcomes in the February 1969 edition of their publication *Kyūtai nyūsu* (Relief News) gives a sense of the methods of fundraising and the scale of the expenditures. Sources of income included fundraising efforts at train stations, collecting funds from attendees at public gatherings, taking donations from the various affiliated factions, and income generated from publications. The costliest expense was retaining the Bengodan, to which Tōitsu kyūtai were initially paying 10,000 yen per detainee in total for their first and second consultations, a figure they noted was in keeping with general expectations for legal fees but which they could not hope to sustain for long (Table 4.1).

For the first few months, the budgets of Tōitsu kyūtai and Zenkyōtō kyūtai were combined. But differences between the component organisations within the support groups soon made this approach untenable. The issue revolved around the question of bail. The political factions had by this time already adopted a strategy of complete rejection of any cooperation with the courts, and as such the question of bail was moot. But Zenkyōtō kyūtai were—and would continue to be—concerned with securing the release of detainees as quickly as possible and as such had focused on fundraising for bail for their members and non-sect aligned students from other universities.[9] Thus, in a reflection of this ideological tension, it was decided that the two budgets would be made independent of each other, and Zenkyōtō kyūtai, which attracted greater funding,

Table 4.1 Income and expenses for Tōitsu kyūtai February 1969[7]

Income		*Expenditure*	
Item	*Amount (yen)*	*Item*	*Amount (yen)*
City based fundraising	1,665,832	Bengodan fees	605,775
Individual donations	583,813	Medical treatment	199,925
Fundraising at student meetings	186,186	Supplies for detainees	478,305
Tokyo Zenkyōtō Support Group donations	510,613	Office Administration	504,705
Income from publications	212,705	Information campaign	457,775
Donations from various organisations	259,398	–	–
Contributions from various factions (tōha)	188,579	–	–
Sales of Shingeki[8]	63,924	Total Expenditure	2,246,485
Total Income	3,671,053	Balance	1,424,565

would allocate a quarter of its income to Tōitsu kyūtai. Individual donations came from people from all walks of life, some of whom donated a percentage of their monthly salaries to one or other of the organisations. A letter from one female supporter, published in *Kyūtai nyūsu* gives a sense of the motivations behind this support, which went beyond the obvious need for funding to encapsulate the importance of donation as a personal political act that brought the struggle into their own daily lives:

> Economic support for the struggle is one thing, but I think what is really necessary for each individual is to be involved in their own situation, such as how the reality of the Tokyo University struggle, other campus and corporate struggles, and anti-war individual struggles are mediated and materialize within themselves in various different environments, and how to universalize their essence [...] At the very least, those who are in a position to support the Tokyo University struggle, including myself, need to be constantly aware of and confirm what this act means to them, in other words, how far it expands within them, and how much of their own blood they are shedding.[10]

Fundraising efforts continued throughout 1969, with revenue streams being added as new publications were released, including the Prison Letters to be discussed later in this book, although donations from individuals such as the anonymous woman quoted above continued to represent the lion's share of income. Legal fees, administrative fees, and the war chest for bail accounted for most of the expenditure (see Table 4.2).

With fundraising efforts up and running, Tōitsu kyūtai and the Bengodan cooperated closely to develop a strategy for coping with the vast challenge of organising support, both legal and personal, for what was now over 700 student detainees. While the minutia of visitation, communication, and relief efforts were strategized, Tōitsu kyūtai and the Bengodan mobilised to survey the physical wellbeing and needs of the detainees, as well as the conditions in which they were being held. Early official reports put the number of injured at Tokyo University at thirty-five: thirty riot police, one student, and four bystanders.[12] When including policing of student actions at Ocha no mizu station the official casualty count rose to sixty-three: forty riot police (of whom two seriously injured), nine students (of which one seriously injured), and fourteen others including one journalist.[13] For a battle that continued over two days and involved upwards of ten thousand people these numbers were extremely conservative; and indeed investigations by the legal team raised serious questions about their veracity. From the evening of the 19th the legal team surveyed 'tens of hospitals', including police medical facilities, and concluded that the number of injured students alone totalled between 269 and 288. The majority of these injuries (109) were burns caused by tear gas which was either fired in canisters or was mixed in with the water used in the riot police's high-pressure water hoses.[14] 'At around 2:30 the riot police came for us', read one of many reports published in *Kyūtai nyūsu*:

> I was hit by a gas canister directly on my glasses. I don't know whether they were aiming for our eyes. It was a distance of 10 metres, but if felt like less. I couldn't open my right eye. My left eye was also blurry. Straight afterwards I took a gas canister to the leg. It hit my trousers and the liquid stuck to me. [The liquid] was then covered with water and soaked in. I was arrested five minutes later. It was dark so I don't know whether anyone witnessed my injuries. You can shoot gas in the air, but it felt like they were shooting horizontally.[15]

In some cases the extent and severity of these burns was such that in even in the deep cold of the Japanese winter students stripped off

Table 4.2 Income and expenditure of Zenkyōtō kyūtai and Tōitsu kyūtai 5/6/1969–28/7/1969)[11]

Income		*Expenditure*	
Item	*Amount (yen)*	*Item*	*Amount (yen)*
City based fundraising	1,315,698	Bengodan fees	1,080,000
Individual donations	4,859,962	Medical treatment	192,288
Fundraising at student meetings	417,988	Supplies for detainees	130,569
Donations from various organisations	650,018	Office Administration	561,093
Contributions from various factions (tōha)	16,500	Bail fund	1,650,000
Sales of Shingeki	106,372	Funds allocated to Zenkyōtō	580,000
General Income	57,894	–	–
		Total Expenditure	4,193,950
Total Income	7,424,432	Balance	3,230,582

Zenkyōtō kyūtai income and expenditure (5/6/1969–28/7 1969)

Income (yen)		*Expenditure (yen)*	
City based fundraising	19,686	Bail fund	1,100,000
Individual donations	2,512,537	Office administration	175,812
Fundraising at student meetings	920	Medical treatment	8,821
Donations from various organisations	229,370	Supplies for detainees	33,880
Other income	357,815	Zenkyōtō struggle fund	337,000
		Bengodan fees	100,000
		Funds allocated to Tōitsu kyūtai	700,000
Total	3,126,328	Total	2,455,513

Tōitsu kyūtai income and expenditure (5/6/1969–28/7/1969)

Income (yen)		*Expenditure (yen)*	
Individual donations	431,345	Bengodan fees	500,000
Fundraising at student meetings	107,733	Supplies for detainees	48,660
Donations from various organisations	8,140	Office administration	564,736

(continued)

Table 4.2 (continued)

Tōitsu kyūtai income and expenditure (5/6/1969–28/7/1969)			
Income (yen)		*Expenditure (yen)*	
Other income	57,897	Funds for the defendant's organisation (hikokudan)	18,710
Funds from Zenkyōtō kyūtai	700,000		
Total	1,305,115	Total	1,132,106

their clothes so that the liquid was no longer touching their skin. In one case documented by journalists for the magazine Asahi Graph, a student presented with what was described as second and third degree burns over 33–35% of their body, which had blistered and were causing intense pain. Investigations by the same journal reported that the chemical used by the riot police was chloroacetophenone (otherwise known as CN), which was (and still is) the most toxic of the range of chemicals used as tear gas for crowd control.[16] Given that some arrested students were unable to wear their clothes due to their contamination, an early priority for Tōitsu kyūtai was supplying new underwear to the detainees.[17]

The injuries sustained by the students also included blunt trauma, lacerations, broken bones, and eye injuries.[18] But perhaps more disturbing were accounts from hospitalised students of post-arrest police violence. It is of course impossible to verify these accounts, of which the students support groups claimed there were seventy-seven, but their records are remarkably detailed and consistent in pointing to a pattern of beatings post-arrest using riot shields, led pipes, and rocks. For example, one of the more egregious, but by no means unique, accounts read:

> Near the Yasuda Auditorium, 10 members of the 4th riot police at the time of the arrest took turns to beat [the student] with iron pipes and pieces of wood, resulting in bruised eyelids and lacerations, approximately 20 stitches.[19]

Students were initially spread over forty-seven police stations before being distributed to detention centres on the western outskirts of Tokyo. As discussed in Chapter 2, the Constitution guaranteed the 'immediate privilege to counsel' for anyone arrested or detained on suspicion of an offence (Article 34) and maintained that right to counsel through the trial process (Article 37). Defendants were also explicitly protected from self-incrimination, and any confession 'made under compulsion, torture or threat, or after prolonged arrest or detention shall not be admitted in evidence' (Article 38). In response to these provisions, the 1949 Attorneys Act (*Bengoshi-hō*) entrusted lawyers 'with the mission of protecting fundamental human rights and achieving social justice', requiring that they perform their 'duties in good faith and endeavour to maintain the social order and improve the legal system' (Article 1). Notwithstanding these Constitutional guarantees, when the lawyers located the students, they found it hard to meet with them. The Bengodan claimed that police employed a range of procedural methods—such as asking for proof that they had been instructed—to maximise the amount of time alone with the suspects: time which was used to convince the students to make a confession. Volunteers who had flocked to the Tōitsu kyūtai Support Centre and then to the holding centres strove to communicate and support a strategy of exercising the right to silence (*mokuhiken*) during interrogation.[20] However, they too reported often finding it impossible to contact their arrested comrades and met with intimidation from the police. One volunteer recounted later that on delivering supplies to women detained at Kikuyabashi and Itabashi police stations the police did all they could to turn her away while also questioning her relationship with the women in custody.[21]

As has been established in the literature on Japan's postwar prosecutors, confessions were and still are the gold standard of evidence for any successful prosecution, to the extent that prosecutors are reluctant to move to trial without them. Given the centrality of confessions it is no surprise that prosecutors have access to a wide range of tools to extract them.[22] Rules governing the admissibility of evidence and confessions are heavily weighted in favour of prosecutors and rules governing interrogation allow for suspects to be held for up to twenty-three days. While suspects have the right to silence they are also required to 'endure' interrogations, that can last tens of hours at a time.[23] Thus as legal scholar Daniel Foote has argued, while there is a right to silence, 'it exists within a framework where the suspect's cooperation historically has been expected and where confessions continue to play a central role in the vast majority of cases.'[24] Moreover, investigators will actively summarise suspects' statements, and in doing so shape them into coherent stories that suspects are then asked to sign.[25] Confessions are penned by prosecutors in a similar manner and will go through many drafts to iron out inconsistencies and contradictions with other sources of evidence before being incorporated into the final court dossier. There is no legal obligation to disclose these drafts to either the courts or the defence.[26] Due to the long periods of pre-indictment detention, lack of legal counsel, and relentless schedules of interrogation, suspects are rendered more likely to sign confessions even if they later deny their veracity in court.[27]

Yet, prior to the events at Tokyo University, standard police practice with students had been to hold them in detention for three days before release without charges. It is evident that the students arrested at Tokyo University expected the same treatment. It quickly became apparent, as their detention dragged on, however, that policy towards students had changed. An article in the Asahi Shimbun described the routine of interrogations as follows:

> Rise at 6 a.m. After washing and eating breakfast, there's a 20-minute workout followed by laundry. Interrogations begin around 10 a.m. and continue until it's time to end at 8 p.m. The classmates who discussed the revolution at the university club are now apart. Inside the cramped cell, there are yakuza, thieves, and perpetrators of robbery. Additionally, it's reported that many have grown hungrier due to the basic bentō [lunchbox] and miso soup served.[28]

Newspapers on both sides of the political spectrum covered these early days of detention and interrogation with a barely concealed sense that the students had finally got what was coming to them. On 25th January, under a headline 'Violent Students', the Yomiuri stated that on realisation that their detention was to be extended, many students expressed a sense of shock. But the paper also reported scenes of resistance at the police stations—singing, shouting slogans etc.,—and widespread resolve to maintain silence. The paper also lingered on the 'smell' of the students, using it to index a state of barbarity that was enough to anger even the other criminals in custody: '…these students had not bathed for a few weeks and were exposed to tear gas for a few hours, or in some cases, over thirty hours. Each student had an unspeakable odour permeating their clothes and bodies, dispersing throughout their surroundings.' Female detainees, who also in these early days refused to cooperate with the police were instead treated with a sense of fascination and bemusement. 'Even when the prosecutor starts the interrogation, they do not break eye contact and just stare' described the paper. '"Your persistent, aren't you?" they would say raising their eyebrows, prompting a bitter smile from the prosecutor'. In general, the students were portrayed uncivilised, irrational, and entitled. The latter was emphasised by noting police surprise at the amount of money (150,000 yen) in one students' bank account and the 60,000 yen he received from his family for living expenses. '"[All this] despite having considerable social status," the investigator said with a sigh.'[29]

By 31 January the newspapers papers started to report that these persistent tactics were bearing fruit. 'Over the past few days,' the Asahi stated 'an unexpected shift has taken place among these students who, without helmets or batons, have relied on complete silence as their sole "weapon" in detention. Their once firmly shut mouths, resembling closed shells, have started to open little by little.' All students at Detention Centre 'A', for example, had for the first two days maintained complete silence, but little by little students began to give their names and addresses. By day four eight had given up this information. The final two, who the paper characterised as 'habitual activists' (*jōshūkatsudōka*) used to the standard 3 nights and 4 days in jail (*sanpaku yokka*) before being released, broke after eight days. For 4th year students, many of whom were in the process of securing, or had just secured, employment, the long detention was clearly unexpected and fear of losing their jobs put pressure on them to break their silence. The paper also reported on students 'coming to their senses' due to their sense of responsibility to their parents. 'They are clearly weak to human emotion (*ninjō*)', claimed the paper. After being told they were causing their mother to worry, a student who had travelled to Tokyo University from the Kansai area was quoted as dropping all pretence of silence and saying 'when I was throwing stones, I didn't think about my mother at all. But now that I am here, being quiet [*shizuka ni shiteiru*], I feel bad for my mother who worked and sent me to university.' The article also reported on the female students. They kept silent for over a week, it was reported, but after they were allowed to bathe for the first time since being arrested and could change into new underwear and sweaters supplied by Tōitsu kyūtai, they began to make small talk. The paper attributed this change in attitude to them being 'refreshed' (*sappari shita*). According to the authorities by January 30th the number of students cooperating with the police at the detention centre had risen from 7 to 20.[30]

The media coverage also hinted at police and prosecutors' endeavours to co-opt parents into the job of getting their children to speak to the police.[31] In fact this was widespread strategy. 'It is the common wish of all adults that young people,' argued the Metropolitan Chief of Crime Prevention Suzuki Ryōichi in a letter to parents, 'that the future leaders of the next generation should not be led astray. The love of parents is the only way to give them comfort, to encourage them, to give them advice, to help them to overcome the differences of age and of thought.' 'Only by working together,' Suzuki continued, 'can these pained and lost souls understand the true meaning of our expectation towards them of responsible action based on reason and self-determination.'[32] The narrative being produced was that these students, who were not yet adults, had been led astray. Their actions were not the extension of a legitimate world view but precisely the opposite: they were a product of (irrational) emotion. It was the responsibility of society to bring them back to the safety of the family as part of the inter-generational national community.

A vignette recounted for the Metropolitan Police Department journal *Jikei* offered an idealised example of the power of the parental involvement in securing the transformation of students. The story told was one of a shared emotional bond between parent and the authorities in recovering the lost innocence of the student radical:

> The refined mother who had flown to the capital and her daughter, S, remained frozen, hand in hand, without brushing away their tears. Their dream of a two-night, three-day stay in custody was abruptly extinguished, and following twenty days of detention, S, a nineteen-year-old female student at Q University, could only cry out, "Mum." Her face held only the expression of a young girl clinging to her mother, devoid of any trace of the warrior-like figure who had been drawn out of the flames of a Molotov cocktail on the rooftop of T University. Despite her repeated silence, S was startled by the twenty-day detention and the relentless investigations of Division Head I.
>
> It was only a few days later when S, under the fatherly and gentle interrogation by Division Head I, began to fully confess. S, the only child of a single mother, had a youthful face that, once she washed the dirt from her hair and face, would inspire anyone to call her "Little S". It was an innocent face that you could hardly believe belonged to the female warrior who, amid a crowd, had worn a helmet, thrown stones at riot police, and occupied a school building.

> Seeing the mother in tears and at a loss, Division Head I consoled her as best he could, sharing about his own daughter who was in the third year of junior high. In doing so, he involuntarily welled up in tears, empathizing with the mother's feelings. Although Division Head I was firmly committed to not overlooking even an inch of the violent students' illegal actions, he was deeply moved by the genuine affection of a mother for her child. The mother held S's hand, put her arm around her shoulder, and looked up at the sky in sorrow. Her actions were purely those of a mother, without any pretence.
>
> Before they knew it, their 15-minute visitation period ended. S was led back to the detention centre in tears, while her mother was guided to a reassuring inn arranged by the staff. During the interrogation the next day, S honestly confessed all the details pertaining to the incident, and gradually started to show a genuine smile, typical of a young girl. Her mother, who visited Tokyo two or three times, found solace in entrusting everything to Division Head I and even consulted him about future matters.[33]

Of course, this was a narrative and process that the students and their support groups would continue to push back on. As a detainee wrote later in a letter to his father after a visitation in detention, for many there was a limit to what conversation between parent and child could achieve:

> ...I didn't blindly follow my friends, I wasn't forced to. I am convinced that it is the right thing to do, which is why I took part in the Tokyo University Struggle and will continue to do so. So there is no shame in meeting you in prison and there is nothing humiliating about it at all. It's not like I'm here for stealing things, or getting drunk and hurting people, or getting caught for electoral fraud. I am here for standing up for the fundamental overthrow of existing society from the outset, and then going toe-to-toe with those who oppose it. X [his younger brother] said, 'There isn't enough talk between parents and children. This may be a reason for [my action], but it is definitely not the direct cause. The corruption of the objectively existing outside world, the crazy mistakes, are the real cause. This is not something that can be solved by a proper dialogue between parents and children. There is a general tendency for parents to persuade their children to stop participating in political activities, as if this were the right thing to do, but it is not. It is also strange that children who have already reached the age of adulthood listen to their parents, and I cannot believe that parents are superior in political and ideological matters.[34]

In these cases of continued resistance, 'love and support' of the family took on a very particular meaning which manifested the psychology of 'tough compassion' formulated and called for by prosecutors and cabinet office researchers in 1968. As the reflections of Tokyo District Public Prosecutor Iwashita Hajime demonstrate, in practice this meant breaking through parents' pre-existing notions of familial obligation to their sons and daughters and convincing parents to accept the authority of the prosecutor as the person who knew best for their child. Iwashita saw parents as falling into three categories: the overwhelmed who could not stop crying and expressing remorse; optimists, who believed that their child had simply fallen into the wrong crowd and could be brought to heel through patient discussion; and fatalists, who were resigned to the path their son or daughter had taken and were simply happy that they were yet to commit a serious crime. With all three types of parents, the prosecutors' position was that the parents were no longer able to control their children and it was therefore imperative that the state intervene and the legal process proceeded unhindered. This was the only way to secure the return of their child to the family. Iwashita would thus say to parents:

> We prosecutors do not hate your children. Your children are an important treasure not only for you, but also for national society. We want to return the children to their parents as soon as possible and send them back to school if possible. But they must be held accountable for their actions. We also want to understand the children as much as possible to ensure that the punishment is appropriate, so if there are any mitigating circumstances that we should consider in deciding the punishment, please do not hesitate to ask.[35]

Iwashita went so far as to give examples of how to help parents in their interactions with their children. He would urge the overwhelmed parents not to show too much emotion during visits and to only express a desire to help if their children 'really want to return to society'. For the optimists, he warned against putting too much faith in conversation and advocated a hard line. Instead of expressing sympathy for their sons and daughters, they should push back. 'Don't be impertinent,' he suggested as a particular line: 'If you want people to listen to you, you'll have to correct your behaviour and come back!' For those fatalistic parents, he would encourage them to believe in the potential for rehabilitation: 'I stress to them that as long as your relationship is one of parent and child, communication is possible.'[36] In all cases he stressed that the physical return of the student to family was not enough to secure the long terms goal of family reintegration. Such an outcome could only come from a fundamental change in the thinking of the student/child, and that change could only be brought about by the state through the legal process.

Within this goal in mind, Iwashita also had a lot to say about dealing with Tōitsu kyūtai, choosing legal representation, and the issue of bail. Some parents he noted with approval broke off communication with Kyūtai organisations as soon as possible. But others might, he argued, feel a sense of obligation given that Kyūtai volunteers were providing support for their children. In these circumstances Iwashita recommend parents meet with the organisation and ask about the type of support they provide and the end goal of that provision. He would suggest the same approach with legal representation. Although it was ultimately up to the defendant to choose their lawyer, he would tell parents there were risks. 'Since it is your child who will bear the burden of a bad outcome and you the parents who will experience the greatest sadness,' he would caution 'you need not worry about anyone else. I hope you will choose a lawyer who will give you and your children a defence you are happy with.' Finally, Iwashita would try to convince the parents that, although it was their right to apply, bail was not in their or their child's best interests. A right, he would argue, was not an obligation. If parents were concerned about their children's health, he would argue that healthcare in prisons was 'near perfect': compared to the unstable (*fukisoku*) life in hostels and dormitories, prisons were far better for their children's health. Moreover, securing bail could destroy a student's positive reflection (*hansei*) on his or her actions. On the outside, Iwashita argued, it was impossible to keep a child away from the influence of the movement. But on the inside, a student could simply choose not to associate with the movement, giving them more agency in their rehabilitation. Thus, it was not enough for students to simply say 'sorry' and ask their parents to pay bail.[37] 'Let us do our best,' he would conclude, 'to keep each other from collapsing due to the slightest lapse of vigilance.'[38]

A Turning Point in Policy Towards Indictment and Detention

Japanese prosecutors have exclusive power to decide whether to charge a suspect, and courts are not permitted to recognise a crime unless the procuracy has made an indictment. Prosecutors, however, have no obligation to proceed with indictment, even if there is enough evidence to do so. This lack of obligation gives prosecutors room to exercise leniency by deferring prosecution in cases where the character of the suspect is deemed salvageable. This has led commentators on the Japanese legal system to argue that rather than operating a system that seeks to control crime through deterrence, the Japanese legal system is predicated on what Daniel Foote calls the 'ethos of specific prevention'.[39] Japanese prosecutors place great emphasis on understanding not only the facts of any criminal acts committed, but also the individual circumstances of the offender and other factors that may have contributed to the offence. Once these facts are established, prosecutors will go to great lengths in exercising leniency to mitigate the impact of criminal justice proceedings on the offender to maximise chances of reintegration and rehabilitation. Leniency, at least at the indictment stage, however, was not on the cards for the students arrest at Tokyo University. On 9th February, while lawyers continued to locate student detainees, the Tokyo District Public Prosecutor's Office announced its intention to indict the overwhelming majority of students arrested between 18 and 19th of January. By the 11th of February, a total of 509 students had been indicted, seven of whom were female, and the case was now firmly the biggest indictment for a single incident in modern Japanese legal history.[40] The majority of indictments were for three crimes, namely: 'unlawful assembly with weapons' (Penal code Article 208 Section 2); 'breaking into a residence' (Article 130) for which students were all rendered joint principle offenders (Article 60); and 'obstructing performance of public duty' (Article 95), again as joint principle offenders.[41] Combined the maximum custodial sentence for these three charges totalled 9 years, with the maximum fine amounting to 900,000 yen.

It should also be noted, however, that since early 1968 there had been some controversy over the applicability of 'unlawful assembly with weapons' to student incidents. The crux of this controversy lay in the law's original purpose, the ambiguity surrounding its scope of application, and the potential for its exploitation by authorities to remove students from the streets with no intention of later indictment. The law's inception had been in response to a series of violent clashes between rival Yakuza organizations from 1956 to 1957, notably the so-called 'Komatsushima War' (Komatsushima kōsō), between the Yamaguchi-gumi and other organized crime families. The legislation was enacted to empower police to arrest potential participants in such clashes pre-emptively, serving as a method of conflict prevention. This original intention (preventing Yakuza brawls), however, raised questions about the law's applicability to other potential conflicts. This issue became salient in January 1968, when Chūkaku-faction students enroute to join protests at Sasebo naval base were unexpectedly stopped, arrested, and allegedly beaten by massed riot police outside Iidabashi station in Tokyo. Authorities arrested 131 students for 'unlawful assembly with weapons,' 'obstructing the performance of public duty,' and violating the Tokyo Public Security Ordinance for failing to register their protest. The case tested the definition of 'weapon' which in the law was ambiguous. For the Yakuza, defining a weapon was relatively straightforward, as they typically employed objects inherently considered weapons, such as Japanese swords and pistols. But students did not carry either. In this regard, police argued that students' placards could easily be converted into weapons since they were made from wooden staves that could be disassembled and used to attack police, who constituted 'another person' (*tanin*) as stipulated in the law's constitutive elements. In effect whether or not a thing became a weapon was based on an interpretaetion of the collective intent of the users within the context of use. The criticism that the law was being abused to remove students from the street with no intention to prosecute, which appeared substantiated by the low indictment figures for the incidents in question (six of 131 at Iidabashi) was, while plausible, difficult to make stick due to the fact that Japan's criminal law recognised the principle of discretionary prosecution. Of course, this issue did not arise at the University of Tokyo as all those arrested were indicted.[42]

The exceptional nature of this mass indictment was borne out by data collected by the Bengodan and statistics published Government White Paper on Crime, which included a detailed section on student unrest (see Fig. 4.1).[43] Prosecutors had previously justified low indictment figures on two grounds: that it was difficult to build a fully evidenced case against the students and that as part of their policy towards indictments prosecutors had factored into consideration the impact on students' futures.[44] The Tokyo University struggle was, therefore, a turning point in prosecutorial policy towards student unrest. Indeed, as Tokyo Chief Prosecutor Takeuchi Takayuki stated to the press in February:

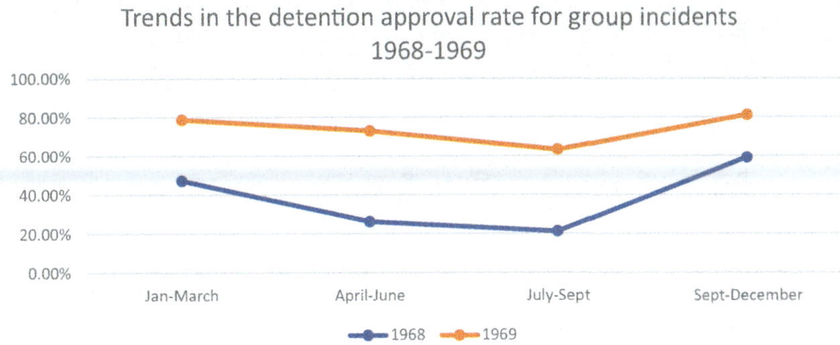

Fig. 4.1 Trends in the detention approval rate for group incidents[52]

> It is unfortunate that recent student movements are prone to resort to violence, particularly in the case of the group violence exhibited during the recent Tokyo University incident. This event is unparalleled in terms of its organization, planning, and the severity of its methods. In light of this, we have felt the urgent need to implement more stringent measures to uphold the rule of law and have subsequently pursued mass indictments. Moving forward, we plan to maintain a strict stance against such offenses. However, at the same time, we hope that students in general will recognize their societal responsibilities, adhere to rationality, and engage in measured actions to avoid squandering their potential by participating in unlawful acts.[45]

The new message was clear. Student unrest would not be tolerated, no special dispensation would be granted, and the mass indictment was to serve as a deterrent to all other students considering joining the movement[46] (Table 4.3).

Similarly, the Tokyo University Incident was remarkable in that not only were the vast majority of those arrested indited, but the courts granted 98% of the prosecution's requests for detention beyond the initial 10-day investigative period. According to Article 60 of Japan's Code of Criminal Procedure, Courts are obliged to release on bail the accused unless there is probable cause to suspect that they may conceal or destroy evidence, there is a risk of flight, or it is not possible to establish a fixed address. Historically the courts tended not to view students as fulfilling any of these criteria and prosecutors did not press the issue (see Fig. 4.1). From the 21 October Shinjuku incident onwards, however, the average

Table 4.3 Detention and indictment figures for student related incidents, 1967–1969[47]

Date	*Name of incident*	*Arrested*	*Detention*			*Indictment*		
			Requested	*Granted*	*Ratio*	*Indicted*	*Not indicted*	*Family court*
08/10/1967	First Haneda Incident	75	65	49	75.4	35	24	16
12/11/1967	Second Haneda Incident	347	237	145	61.2	45	216	86
15/01/1968	Iidabashi Incident	131	126	30	23.8	6	90	35
18/01/1968	Yūrakuchō Incident	108	66	35	53	4	73	31
19/01/1968	Foreign Ministry Incident	89	41	7	17.1	4	74	11
19–21/1/1968	Sasebo Incident	70	66	48	72.7	17	40	13
26/2–31/3/1968	Narita Incident	259	127	88	69.3	39	180	40
3/3/1968	Third Ōji Incident	50	28	7	25	2	37	11
8/3/1968	Fourth Ōji Incident	158	128	75	58.6	22	107	29
28/3/1968	Sixth Ōji Incident	181	158	76	49.1	68	76	36
1/4/1968	Eighth Ōji Incident	121	77	42	54.5	24	67	30
26/4/1968	International Anti-War Demonstration Incident	95	67	15	22.4	5	71	20

			Detention			Indictment		
Date	*Name of incident*	*Arrested*	*Requested*	*Granted*	*Ratio*	*Indicted*	*Not indicted*	*Family court*
27/4/1968	Okinawa Day Demonstration Incident	213	121	10	8.3	0	156	57
7/6/1968	US (possibly referring to US-related incident)	210	22	4	18.2	2	142	60
27/6/1968	Tōyō University Confinement Incident	172	75	8	10.7	2	118	48
27/7/1968	Asia Pacific Council (ASPAC) Incident	65	33	5	15.2	3	35	18
1/8/1968	Anzen Station US Tank Prevention Incident	69	17	2	11.8	2	64	3
2/9/1968	Kakumaru-faction Incident	57	44	5	11.4	1	No data given	3
4/9/1968	Nihon University	132	117	43	36.8	6	55	19
7/9/1968	Nihon University	129	71	13	18.3	3	No data given	50
12/9/1968	Nihon University	154	84	6	7.1	3	No data given	33
22/9/1968	Tachikawa Base Incident	111	75	6	8	1	92	18
22/9/1968	US Tanker Incident	83	64	12	18.7	7	49	27
8/10/1968	First Shinjuku Incident	156	126	75	59.5	22	No data given	28

(continued)

Table 4.3 (continued)

Date	Name of incident	Arrested	Detention			Indictment		
			Requested	*Granted*	*Ratio*	*Indicted*	*Not indicted*	*Family court*
21/10/1968	Shinjuku Station Incident	532	319	158	49.5	32	No data given	72
21/10/1968	Defence Agency Incident	336	294	212	72.1	41	76	45
21/10/1968	International Anti-War Demonstration Incident	105	65	45	69.2	34	32	37
7/11/1968	Prime Minister's Office Demonstration	467	289	132	45.7	34	92	119
12/11/1968	Japan Art University Incident	53	48	48	100	19	23	11
21/12/1968	Sophia (Jōchi) University Incident	59	59	47	79.7	15	No data given	5
09/01/1969	University of Tokyo Incident	51	46	37	80.4	14	34	3
10/01/1969	University of Tokyo Incident	149	143	124	86.7	41	No data given	19
18/01/1969	University of Tokyo Incident	325	295	288	97.6	208	60	42
19/01/1969	University of Tokyo Incident	459	447	438	98	340	40	52
7–12/2/1969	Kwansei University Incident	80	55	54	98.2	48	23	7

			Detention			*Indictment*		
Date	*Name of incident*	*Arrested*	*Requested*	*Granted*	*Ratio*	*Indicted*	*Not indicted*	*Family court*
21/2/1969	Chuo University Incident	222	124	26	21	7	187	28
27/2/1969	University of Electro-communications Incident	129	74	23	31.1	No data given	No data given	No data given
3/3/1969	University of Kyoto Incident	61	35	9	25.7	2	57	2
10/4/1969	Tokyo University of Foreign Studies Incident	128	103	19	18.4	No data given	No data given	No data given
12/4/1969	Take-back Japan struggle Incident	115	24	5	20.8	No data given	No data given	No data given
28/4/1969	Okinawa Day Incident	979	934	826	88.4	189	No data given	45

request-to-detention ratio rose to 68%. And amongst the statistics the Tokyo University Incident stood out with a ratio of 98%. The prosecution's take on these eyebrow-raising detention figures was that they were only strange in the context of policing student unrest, not in policing generally. Ministry of Justice Prosecutor Kawasaki Kensuke, for example, argued that the detention request-to-detention ratio of students between the Narita Incident and the events at Tokyo University was 54.1%, which was significantly lower than for 'general prosecutions' (*ippan keijijiken*) of 98%. In effect then, for the prosecution it was the court's previous lenient approach to student unrest that was the anomaly to be corrected. Moreover, prosecutors argued that given student crime was extremely (*kiwamete*) organised and pre-planned, and most students refused to cooperate with the authorities or even acknowledge their crimes, student crime was precisely the sort of case where there was a risk that defendants released on bail would tamper with evidence. Student activists tended not to have a fixed address and were as such a flight risk, they argued. More generally prosecutors maintained that many students were habitual criminals (*jōshūteki hankō*) and as such their right to bail was significantly limited.[48] The courts, at least until August when there was a change in policy (see Chapter 5), now agreed with this position (see Table 4.2).[49]

There was the further question of bail. Traditionally bail had been set at between 40 and 50,000 yen for students, and had usually been granted within a few days of application. Now bail was set at 100,000–150,000 yen and the courts appeared to be in no rush to process applications (see Table 4.5).[50] But this doubling of the bond was mostly irrelevant, as bail simply was not granted. Indeed, due to the fact that the Bengodan did not have the resources to complete the monthly bail applications, the detainees themselves were trained on formatting and submitting the document, which became part of their routine while awaiting trial; so too did the disappointment of receiving the official notice that their application had been declined. A student from Kobe University mused about a calendar on his cell door on which there was a picture of a smiling women in a white dress holding out something that looked like a present. 'Every time I look at it,' the student wrote, 'I wonder what is in that present. Up to now it hasn't been anything good, but perhaps sometime soon she will give me my notice of bail'[51] (Table 4.4).

The Tokyo University indictments were over double that of the 1952 May Day case, which at the time held the record with 261 indictments. Why though didn't the prosecution charge them with rioting as had

Table 4.4 Number of bail applications granted by month based on a survey of 276 students included in documents submitted to the court by the students' legal representation[53]

Date	*Number of individuals granted bail*
February 1969	1
March	12
April	31
May	9
June	7
July	No data
August	52
September	24
October	23
November	44
December	35
January 1970	6
February	2
March	1
Still in detention as of March 1970	9

Table 4.5 Bail bond based on a survey of 263 students included in documents submitted to the court by the students' legal representation[54]

Cost of bail (Yen)	*Number of individuals*
30,000	1
50,000	5
100,000	12
150,000	219
180,000	3
200,000	22
250,000	1

been the wishes of politicians in 1968? First, prosecuting for rioting simply had not been effective. The Shinjuku Incident, which had only resulted in 32 indictments, served as a negative example in this regard. Indicting for comparatively simpler crimes, which could be prosecuted more easily allowed prosecutors to move swiftly into action such that over 500 activists were taken off the streets in a de facto act of preventative policing. And the granting of extension requests by the courts enabled prosecutors to make full use of the 'paradise' conditions they enjoyed when dealing with non-student offenders for a full 20 days. If trials could be concluded quickly students would either be serving sentences during the renewal of the Anpo in 1970, or in the case of suspended sentences would know taking part in demonstrations would lead to a custodial sentence. And as per Tokyo Chief Prosecutor Takeuchi Takayuki's statement to the press, the indictments sent a strong signal that the state was willing to prosecute student activists en masse, which would deter future students from joining activist organisations.

Second, the Bloody May Day trial, which was by 1969 was lumbering towards its first verdicts, served as a warning to prosecutors about the potential dangers in the courtroom of indictment for rioting. According to Tokyo Public Prosecutor Takeda Shōzō, prosecuting for rioting was challenging due to the law's "double" structure, which targeted the group while only allowing for the investigation of individuals for criminal liability. This required prosecutors to establish both the specifics of the group disturbance and collect two distinct types of evidence for appraisal. Additionally, this broad scope had enabled lawyers to expand their arguments in court to encompass postwar social and political developments, framing the case in terms of suppressing the Communist Party and student activists. Takeda argued that the outcome was a "political quagmire," distracting from the prosecution's objective of establishing the case's facts. Furthermore, Takeda contended that while these tactics may have been advantageous for the unified group, which sought to challenge the case's political aspects, those who opted for a small group trial were disadvantaged, as the courts would not issue a verdict until all evidence for both sets of defendants had been heard.[55] In this regard, however, some commentators saw a more calculated approach from prosecutors to maximise the penalties that could be secured against the students. According to the analysis of legal scholar Saeki Chihiro and former judge and lawyer Yoneda Yasukuni, had rioting been the charge, it was likely the majority of students would have been viewed as simply going along with the crowd (*fuwazuikō*) and only receive a fine of less that 2,500 yen. And in their estimation, even though there were legal precedents in which harsher punishments were meted out due to differences in interpretation, the defendants would have been in a strong position when arguing their case for such treatment.[56]

There is also the question of why the courts changed their stance on detention and bail. Contemporary accounts from the left simply put the change down to the courts showing their real colours as agents of public security. This assessment, however, did not explain prior decision-making policy. The answer is more likely the courts' sensitivity to political encroachment on its authority. Although there is no evidence of direct political interference in the court's decisions to grant such requests in the Tokyo University case, it is plausible that the judiciary, ever sensitive to threats to its autonomy, pre-empted such political interference by changing its policy towards students of its own accord.[57] Indeed, as was shown in the previous chapter, since the Shinjuku Incident, students came to be seen as a major threat to national security in the run up to renewal of the Anpo in 1970. Policing of the Shinjuku incident was a great experiment, with considerable preplanning, in managing this threat through the application of anti-rioting laws to students. But that experiment, as demonstrated by the very low indictment figures, had failed. The outcome was a storm of criticism from politicians and commentators on the right, who alleged the courts were to blame due to their reluctance to grant prosecutors' requests for extended detention. The incident had also raised fears that unrest by students would be capitalised upon by violent bystanders, leading to mass insurrection and rioting. In the aftermath public security officials, and the courts, were criticised for application of the law being too little too late and called for more proactive, preventative approaches to managing unrest. The courts in particular were singled out for their lenient approach to detention and bail.

There was however a further strand of criticism of the courts that was shaping public sentiment around them that may have contributed to the hardening of attitudes towards students. In 1967 the right-wing magazine Zenbō, known for its virulent anti-communist agenda, published a special edition arguing that the courts had been infiltrated by the left, and that left-wing bias in administrative decision making and court rulings was a clear and present danger to the rule of law in Japan. Zenbō's *bette noir* was the Young Lawyers Association (*Seinen hōritsuka kyokai*), which they viewed as under the control of the JCP and to which 250 sitting judges claimed membership. At study sessions and away days, it was claimed, these judges would mix with radical left-wing lawyers, and listened to lectures that pushed a 'left-wing agenda' on constitutional matters. Furthermore, the courts were surrounded by other JCP sponsored and other left-wing organisations (such as the Japan Civil Liberties Union and the Japan Lawyers Association for Freedom) who continued to exert pressure on legal outcomes.[58]

Chief Justice of the Supreme Court of Japan Yokota Masatoshi 1969 New Year's statement demonstrated that the Supreme Court was taking such criticism seriously. While noting that denunciation of the courts was nothing new, such criticism tended to emanate from people with 'left-wing tendencies.' The situation, argued Yokota, was now more complex:

> On one hand, there are criticisms that courts, particularly the Supreme Court, are pandering to the executive and legislative branches, neglecting their responsibility as guardians of the Constitution. On the other hand, there are criticisms that recent judges, especially younger ones, are overly sympathetic to defendants, suspects, and people with left-wing tendencies in their judgments, with particular concerns regarding rulings of unconstitutionality and warrant handling in lower courts.

What were the courts to do? Rather than dismiss all these criticisms as simple noise (*zatsuon*), as his predecessor Tanaka Kōtarō had argued with regard to left-wing criticism in the 1950s, Yokota now called for judges to listen:

> ...we as judges should be willing to listen humbly to sincere criticisms from the public and outsiders and have the room for self-reflection. After all, the authority entrusted to us by the Constitution is extremely important, and the existence of such authority within the courts is essential to truly protect the human rights of the people and rectify the political posture of our country. To fulfil our responsibilities, we must engage in considerable study and effort, and strive to improve our individual qualities. Moreover, we must not be misled by so-called "noise," but rather, in the face of sincere criticism from outside, we must correctly respond to that criticism by clarifying the proper form of the Constitution and other laws through specific cases.

If the message here was not enough it was also reported that the Secretariat of the Supreme Court used its own resources to buy 170 copies of the Zenbō special edition, which was sent out to courtrooms across Japan.[59] It is therefore likely that a combination of these varied forms of criticism shifted attitudes towards detention and bail policy for students.

Challenging the Courts Governance

Responding to this changing legal environment, the Bengodan challenged the extended detention of their clients by pointing out that the argument students would destroy evidence rested on shaky ground. The most obvious counterargument to the prosecutors' reasoning was that the students had been caught red-handed by the police during the struggle; the charges against the students all related directly to the actions of 18 and 19th of January and it was difficult to see what evidence the students might destroy. As Bengodan lawywer Ishikawa Hiromitsu wrote in the journal *Sekai*, up until the October 21 1968 Shinjuku Incident the courts released students on the principle that testimony from riot police witnesses to the crime was evidence enough for a conviction.[60] Moreover, given that the students had already been indicted based on the evidence gathered, it was again unclear what this extra evidence might be and how it might be used. In fact, the courts had themselves developed the precedent that the abstract notion that defendants might tamper with evidence was not sufficient cause to deny bail.[61] There needed to be a concrete, specific and demonstrable fear that tampering would occur. In this regard the courts argued that once released on bail students might coerce other defendants, who had been granted bail, into changing their statements to the police. But there were plenty of people outside detention centres that could do this already; again, it was unclear what extra evidence was needed to prove the students had committed the crimes they were charged with, and any witness who did change their statement faced perjury charges.[62] Finally, this argument did not explain why the same sorts of students as had participated in protests before the Shinjuku incident were now subject to a different appraisal.[63]

The answer, at least in the eyes of the Bengodan, was a shift in the Court's role from passive adjudicator to active participant in the management of the case. The defence team reported that when they took up with the Tokyo district court these changes in detention and bail outcomes Judge Yokogawa responded that 'you [the legal team] should recognise that the circumstances have changed…Recent student movements have become more spontaneous and violent. In response, the judiciary has its own methods of governance.'[64] This 'governance' seemed to indicate that the function of detention and bail had morphed from a legal process to a tool for managing public order. And indeed, the criteria for allowing bail now appeared to be the extent to which the defendant acquiesced to the court's approach to trying the case. The Bengodan reported visiting a judge accompanied by a student defendant's mother in the hopes that bail could be secured. After pleading their case the judge was quoted as replying:

> Your son has said nothing so [release on bail] is impossible...If we don't know anything there is nothing we can do. If you really want to see him released convince him to speak. Go with your lawyers and have them convince [your son].[65]

'Speaking', however, invariably meant acquiescing to the Court's group trial process, changing legal representation, and submitting documentation that evidenced a 'change in mind' regarding the movement and its actions. When these things happened, students were very quickly released into the custody of their parents. Yet these criteria had no impact on the substance of the crimes the students were accused of and had no bearing on the public prosecutor's continued request for detention. When students refused to comply with the Courts, the decision regarding bail lay with the prosecutor. But when students did comply, the Court took back its authority in what can be seen as an act of conditional paternal benevolence. In this sense, legal appeals by the lawyers against prolonged detention only demonstrated continued lack of remorse. As one judge put it: 'the way you write your appeal is different. The question is whether he is remorseful or not. If he is remorseful, he will be released, if not, he will be kept in jail for as long as he wants.'[66] Demonstration of remorse was thus the precondition for reintegration into the national community, which happened via the family as that community's basic social unit. In adopting the Court's trial process students were therefore acknowledging that their actions transgressed the moral norms of the national community and showed that they were ready to re-establish their membership to the nation.

On 13th March, stating that denial of bail was 'politically motivated oppression of the Tokyo University struggle', the defence team submitted a collective request for disclosure of the reasons for detention (*kōryū riyū kaiji*) covering 372 students.[67] In doing so they knew the request would put the courts in an impossible position, as according to the Rules of Criminal Procedure (*Keiji soshō kisoku*, RCP) the courts were obliged to disclose these reasons within five days of the request. After missing this window, however, the courts stated on 19 March that it was simply 'impossible' to hold the hearings within the time frame stipulated and, using a clause within the RCP guidance that allows for disregarding the five-day timeframe when 'unavoidable' (*yamu wo enai toki*), opted instead to disclose the reasons for detention in separate hearings of around 30 cases spread across seven courtrooms.[68] Despite a spirited petition from the lawyers to the Supreme Court seeking intervention into this process, the disclosure hearings slogged on.[69] As is perhaps unsurprising, for the students and their lawyers these hearings felt perfunctory at best and at worst downright hostile. Reports were soon heard of strict limits placed on the time allocated for statements by the defence, students' questions being cut off by judges, and courtrooms routinely cleared due to interjections from the gallery. Judges were wont to simply restate the reasons for detention—fear of destruction of evidence—and not the evidence to support their suspicions.[70]

As legal scholar Yokoyama Keiichirō observed at the time, the courts' attitude towards disclosure of reasons for detention was not so much a break with past practice as a continuation of a trend of emptying the process of disclosure of any substantive meaning.[71] Around the time of the 1952 May Day trials judges were committed to the idea that it was not enough to simply restate reasons for detainment at such hearings, but it had to be evidenced once again why detention was necessary. However, in the context of rising levels of organised civil unrest in the 1950s, attitudes began to shift, and courts ushered in strict measures to limit the actions of defendants and their lawyers, as well introduced more robust courtroom security.[72] More significantly, however, by the mid-1960s judges seem positively sceptical of the process all together. For example, Kumagai Hiroshi, who would later play a lead role in the trial, stated in the opening to a 1966 roundtable discussion on detention hearings that:

> ... as a judge, [disclosing the reason for detention] is a terrible job... and when I think about why it is such a terrible job, it is because the hearing tends to turn into a courtroom battle. Even if the judge does his best to follow the rules of disclosure and explain the reason for detention, [the defendants] are never convinced. This is because there is a tendency to attack the court with requests for explanations...[73]

In this spirit, most of the panel discussion focussed on techniques (*gijutsu*) for limiting discussions around the reasons for detention and the evidence backing up that necessity. The general approach was to state the reason as given at the time of indictment and refuse to give further explanation for fear that the defence teams begin to argue with the judges. As one judge said plainly 'you give specifics, so they bite back. It is better if you don't say anything.'[74] This did not mean, however, that the judges saw the system itself as having no value. The judges noted that most requests for disclosure do in fact result in the release of defendants on bail, but that this happens before any hearing can take place due to the prosecutor withdrawing the request for detainment.[75] Not all the judges agreed with such an interpretation, however. In a telling exchange, panellist Izumi Tokuji attempted to argue that rules on disclosure of evidence should be read in the context of the intentions of the framers of the Constitution, who wished to prevent detention and trial happening behind closed doors. And indeed, he continued, the German legal principles (from which much of Japanese jurisprudence drew) governing detention stated that such a hearing was an opportunity for the court to either maintain or discontinue detention based on the validity of the reasons given by the prosecution. While some of the panel remained unconvinced by this argument it did prompt speculation on the substantive basis of this minimalist interpretation of the law. Yet Kumagai effectively shut down this line of reasoning. By the procedural logic that a prosecutor will withdraw their detention request if they believe it now undefendable, a prosecutor who maintained the detention request must be sure of the validity of the request, which was enough evidence for Kumagai that the original reasoning was still valid. According to this logic, once the courts agreed to a request for detention, the prosecutor was in the driving seat.

The first verdict in the trials, of students that came to be known as the 'repentant group' (*hansei gumi*) came on March 6th. During the trial the defendant—an ML (Marxist-Leninist League)-faction Tōyō University student, who had joined the defence of the University of Toyko in its final stages—expressed both his remorse and a lack of agency in his actions:

> I was designated to the remaining unit (*zanryū butai*) and was not allowed to return home for personal reasons. I knew that my actions would break the law, but I was helpless. Now, I deeply regret my actions and believe that behaviour beyond the legal framework should not be tolerated.

Finding the defendant, guilty of all charges Judge Goto Isamu read out the following assessment his actions, but also an appraisal of the defendant's remorse:

> The actions of the defendant have ignored the existing order, shattered democratic principles, and sought to revive a savage era of darkness. Given the consequences on society, their liability is significant; however, there is room for discretion in light of their profound self-examination...

As such, while Judge Goto sentenced the student to the full two years requested by the prosecution, he suspended the sentence for two years. The courtroom was empty except for his parents.[76]

On March 11th, the Yomiuri published an article discussing the prosecutor's intention to pursue an 18-month custodial sentence for a female student (M) belonging to the same group of ML-faction students as the case above. The prosecutor justified this decision by stating, "Though she remains unmarried, she bears considerable responsibility for her actions." Unlike the Tōyō student, M was portrayed in the press as contesting charges she disagreed with (admitting to throwing stones at the police but not Molotov cocktails) and demonstrating greater resolve in defending her decision to stay and fight. However, M also indicated to the court that she had applied to leave university and would return to her hometown to find a job. Two days later Judge Monma Yoshio read out his verdict: 'The defendant has one count of arrest on her record, and as such I cannot take her actions in this case lightly. However, her role was predominantly supporting others and preparing food, and she has since applied to leave university and is to return home to her parents. She shows adequate remorse for her actions.' M was sentenced to the full 18 months, with the sentence suspended for three years, and while she still maintained that her actions were legitimate, her commitment to reintegrate herself into her local community and become a productive member of society had been enough to avoid prison.[77]

In both instances, the trials were swiftly concluded within a few hearings, resulting in the resolute conviction and sentencing of students to custodial terms. These outcomes were accompanied by displays of benevolence contingent upon sufficient expressions of remorse, either verbally or through actions taken after the conviction. The new approach was evidently achieving the intended effect. However, any optimism held by prosecutors or the judiciary regarding the smooth progression of the remaining trials was soon to be challenged. A contentious struggle over procedure, as well as the fundamental purpose of the trial, the legal profession, and the very essence of the rule of law, was about to unfolded in earnest.

Notes

1. Daniel H Foote, "The Benevolent Paternalism of Japanese Criminal Justice," *California Law Review* 80, no. 2 (1992): 317.
2. "Kyūen katsudō genkyō," *Kyūtai nyūsu*, February 1, 1969, 1.
3. Tōdaitōsō bengo-dan, *Tōdai saiban: towareteiru mono wa nani ka* (Tokyo: Tabata shoten, 1969), 19. Sakamoto denied this version of events in a letter to the Asahi Journal. "Dokusha kara," *Asahi Jānaru*, June 8, 1969.
4. The lawyers refer to Hirano as the Dean of the Faculty of Law. However, at this point acting President Katō was still the Dean. Hirano succeeded Katō after the latter demitted office on 22nd January. "Hōgakubuchō ni hirano kyōju," *Asahi Shimbun*, January 23, 1969, 15.
5. *Tōdai saiban: towareteiru mono wa nani ka*, 16–22.
6. Shigehide Kōbe, "Tōdai zenkyōtō kyūtai no undō keika," *Kyowakoku* 3 (1970): 207–8.
7. "Kyūtai zaisei jōhō hōkoku," *Kyūtai Nyūsu*, February 20, 1969.
8. Shingeki was the official publication of Tokyo Zenkyōtō.
9. Hiroshi Watanabe, "Tōdai saiban tōsō wo furikaette – kyūtaibu no tachiba kara," in *Shiryō: Tōdai saiban tōsō*, ed. Tōdaitōsō tōitsu hikoku-dan (jiritsu-sha) shiryō henshū iinkai (Tokyo: Tōdaitōsō tōitsu hikoku-dan (jiritsu-sha) shiryō henshū iinkai, 1978), 251–53.
10. "Zaisei hōkoku," *Kyūtai nyūsu*, April 15, 1969.
11. "Shūchū-teki kanpa o! yosō sa reru tairyō hoshaku," *Kyūtai nyūsu*, August 15, 1969.
12. "Over 370 Students Arrested in Battle at Hongo Campus," *Japan Times*, January 20, 1969, 1.
13. "63nin Ga Kega," *Yomiuri Shimbun*, January 20, 1969, 16. These ratios are repeated in the official casualty statistics for student unrest in the 1969 Crime White Paper, which puts casualties across all incidences of student unrest between 26 February 1967 and 12 April 1969 at 9519 police, 977 students and 334 bystanders.

Ministry of Justice, "Shōwa 44-Nenban Hanzai hakusho: hanzai no dōkō to hanzai-sha shogū o meguru shomondai," 1969, https://hakusyo1.moj.go.jp/jp/10/nfm/mokuji.html.

14. *Tōdai saiban: towareteiru mono wa nani ka*, 49–52.
15. "Kanken no kyōbō na danatsu no jittai," *Kyūtai nyūsu*, February 4, 1969, 2.
16. For a discussion of the toxicity of various chemicals used as tear gas see Leo J Schep, R J Slaughter, and D I McBride, "Riot Control Agents: The Tear Gases CN, CS and OC—a Medical Review," *Journal of the Royal Army Medical Corps* 161, no. 2 (2015): 94. The *Asahi Graph* articles mentioned were reprinted in *Tōdai saiban: towareteiru mono wa nani ka*, 34–46.
17. "Kyūen katsudō genkyō," 1.
18. *Tōdai Saiban: Towareteiru Mono Wa Nani Ka*, 24–48. It is worth noting that Zenkyōtō's own collection of sources contains a table that puts these numbers at 369, as does lawyer Ishikawa Hiromitsu's account published in *Sekai*. See Tōdaitōsō zengaku kyōtōkaigi, ed., *Toride no ue ni wareranosekai o: dokyumento tōdaitōsō* (Tokyo: Aki shobō, 1969), 539; Ishikawa Hiromitsu, "Bōryoku gakusei ni jinken ga nai no ka - bengonin kara no repōto," *Sekai*, no. 281 (April 1969).This number however appears to be a misprint copied over from a table that appeared in Kyūtai news: when the data in that table is tallied the overall number of injured amounts to 269 with 76 of that number being considered seriously injured. See "Kanken no kyōbō na danatsu no jittai." The figure of 269 is also closer to 288 given by the lawyers in their collection of materials.
19. Tōdaitōsō bengo-dan, *Tōdai saiban: towareteiru mono wa nani ka*, 37.
20. As Steinhoff has discussed, the Kyūen Centre would later produce a booklet entitled 'Kyūen nōtō' which documented police techniques and discussed methods of resistance. This booklet, however, only became available from September 1969 and was thus not available for students arrested during the Tokyo University struggle.
21. Kikuyabashi Police station was reserved for women detainees. Nakashima Chiyo, "Tōsō hatten to shien katsudō," *Kyūen Sentā*, February 10, 1970, 4.
22. David T. Johnson, *The Japanese Way of Justice: Prosecuting Crime in Japan*, Studies on Law and Social Control (Oxford University Press, 2002).

23. Ibid., 36–37. Miyazawa Setsuo, *Policing in Japan: A Study on Making Crime*, trans. Frank G. Bennett and John O. Haley (State University of New York Press, 1992), 16–18.
24. Daniel H Foote, "Confessions and the Right to Silence in Japan," *The Georgia Journal of International and Comparative Law* 21, no. 3 (1991): 415.
25. Miyazawa, *Policing in Japan: A Study on Making Crime*, 21.
26. Johnson, *The Japanese Way of Justice: Prosecuting Crime in Japan*, 251.
27. Patricia Steinhoff, "Introduction," in *Going to Court to Change Japan: Social Movements and the Law in Contemporary Japan*, ed. Patricia Steinhoff (Ann Arbor, MI: University of Michigan Press, 2014), 7.
28. "Katai kuchi mo hogureru tōdai jiken kōchi gakusei 'furusato no haha' ni horori - tōdaifunsō," *Asahi Shimbun*, January 31, 1969, 8.
29. "Bōryoku gakusei: kibishiku tsuikyū," *Yomiuri Shimbun*, January 25, 1969, 15.
30. "Katai kuchi mo hogureru tōdai jiken kōchi gakusei 'furusato no haha' ni horori - tōdaifunsō.".
31. See Patricia Steinhoff, "Mass Arrests, Sensational Crimes and Stranded Children: Three Crises for Japanese New Left Activists' Families," in *Imagined Families, Lived Families: Culture and Kinship in Contemporary Japan*, ed. Akiko Hashimoto and John W Traphagan (Albany, N.Y.: SUNY Press, 2008), 86.
32. Tōdaitōsō bengo-dan, *Tōdai saiban: towareteiru mono wa nani ka*, 59–60.
33. Jō Umihiko, "Aru episōdo," *Jikei* 51, no. 5 (May 1969): 141–42.
34. "Gokuchu de tatakau gakuyu kara: oyako no taiwa" ni mo genkai – menkai de atta chichi ni uttaeru," *Kyūtai nyūsu*, April 15, 1969, 1.
35. Hajime Iwashita, "Kenkyo gakusei ryōshin to kenji to no taiwa," *Hōritsu No Hiroba* 23, no. 4 (April 1970): 14.
36. Iwashita, "Kenkyo gakusei ryōshin to kenji to no taiwa.".
37. Note this was written in 1970 when applications for bail would be more successful.
38. Ibid.
39. Foote, "The Benevolent Paternalism of Japanese Criminal Justice," 241.

40. "Sara ni 320 nin kiso. Tōkyō chiken gōkei 509 ni," *Asahi Shimbun*, February 11, 1969. This was the first time women had been indicted in student unrest cases.
41. These articles of the penal code read in full: *Unlawful Assembly with Weapons*:
    Article 208–2(1)—When two or more persons assemble for the purpose of jointly harming the life, body or property of another person, any participant of the assembly who has prepared weapons or knows that weapons have been prepared, is punished by imprisonment for not more than 2 years or a fine of not more than 300,000 yen. (2) In the case referred to in the preceding paragraph, a person who having prepared weapons or knowing that weapons have been prepared, causes others to assemble, is punished by imprisonment for not more than 3 years. *Breaking into a Residence*: Article 130—A person who, without just cause, breaks into a residence of another person or into the premises, building or vessel guarded by another person, or who refuses to leave such a place upon demand is punished by imprisonment for not more than 3 years or a fine of not more than 100,000 yen. *Obstructing or Compelling Performance of Public Duty*: Article 95(1)—A person who assaults or uses intimidation against a public employee in the performance of public duty is punished by imprisonment or imprisonment without work for not more than 3 years or a fine of not more than 500,000 yen. *Co-principles*: Article 60—Two or more persons who commit a crime in joint action are all principals. See "Penal Code" (1907), https://www.japaneselawtranslation.go.jp/ja/laws/view/3581#je_pt1ch11at1.
42. Hayama Takeo, "Kenryoku no wana – kyōki junbi shūgō-zai (tokushū "sasebo" no shōten)," *Gendai No Me* 9, no. 3 (March 1968): 196–202.
43. There are slight discrepancies, but they are accounted for by the fact that the White Paper only presents information on cases of student unrest in which 50 of more students were arrested.
44. Kitamura Tetsuo, "Shūdanteki kōan soshō no mondaiten–gakusei jiken wo chūshin ni," *Jurisuto*, no. 424 (June 1969): 75.
45. "Zenrei no nai keikaku-teki bōryoku," *Asahi Shimbun*, February 10, 1969.
46. Government statistics demonstrate that the three laws applied in the Tokyo University case, and in particular 'unlawful assembly

with weapons', were the primary charges used in the management of student unrest throughout 1969. Of the 3961 individual indictments for student unrest related incidents surveyed for the 1969 White Paper on Crime, 2349 (72.7%) were for 'unlawful assembly with weapons', 1658 (52%) were for 'obstructing performance of public duty' and 1054 (32.6%) for 'breaking into a residence.' In contrast, there were no indictments for rioting and only 4 (0.1%) under the Habōhō. Percentages given exceed 100% due to the fact that students were often prosecuted for more than one offence. See Hōmushō, "Hanzai hakusho: higi-sha no zaimei, zenreki nado," 1970, https://hakusyo1.moj.go.jp/jp/11/nfm/n_11_2_3_2_2_3.html.
47. Hōmushō, "Shōwa 44-nenban hanzai hakusho: jiken no juri to shori," 1969, https://hakusyo1.moj.go.jp/jp/10/nfm/n_10_2_1_5_2_0.html.
48. Kawasaki Kensuke, "Saikin ni okeru gakusei jiken kōhan no jitsujō," *Hōritsu No Hiroba* 22, no. 4 (April 1969): 7. In 1969 Kawasaki was a public prosecutor attached to the Ministry of Justice.
49. "Chisai, 5nin no hoshaku kettei: chiken wa teishi mōshitate," *Asahi Shimbun*, July 5, 1969.
50. "Nagabikuka gakusei no kōchi. hoshakukin chōtatsu ni nayamu," *Asahi Shimbun*, February 15, 1969. The defence team give bond figures of 10 – 70,000 yen before 1969 and 150,000 yen after.
51. Gokuchū shokan hakkan iinkai, ed., *Tōdai tōsō gokuchū shokanshū 1* (Tokyo: Mitani Shobo, 1970), 231.
52. Hōmushō, "Hanzai hakusho: higi-sha no kōryū no jōkyō," 1970, https://hakusyo1.moj.go.jp/jp/11/nfm/n_11_2_3_2_2_2.html.
53. Tōdaitōsō bengodan, *Tōdai 1. 18, 19 tōsō saiban bōtō chinjutsu-sho* (Tokyo: Jiritsu-sha, 1970).
54. Ibid.
55. Takeda Shōzō, "Mēdē sōjō jiken no shinri to hanketsu," *Hōritsu No Hiroba* 23, no. 4 (April 1970): 6–12.
56. Saeki Chihiro and Yoneda Yasukuni, "Shūdanjiken no keiji tetuzuki," *Hōritsu Jihō* 42, no. 8 (June 1970): 66.
57. The debate on Judicial independence in Japan has been analysed by Frank Upham, who concludes that 'perhaps the strongest lesson to be taken from the Japanese experience is that all judiciaries are profoundly political and their performance entirely contingent on

both their own institutional culture and the political culture in which they operate.' See Frank K. Upham, "Political Lackeys or Faithful Public Servants? Two Views of the Japanese Judiciary," *Law & Social Inquiry* 30, no. 2 (2005): 421–55.

58. These allegations were published in book form in 1969. Shisō undō kenkyūjo, *Osorubeki saiban* (Zenbōsha, 1969).
59. Seinen hōritsuya kyōkai and Seinen hōritsuya kyōkai bengoshi gakusha gōdō bukai, *Seihōkyō: kenpō to tomoni 35-nen* (Nihonhyōronsha, 1990), 108.
60. Ishikawa, "Bōryoku gakusei ni jinken ga nai no ka - bengonin kara no repōto," 174.
61. Ishikawa, "Bōryoku gakusei ni jinken ga nai no ka - bengonin kara no repōto.".
62. Tōdaitōsō bengo-dan, *Tōdai saiban: towareteiru mono wa nani ka*, 72–80.
63. Yokoyama Keiichirō, "Kōryū, tokuni kōryū riyū kaiji o megutte," *Hōritsu Jihō* 41, no. 8 (July 1969): 13.
64. Tōdaitōsō bengo-dan, *Tōdai saiban: towareteiru mono wa nani ka*, 70.
65. Ibid., 81.
66. Ibid., 82.
67. "Tōdai jiken de manmosu seikyū," *Yomiuri Shimbun*, March 15, 1969.
68. Ibid.
69. Yokoyama, "Kōryū, tokuni kōryū riyū kaiji o megutte," 14.
70. See for example the discussion in Hisa Aoki, "Shihōkisha zadankai: tōdai saiban," *hōgaku seminā*, no. 163 (September 1969): 138–39.
71. Yokoyama, "Kōryū, tokuni kōryū riyū kaiji o megutte," 14.
72. Kumagai Hiroshi, "Kōryū riyū kaiji no jitsumu ue no shomondai," *hanrei taimuzu*, no. 184 (1966): 64.
73. Ibid., 62.
74. Yokoyama, "Kōryū, tokuni kōryū riyū kaiji o megutte," 18.
75. Kumagai, "Kōryū riyū kaiji no jitsumu ue no shomondai," 67.
76. "Tōdai jiken, hatsu no hanketsu: hansei no tōyōdai nama, shikkō yūyo," *Yomiuri Shimbun*, March 6, 1969.
77. "Joshi gakusei ni hatsu no hanketsu: hansei mitome no shikkō yūyo," *Yomiuri Shimbun*, March 13, 1969.

References

Aoki, Hisa. "Shihōkisha zadankai: tōdai saiban." *Hōgaku Seminā*, no. 163 (September 1969): 136–51.

Asahi jānaru. "Dokusha kara." June 8, 1969.

Asahi Shimbun. "Chisai, 5nin no hoshaku kettei: chiken wa teishi mōshitate." July 5, 1969.

Asahi Shimbun. "Hōgakubuchō ni hirano kyōju." January 23, 1969.

Asahi Shimbun. "Katai kuchi mo hogureru tōdai jiken kōchi gakusei 'furusato no haha' ni horori - tōdaifunsō." January 31, 1969.

Asahi Shimbun. "Nagabikuka gakusei no kōchi. hoshakukin chōtatsu ni nayamu." February 15, 1969.

Asahi Shimbun. "Sara ni 320 nin kiso. tokyo chiken gōkei 509 ni." February 11, 1969.

Asahi Shimbun. "Zenrei no nai keikaku-teki bōryoku." February 10, 1969.

Foote, Daniel H. "Confessions and the Right to Silence in Japan." *The Georgia Journal of International and Comparative Law* 21, no. 3 (1991): 415–88.

———. "The Benevolent Paternalism of Japanese Criminal Justice." *California Law Review* 80, no. 2 (1992): 317.

Gokuchū shokan hakkan iinkai, ed. *Tōdai tōsō gokuchū shokanshū 1*. Tokyo: Mitani shobo, 1970.

Hayama, Takeo. "Kenryoku no wana – Kyōki junbi shūgō-Zai (Tokushū "sasebo" no shōten)." *Gendai no me* 9, no. 3 (March 1968): 196–202.

Hōmushō. "Hanzai hakusho: higi-sha no kōryū no jōkyō," 1970. https://hakusyo1.moj.go.jp/jp/11/nfm/n_11_2_3_2_2_2.html.

———. "hanzai hakusho: higi-sha no zaimei, zenreki nado," 1970. https://hakusyo1.moj.go.jp/jp/11/nfm/n_11_2_3_2_2_3.html.

———. "shōwa 44-nenban hanzai hakusho: jiken no juri to shori," 1969. https://hakusyo1.moj.go.jp/jp/10/nfm/n_10_2_1_5_2_0.html.

Ishikawa, Hiromitsu. "Bōryoku gakusei ni jinken ga nai no ka - bengonin kara no repōto." *Sekai*, no. 281 (April 1969).

Iwashita, Hajime. "Kenkyo gakusei ryōshin to kenji to no taiwa." *Hōritsu no hiroba* 23, no. 4 (April 1970): 13–18.

Japan Times. "Over 370 Students Arrested in Battle at Hongo Campus." January 20, 1969.

Jō, Umihiko. "Aru episōdo." *Jikei* 51, no. 5 (May 1969): 141–42.

Johnson, David T. *The Japanese Way of Justice: Prosecuting Crime in Japan*. Studies on Law and Social Control. Oxford University Press, 2002.

Justice, Ministry of. "Shōwa 44-nenban hanzai hakusho: hanzai no dōkō to hanzai-sha shogū o meguru shomondai," 1969. https://hakusyo1.moj.go.jp/jp/10/nfm/mokuji.html.

Kawasaki, Kensuke. "Saikin ni okeru gakusei jiken kōhan no jitsujō." *Hōritsu no hiroba* 22, no. 4 (April 1969): 6–12.

Kitamura, Tetsuo. "Shūdanteki kōan soshō no mondaiten--gakusei jiken wo chūshin ni." *Jurisuto*, no. 424 (June 1969): 62–77.

Kōbe, Shigehide. "Tōdai zenkyōtō kyūtai no undō keika." *Kyowakoku* 3 (1970): 207–8.

Kumagai, Hiroshi. "Kōryū riyū kaiji no jitsumu ue no shomondai." *Hanrei Taimuzu*, no. 184 (1966).

Seinen hōritsuka kyōkai, and Seinen hōritsuya kyōkai bengoshi gakusha gōdō bukai. *Seihōkyō: kenpō to tomo ni 35-nen*. Nihon hyōronsha, 1990.

Kyūtai Nyūsu. "Gokuchu de tatakau gakuyu kara: oyako no taiwa" ni mo genkai - menkai de atta chichi ni uttaeru." April 15, 1969.

Kyūtai nyūsu. "Kanken no kyōbō na danatsu no jittai." February 4, 1969.

Kyūtai nyūsu. "Kyūen katsudō genkyō." February 1, 1969.

Kyūtai nyūsu. "Kyūtai zaisei jōhō hōkoku." February 20, 1969.

Kyūtai nyūsu. "Shūchū-teki kanpa o! yosō sa reru tairyō hoshaku." August 15, 1969.

Kyūtai nyūsu. "Zaisei hōkoku." April 15, 1969.

Miyazawa, Setsuo. *Policing in Japan: A Study on Making Crime*. Translated by Frank G. Bennett and John O. Haley. State University of New York Press, 1992.

Nakashima, Chiyo. "Tōsō hatten to shien katsudō." *Kyūen sentā*, February 10, 1970.

Penal Code (1907). https://www.japaneselawtranslation.go.jp/ja/laws/view/3581#je_pt1ch11at1.

Saeki, Chihiro, and Yasukuni Yoneda. "Shūdanjiken no keiji tetuzuki." Hōritsu jiho 42, no. 8 (June 1970): 61–69.

Schep, Leo J, R J Slaughter, and D I McBride. "Riot Control Agents: The Tear Gases CN, CS and OC—a Medical Review." *Journal of the Royal Army Medical Corps* 161, no. 2 (2015): 94.

Shisō undō kenkyūjo. *Osorubeki saiban*. Zenbōsha, 1969.

Steinhoff, Patricia. "Introduction." In *Going to Court to Change Japan: Social Movements and the Law in Contemporary Japan*, edited by Patricia Steinhoff, 1–16. Ann Arbor, MI: University of Michigan Press, 2014.

———. "Mass Arrests, Sensational Crimes and Stranded Children: Three Crises for Japanese New Left Activists' Families." In *Imagined Families, Lived Families: Culture and Kinship in Contemporary Japan*, edited by Akiko Hashimoto and John W Traphagan. Albany, N.Y.: SUNY Press, 2008.

Takeda, Shōzō. "Mēdē sōjō jiken no shinri to hanketsu." Hōritsu no hiroba 23, no. 4 (April 1970): 6–12.

Tōdaitōsō bengodan. *Tōdai 1. 18, 19 tōsō saiban bōtō chinjutsu-sho*. Tokyo: Jiritsusha, 1970.

Tōdaitōsō bengo-dan. *Tōdai saiban: towareteiru mono wa nani ka*. Tokyo: Tabata shoten, 1969.

Tōdaitōsō zengaku kyōtōkaigi, ed. *Toride no ue ni wareranosekai o: dokyumento tōdaitōsō*. Tokyo: Aki shobō, 1969.

Upham, Frank K. "Political Lackeys or Faithful Public Servants? Two Views of the Japanese Judiciary." *Law & Social Inquiry* 30, no. 2 (2005): 421–55.

Watanabe, Hiroshi. "Tōdai saiban tōsō wo furikaette -- kyūtaibu no tachiba kara." In *Shiryō: tōdai saiban tōsō*, edited by Tōdaitōsō tōitsu hikoku-dan (jiritsu-sha) shiryō henshū iinkai, 251–53. Tokyo: Tōdaitōsō tōitsu hikoku-dan (jiritsu-sha) shiryō henshū iinkai, 1978.

Yokoyama, Keiichirō. "Kōryū, tokuni kōryū riyū kaiji o megutte." *Hōritsu Jihō* 41, no. 8 (July 1969): 10–19.

Yomiuri Shimbun. "63nin ga kega." January 20, 1969.

Yomiuri Shimbun. "Bōryoku gakusei: kibishiku tsuikyū." January 25, 1969.

Yomiuri Shimbun. "Joshi gakusei ni hatsu no hanketsu: hansei mitome no shikkō yūyo." March 13, 1969.

Yomiuri Shimbun. "Tōdai jiken de manmosu seikyū." March 15, 1969.

Yomiuri Shimbun. "Tōdai jiken hatsu no hanketsu: hansei no tōyōdai nama, shikkō yūyo." March 6, 1969.

CHAPTER 5

Establishing and Contesting Procedure

In a discussion of the Tokyo University trial that appeared in the June 1969 edition of the legal journal *Juristo*, lawyer, legal scholar, and expert on Japan's Code of Criminal procedure Tamiya Hiroshi reflected on the novelty inherent in the case:

> When dealing with classic or traditional crimes, the role of the criminal courts and their areas of investigation are relatively clear and mutually understood. With public security cases and other new crimes, however, we are forced to reflect on new substantive legal theories of crime and are also forced to confront new and fundamental procedural questions one after the other.[1]

This chapter uses Tamiya's observation as a starting point for exploring how the courts and the Bengodan grappled with 'these fundamental questions of procedure'. As outlined in chapter three, Zenkyōtō was not a traditional political movement advocating for institution reform within Japan's pre-existing norms of political practice. It was instead a movement defined by anti-formalism and the rejection of separation of thought and action; an organisation that adopted radical negation as its method and embraced emotion as a legitimate foundation for action. Furthermore, Zenkyōtō's politics was emergent and rooted in the present—a process of creative destruction that attempted to create breaches in order (*chitsujo*)

C. Perkins, *The Tokyo University Trial and the Struggle Against Order in Postwar Japan*, New Directions in East Asian History,
https://doi.org/10.1007/978-981-99-7043-8_5

to allow new political potential to emerge. Within this movement the individual and the collective were seen in a process of mutual transformation, as collective action fuelled changes in individuals that fed-back into the collective as part of a shared cognitive framework.[2] In contrast, the logic of the courts was, and is, held as the apotheosis of procedural rigour: a space of rules, norms and atmospheres that regulate both conduct and emotions, and in so doing legitimate trial outcomes as socio-legal truths. It is also a space that makes distinctions: between thought and action, individuals and collectives, and of course legal and illegal acts.

With these points in mind, this chapter analyses the contest of trial procedure not just as a technical matter, or an attempt at stalling the trial, but as a fundamental clash of worldviews. As such I ask questions about how the courts approached the new logistical challenge presented by the Tokyo University struggle indictments, and how the courts and the students' legal team tried to establish the legitimacy of their arguments about how the trial should proceed. On what basis, what moral authority, did that legitimacy rest? And how did the Bengodan contest the case? What was their strategy and on what theoretical ground did it stand? To answer these questions, this chapter examines the process through with the structure of the trials was contested, paying particular attention to how documents produced by the courts and by the Bengodan attempted to shape the relationship between the courts and the students and their lawyers. Both the courts and the Bengodan sought to frame their approaches in terms of safeguarding the rights of the students on trial, although the ways in which those rights were conceived were radically opposed. For the courts, securing rights was about focus on the individual, and expediting the trial so that the futures of those individuals could safeguarded. For the Bengodan, the rights of the students remained firmly in the here now as part of a struggle to maintain the irreducibility of the students' actions, and treating the students as atomised individuals before the state took away from them the framework needed to maintain that position. The two sides also took very different perspectives on questions of truth. The courts fought to restrict truth in the courtroom to framework of the Code of Criminal Procedure while the Bengodan argued for the introduction of a more expansive, and more destabilising form of truth seeking aligned with the goals and methods of the Zenkyōtō movement. As will be shown, however, the Bengodan faced significant challenges in this regard, not only due to the arguments of the courts, but also due to internal tensions in their own thought, which was never able to fully reject the source of the 'bourgeois jurisprudence' they contested, namely the post-war Constitution itself.

The main sources for this discussion is a collection of documents that crystallised the positions of both sides, the most important being the lawyers' Prospectus (*kessei'isho*) and their Written Opinion (*ikensho*), and the Court's two stage response: The Basic Policy on the Handling of Tokyo University Incident-related Cases (*Tōdai kankei jiken no toriatsukai ni kan suru kihonhōshin*, hereafter the Basic Policy) and a separate addendum entitled A Proposal on the Policy for the hearing of the Tokyo University case (*Tōdaijiken no shinrihōshin ni kansuru ichi teian*, hereafter Proposal). All three documents were publicised widely and became key reference points for the swirling discourse around the trial as it unfolded. The final section draws on roundtable discussions with Bengodan representatives and constitutional law scholars in which the Bengodan's theoretical position was pushed to its limits.

The Bengodan's Declaration of Intent

On 13 February, the Bengodan issued a public statement setting out their approach to the trial.[3] The statement was notable for its complete lack of reference to the crimes for which the students had been indicted. Instead, the legal team used the document to draw battlelines around procedure, which acted a proxy for distinct worldviews. They would pursue a collective trial for the students and in this they were unwavering. But this approach, they argued, was more than a legal strategy of defence or a simple strategy to paralyse the courts. It was in fact fundamentally related to the philosophy of the movement they were defending, and the implications of that philosophy for the lawyers' legal practice.

In this regard, the statement was a damning indictment of Japan's postwar legal structure. As the Bengodan saw it, the defence were traditionally considered inseparable from the three-part system that constituted Japan's 'unified view of the legal profession' (*hōsō ichigenkan*). Within this system, it was presumed that the defence shared a responsibility with the courts and the prosecution to ensure trials ran smoothly. In practice this meant that defence lawyers should make as little trouble as possible in the trial to ensure that cases were concluded quickly. Yet the Tokyo University struggle, which the lawyers argued had 'fundamentally questioned the nature of academia, the law, and the state within the context of 100 years of Japanese capitalism,' now compelled them to ask similar questions about their position as defence council.[4] 'Could lawyers become more than simply "shameful adjuncts to the court"? Could they overcome their complicity within a system designed to maintain the political status-quo?' they asked at the outset of the statement. Their response to this question was categorical. 'This time,' they declared 'there would be no cooperation with the courts.'[5]

The lawyers' philosophical orientation to the trial put them on a collision course with the most fundamental tenets of modern legal practice. Drawing on Jean Paul Sartre's introduction to the first edition of the French leftwing journal *Les Temps Modern*, the legal team framed the trial not in terms of guilt or innocence, but as a battle against what they identified as 'bourgeois jurisprudence' (*burujoa hōron*). The primary nature of this orientation to the law, they argued, was that it applied the 'analytical mind' (*bunseki teki seishin*) to all human endeavours, and in so doing broke down human actions into their respective constituent parts, just as modern science reduces matter into its constituent elements. For Sartre, this analytical orientation was an important weapon for the masses in overthrowing the unquestioned structures of the *ancien régime*. In opposition to that regime's structures of worth—birth right, blood, eldership and so on—man was now seen as the fundamental component of society: individual, indivisible, and equally deserving of human rights. All men were equal before the law. Yet in Sartres view equality, universality, and the analytical mind now functioned as a defensive weapon for the bourgeoise. Universalism was the new myth through which the bourgeois governed: it blinded society to real differences in power and resources, and emergent forms of collectivity based around those inequalities—such as class consciousness and the emergent Zenkyōtō community—could be analysed away.

The Bengodan applied Sartre's views to the trial by arguing the analytical mind of the courts posed a similar threat to the students' community. 'The power of the courts, which is based on bourgeois jurisprudence,' they argued '… analyses acts into fragments, separates the accused into a number of tribunals and tries to maintain the bourgeois order.' The real threat of the trial, then, was not that the students could be convicted, but that the analytical mind, as manifest in the process of the trial, would destroy the students' emergent community and values by reducing them to individuals before the law. To avoid this fate, the lawyers avowed to pursue a joint trial not as a legal tactic, but to negate the fragmentation of the Tokyo University struggle which they argued would prevent the significance of the event from being grasped in its entirety.[6] In essence, with this statement the legal team challenged the very basis of modern jurisprudence, arguing that it was fundamentally hostile to any mode of belonging other than to the hegemonic community of the (capitalist) state. In doing so, they forcefully declared they would not 'play by the rules of the game' necessary to produce the Tokyo University struggle into crime, and in so doing surfaced the question of the trial's legitimacy.[7] Thus, the reason for the lack of reference to the students' crimes was that for the defence they were incidental to the main goal of putting the trial itself on trial.

This position translated to three broad goals. First the trial, by virtue of the nature of the Tokyo University struggle, was conceptualised as moving beyond the boundaries of traditional courtroom battles. In this the Bengodan saw previous courtroom battles as focussed on vigorous defence of defendants but unwilling to go beyond the norms of bourgeois jurisprudence. Second, and related to this first point of overcoming traditional courtroom battles, the trial was viewed as an extension of the Tokyo University struggle itself. The goal was then not to contest the crimes in terms of guilt or innocence, but to radically negate the logic that produced the students' actions as crimes in the first place. The third goal was to use the trial as a vehicle for strengthening the resolve to fight in the face of oppression of the movement. The trial was to be a new front for the struggle embedded deeply within the legal system itself whose goal was to expose the naturalisation of violence in the courtroom under the guise of legal order, and in so doing erode that system's authority in the eyes of the public.

Tōitsu kyūtai, the Defendants Organisation (*Hikokudan*), the Bengodan, and the Families Association all signed up to this strategy. This did not mean, however, that consensus was easily reached. Within the Bengodan three broad opinions as to how to proceed with the case had emerged. First, in keeping with the tradition of courtroom battles there was the option of contesting the case within the framework of 'bourgeois law' as one concerning protection of the students' fundamental rights as guaranteed by the postwar Constitution. Second, consistent with the Bengodan's Proposal, was the option of transforming the trial into an instance of mass-negotiation modelled on the approach taken by Zenkyōtō at Tokyo University, in which the lawyers would focus on their own position within the legal system. And finally, there was the opinion that above all else securing the quick release of the defendants was paramount, and this would require cooperating with the trial process and allowing, with qualifications regarding their constitution, the small group trials to go ahead. These positions were reflected in Tōitsu kyūtai, and can be summarised as boiling down to the positions of mitigating the severity of sentencing, pursuing a joint trial at all costs, and securing the early release of the students. Ultimately, after heated discussion the basic strategy of pursuinig a unified trial was decided upon, although there was no real conclusion as to how that would translate into legal tactics.[8] According to the later assessment of Watanabe Hiroshi, who had been a postgraduate student at Tokyo University in 1968/69 and was a member of the Zenkyōtō support group, for hardliners in the Bengodan, the trial was an opportunity to extend the struggle into the courtroom, where the 'full picture' of the struggle could be painted, and where Zenkyōtō methods could be used to interrogate the basis of bourgeois law. But for many, if not all, members of Zenkyōtō kyūtai, whose primary goal was to secure the release of their fellow students, this approach raised more questions than it answered. It was clear that complete non-cooperation with the courts would almost certainly make it far more difficult to secure bail for the detainees. Furthermore, some worried that the debate over direction had taken place mostly within the legal section of Zenkyōtō, at the expense of wider mass debate with the broader support movement. Raising these issues, however, would invite being labelled pejoratively as cleaving to a simple 'post-incident processing' (*jikogo shori*) approach.[9] It was thus on the basis of the Prospectus that the Bengodan entered into negotiations with the Tokyo District court over procedure.

(Non)negotiations with the Court

The first question facing the Tokyo District court was the basic form in which it would hear the cases. There were two options. Option one, which is designed to try simple cases quickly, would treat each student as an independent case (*tandokujiken*) and distribute those cases to individual judges. In contrast the courts could opt for the 'panel system' (*gōgitai*), whereby cases are heard by a panel of three judges, and which is reserved for cases that carry potentially heavy punishment (the death penalty, life imprisonment or custodial sentences for more than one year), or which are particularly complex.[10] Since 1952 this decision had been made by a five-person panel (*saitei gōgi i'inkai*), which at the time of the Tokyo University Trial was headed by Chief Judge Yokogawa Toshio.

After its deliberations the committee reached the conclusion that, given most of the students were accused of independent incidents and had been indited on that basis, their cases should be classified *tandokujiken* and allocated to individual judges for hearing. This approach had the drawback of rendering onerous communications between the defence and the vast array of judges required to hear all the cases. To solve this problem, Yokogawa assumed the role of intermediary (*madoguchi*), listening to the requests of the defence, liaising with relevant judges, and communicating back outcomes. This arrangement, the courts argued, had now become standard practice for managing the rise in indictments of student unrest.[11]

Yokogawa, accompanied by Judge Toda Hiromu, proceeded to consult with the legal team between 21 February and 19 March, in the end meeting with them on four separate occasions.[12] The nature of this process became a sticking point in the trial, with both sides accusing the other of negotiating in bad faith and, subsequently, misrepresenting the discussions to the public. In the court's view the discussions never got off the ground: the lawyers simply argued for a joint trial against all reason. But while it was always unlikely, given the already polarised positions taken by the courts and the lawyers, that negotiations could ever be constructive, the story is more nuanced than simply one of defence obstinacy. This was because while the courts viewed questions of process as practical problems to be solved, for the Bengondan that process was, in the name of expediency, being wielded by the courts in ways that resonated uncomfortably with prewar inquisitorial practice.

The first meeting ended in the legal team reaffirming their public statement against separate group trials, a position rebuffed in short order by the court committee. Yokogawa and Toda then invited the Bengodan to submit a proposal for a unified trial, which the legal team did as a formal written Opinion (*ikensho*) on 6 March. The Opinion opened with the assertion that 'the 18/19 January actions of the young men and women prosecuted for the Tokyo University Struggles were those of one group with a shared objective, acting as a whole'.[13] With this in mind, the Bengodan had petitioned the courts to dispense with individual trials, and instead try the students as one group. The legal team's argument rested on three pillars. The first was procedural. The Bengodan argued that the choice to break the students into small groups for trial had proceeded as if this method was established precedent. The Bengodan stated, however, that this was in fact backwards: the precedent in cases where many defendants were to be tried for participation in the same offence was to assume one single trial and then, if necessary, make the case for a different approach. The courts had in effect pre-empted standard procedure by moving ahead with small group trials, which were the exception not the rule, and in doing so had put the defence and the students in the strange position of having to appeal for what normally would have been standard procedure. The Bengodan were also scornful of any notion that the limitations of the court estate should influence the format of the trial. These physical limitations, they argued, should have no bearing on the content of the trial itself, and they should certainly not be allowed to distort the pursuit of truth (*shinjitsu no tsukyū wo waikyokuka suru*).

The Bengodan' second point addressed directly one of principle norms of Japanese jurisprudence, namely what it meant to arrive at the truth of the incident. As the literature on Japanese prosecutors has shown, for prosecutors the norm of precise justice (*seimitsu shiho*) compels them to produce extremely detailed dossiers of evidence that not only contain the minutiae of the acts in question, but also the personal circumstances of the accused. This narrative is written to meet the constitutive requirements (*kōsei yōken*) of the crime in question, and the inclusion of a confession of guilt (with expression of remorse) grants that narrative its legitimacy by establishing responsibility (*sekinin*).[14] For the Bengodan, however, this method of ascertaining the truth (*jijitsu nintei*) was problematic in that it could only speak to the truth of acts as already defined in the penal code (*kōsei yōken teki jijitsu*). Trying such a case based on ascertaining whether 'a stone was thrown' would, in their eyes, make it impossible to correctly understand the meaning and social importance of the incident. In contrast the Bengodan argued that:

> There is a truth here that must be explored in this trial. The meaning of the actions of these young people does not lie in the fragments of action left over from the dissection of their bodily movements. The meaning only becomes clear when we understand the actions of the young people as part of a unified whole. Without this, we cannot see the state as a constituent element [*kōsei'in*] and we cannot ask questions about the culpability of the youth who bear responsibility for our future.[15]

In fact, for the Bengodan there was a double fragmentation at work. Not only was the collective action of the students subject to 'dissection' through application of the constitutive requirements of the penal code to frame their actions, but by distributing hearings across different court rooms, the Bengodan argued, witness statements and other evidence would also become disconnected from the whole. To go ahead with this method of trying the students would result in an incalculable disadvantage for the students; both in the context of the outcome of their individual cases, and also in their ability to express the legitimacy (*seitōsei*) of their actions. Such an approach, they argued, amounted to infringement of the students' right to defence. It also put great strain on the Bengodan's team itself as they would be stretched across several courtrooms rather than being able to focus their attention on one legal battle.

Finally, in contrast to the arguments emanating from the courts, the Bengodan maintained that the majority of students wished for their cases to be seen as part of a wider movement: they wanted to express themselves with their peers and sought for their actions to be judged as a whole. Should the case be allowed to proceed as separate trials, not only would the students' wishes be contravened, but there would be a proliferation of 'understandings of the whole' (*zentai ninshiki*). This outcome, the defence argued, would be worlds away from grasping the truth in a trial that warranted a single judgment from the state. The opinion ended with a plea which again raised the question of truth:

> We urge the court to hear the Tokyo University trial in a single forum, without prejudice or bias, and to recognise the true meaning of the actions that the Japanese youth have dared to take.[16]

Stepping back from the detail of the Opinion, a few key themes, all related to various forms of fragmentation, permeate the argument. The first was that procedure mattered. While the courts argued on the basis of practical solutions to the challenge of hearing such a large case, the Bengodan maintained that such pragmatism was not ideologically neutral. Choices born of physical or procedural limitations—the size of a room, methods of liaising with defendants—would necessarily impact the substance of the case and could not simply be worked around. The reason these pragmatic decisions mattered was related to the ideological foundations of the law itself. Consistent with their Prospectus, the Bengodan argued that the structure of the law, in particular the doctrine of constitutive elements, was only capable of uncovering an impoverished version of the truth of events by reducing them to a simplistic sum of their parts. Such a reduction, however, was for them impossible. The meaning of acts was not only born out of context but was inseparable from the intentionality behind them. And importantly, that intentionality was for the students at Tokyo irreducibly collective. Their actions only had meaning as part of the whole, and it was only through the whole that they could assert their legitimacy.

The importance of the group presented in Bengodan's Opinion resonates with a particular facet of Jean-Paul Sartre's philosophy: his perspective on varying forms of collectivity and the distinct freedoms they enable as outlined in his *Critique of Dialectical Reason*.[17] Although, in contrast to the Prospectus, the Opinion did not mention him explicitly, Sartre's conceptual paradigm for thinking through different forms of collective freedom was circulating amongst those in the movement at the time, and an overview of this framework helps deepen further interpretation of the significance of the fight for a unified group trial.[18] Of particular note is Sartre differentiation between group structures—which he labelled 'serial collectives,' 'groups in fusion,' 'organized groups', and 'institutions'. Sartre posited that each of these structures offered varying degrees of individual expression and that consequently, certain group formations offered individuals a greater degree of practical freedom than others.

For Sartre, the most basic of all collectives was the 'atomised crowd', which he referred to as a 'serial collective'. In this sort of collective, while all the members of the group may be working towards the same or similar goals, they are not conscious of each other and work independently. Sartre used the image of Parisians waiting for the bus to illustrate seriality. From the outside the would-be bus-riders appear as a collective. But, in fact, each is an isolated individual pursing their own goals with no connection to the others in the queue. What is more, argued Sartre, individuals in the serial collective may come to see each other as a threat: in the bus-stop example others in the queue might get in the way, or might be the person who pushes in and takes the final place. The others in the series thus become a threat to the practical freedom of the individual subject. Sartre argued that serial being is always produced by an external object, in this case the bus stop, that 'unifies each individual's intentional activity without creating an organic common bond between the individuals.'[19] The outcome is alienation and 'unfreedom': the individual is alienated from their freedom, from others around them, and is unable to express themselves organically in the world. They are passive actors, experiencing events as external forces that happen to them with no potential for shaping those forces' outcomes.

The serial collective was in Sartre's thought contrasted with 'the group in fusion' and its extension 'the organised group.' In contrast to the passivity of the serial collective, the group in fusion is active in fighting against a common external threat. Individuals recognize each other's subjectivity and work together, creating a sense of solidarity and mutual recognition. This group is marked by genuine communication and shared intentionality, leading to a form of 'freedom' as individuals are actively engaged in shaping their collective reality. To use the words of Gavin Rae: 'While the mass of individuals of seriality and the group formation called the institution constrain the individual's practical freedom, the democratic, organic, and spontaneous group formations called the group-in-fusion and the organized group enhance his practical freedom.'[20] It is thus only in organic collectives that individuals can achieve freedom; externally constituted serial collective could only ever lead to alienation, passivity, and social unfreedom.

The final type of group formation discussed by Sartre was the 'organised group.' The organised group is a way of thinking about the how the group in fusion maintains itself over time. Given that the group is fusion is always constituted by threat or crisis, it is always destined to dissolve once that crisis is either overcome, dissipates of its own accord, or becomes implicit rather than explicit. In these circumstances the group in fusion can put in place organisational measures to maintain the group and its commitment to caring for and affirming the group's guarantee of the practical freedom of individuals. They do this through a promise, in Sartre's words 'a pledge', either implicit or explicit, to 'affirm practical freedom from external threat.' Such a pledge:

> ...brings each member of the organized group to recognize and express solidarity with the other's practical freedom. The result of this reciprocated solidarity is a close knit group in which each member comports himself freely in relation to the other, supports the other's independent projects, and perceives the other to be an extension of, rather than a constraint on, his own practical freedom. For this reason, 'members [of the organized group] act in concert as a "we"'[21]

Sartre however also acknowledged that the organised group could, over time, atrophy into his final type of organisation that will again limit the practical freedom of its members: the institution. Institutions arise when the roles individuals play within the organisation become seen as more important than the individuals themselves. The individual ceases to be seen as unique and becomes 'trapped by the dictates and norms of the function he fulfils in the institution.'[22] As per the discussion in Chapter 3, it is clear that the principles of Zenkyōtō were codified as to avoid such institutionalisation coming about, although as will be discussed in later chapters the threat of institutionalization and the objectification of the movement—and the detainees within it—became very real as time passed. But in the context of this discussion of process, when put in the context of Sartre's framework the Bengodan's claim for the importance of being tried as a collective can be seen as an appeal to maintain their organised group, which in turn was their guarantor of meaningful practical freedom. Appearing in small groups as individuals would signal the reduction of the students' organised group to a serial collective constituted by the external force of the judge. At such a moment the students would lose their practical freedom and, in their confessions and testimony, become a potential threat to each other. The Bengodan's position therefore was that only through a unified trial could the rights of the students be upheld, as it was only in the collective that they were able to exercise their practical freedom.

The Basic Policy

One month later, on 3rd April, the Courts responded to the Bengodan with their *Basic Policy on the Handling of the Tokyo University Incident-related Cases*.[23] As noted above, this document, along with a separate addendum entitled *A Proposal on the Policy for the hearing of the Tokyo University Case,* set out the court's response to the Opinion. Both documents were performative assertions of legitimacy of the state to reproduce this order, grounded in the moral authority of paternalistic obligation to the future rights of the students. That performance began in the opening paragraph with a statement of the problem facing the courts:

> In the recent Tokyo University case, the largest number of students have been prosecuted since the courts began, and most of them are currently in custody. As a result, the judges of the Tokyo District Court's Criminal Division have been struggling day and night to find a proper and speedy [*tekisei jinsoku*] way to try this case.[24]

This short opening paragraph contained key themes that recurred throughout the document. First the unprecedented conditions of the mass prosecution was framed as a technical problem to be solved by the court, not one they themselves had a hand in creating. The fact that the students were mostly in custody was presented as an issue external to and wholly separate from the court's judicial remit, although as we have seen above the necessity of prolonged detention, and the courts' role in its sanction, was heavily disputed. Yet with the issue of detention externalised the court framed itself in the public eye as working in the best interest of the students by striving to resolve the trial as quickly as possible, and as such enable the detainees to continue with their lives. The attentiveness and diligence of the courts in pursuit of this aim was reinforced throughout the document. As well as the 'struggle night and day' noted in the first paragraph, Yokogawa explained that after they received a copy of the Opinion, the courts spent 'long hours' listening to the lawyer's detailed arguments for a unified trial, after which the Tokyo District Court Judges engaged in multiple debates that stretched into the night as they interrogated the very principles of criminal trial. The cumulative effect of this framing was to create the impression that the *Basic Policy* was a sincere attempt by a judiciary embattled on all sides to solve a problem not of their making but to which they were wholly committed.

The Basic Policy was structured around a dichotomy between *ideals and emotion* and *practical judgement borne of experience*, and this contrast provided the basis for the Court's rejection of the *ikensho* proposals. Yokogawa used the language of sentiment to acknowledge how it may *feel* (*shinjō toshite*) that due to the shared nature of the incident the students should be tried together, the practical considerations inherent in carrying out a trial cannot be 'resolved through *mere idealism*' (*tan naru risōron*, my italics). Experience had taught the courts how best to balance the demands of 'safeguarding human rights', finding 'the factual truth' of events, and the need for the 'implementation of criminal laws and regulations quickly and appropriately.'[25] In fact, to go against the legal foundations produced by these years of experience (*tanen no keiken*) would be dangerous and wholly irresponsible of the court. Thus 'after careful discussion from all theoretical and practical perspectives,' the courts concluded there was no alternative other than to proceeded with separate small group trials.[26] In further justifying this position the courts maintained three lines of argument: the limits of attentiveness (*ninshiki nōryoku no genkai*), the smooth running of the court, and that the concern of the court must be limited to the adjudication of guilt or innocence in respect to the charges levelled.

To begin with Yokogawa argued that a single group trial would prevent the courts from fulfilling their obligations due to the judges' inability to pay proper attention to each individual defendant. In a unified trial it would be simply impossible, he argued, for the courts to 'accurately judge and evaluate the existence and degree of individual and specific guilt through human contact and interaction with individual defendants who have individuality and subtle nuances in their actions.' With this argument Yokogawa claimed for the courts a key plank of the Bengodan Opinion. While the Bengodan may have maintained their approach best enabled the students to represent themselves, the court maintained that their approach was inherently more human (*ningenteki*) in that it would pay proper respect to the individuality of each defendant and the specifics of their equally individual actions. The courts were thus safeguarding the students from being lumped together and dealt with indiscriminately (*juppa hitokarage*). The size and composition of those groups, of course, was an open question but in that respect the courts could again draw upon their experience.[27]

The second distinction Yokogawa made was between the norms that govern the courts and the norms that govern other public spaces. This was a question of producing in the court an appropriate atmosphere. As anthropologists of the law have argued atmosphere of the courts is not only about order in the physical sense, but also about producing conditions in which emotional dispositions are regulated within a dichotomy legal reason and emotional unreason. As Leif Dahlberg argues maintaining this reason/emotion dichotomy is fundamental to modern law:

> The control and regulation of the display of affect and emotion in the courtroom should be seen in relation to the fundamental opposition between emotion and law (denoting both legal procedure and legal statutes), where emotion stands for disorder and unreason and law stands for order and reason, and hence where emotion is seen as exterior to law.[28]

Working within this dichotomy, Yokogawa argued that as the number of spectators grew (the implication being the audience would be large for a single trial) there was the danger that outbursts would be amplified by the effects of group psychology, and that in such a situation it would be impossible to maintain an atmosphere (*fun'iki*) appropriate for the justice system. Yokogawa contrasted the atmosphere of the court with that of the public event. The correct atmosphere of the courts, which as quiet and solemn (*seishuku*), contrasted with 'public speeches where applause and shouting are common.' Justification for this position was both practical and bound up with Japan's status as a modern nation state. In practical terms the strife internal and external to the courtroom caused by a unified trial would, in the view of the courts, raise the problem of safeguarding the defendants: a responsibility placed on the courts by society. But more importantly, to allow the atmosphere of the court to be anything other than peaceful would be to betray Japan's status as a modern nation. For as Yokogawa wrote: 'This is a principle established by the wisdom and experience of many years of mankind, and a fact strictly adhered to by all nations that consider themselves modern.'[29]

Third, Yokogawa addressed the question of truth raised by the Bengodan. In a display of what can be described as paternalistic empathy for the Bengodan' position, the court agreed it was vital to place the actions of the students within their proper context. 'As a criminal judge it goes without saying' argued Yokogawa, 'that we must view the defendants' actions holistically'. Indeed, for this case it would be very difficult to make a 'legitimate judgement and assessment of the defendants' culpability' without 'a certain level of historical and social background'. But in the same breath Yokogawa made it clear that the remit of the court must be defined by the Code of Criminal Procedure, and within that remit the focus of the trial must be the extent of culpability of the defendants. As such, use of background material must always be directed toward better understanding of defendants' actions for the purpose of rendering a sound verdict. The trial could not be allowed to pass judgement on the 'political system and education system', Yokogawa stated, nor 'the arguments and thought of the students.' He cautioned that allowing the trial to become a mass negotiation aimed at passing judgement on the Tokyo University Problem (*Tōdai mondai*) would violate the students' constitutional right to freedom of speech, thought, and belief as guaranteed by the postwar Constitution. And in a subtle nod to the ever-present fear of political threats to judicial independence, Yokogawa warned that such a trial would also likely bring upon the courts harsh sanction on 'several levels.' In sum, Yokogawa denied the courts harboured malicious intent to define and try the case in the narrowest possible terms. Instead, they would listen impartially to the students while working 'from the basis of a broad holistic perspective' to 'establish the correct meanings and evaluations of individual specific actions.'[30]

Finally, in addressing the Bengodan' argument that once separated from their peers the students would not be able to adequately assert themselves and the legitimacy of their actions, Yokogawa returned to the connection between emotional regulation and atmosphere. First, he reframed the Bengodan concern for solidarity as an issue of psychological isolation (*shinriteki kodoku*) and then pledged to reduce this situation to the greatest extent possible. However, once more he asserted that the court must not take on the atmosphere (*fun'iki*) of a public negotiation:

> [i]f the statements made by the parties involved end up as one-sided declarations that are thrown back and forth without any path of mutual understanding, this would be far from the ideal situation of a court where calm reason prevails, and there would be a great risk that the fundamental rights of the accused could not be guaranteed.

Regarding the necessity of the group to assert oneself, Yokogawa countered that such an argument was equally dangerous. 'A person's character, individuality, ways of thinking and ways of feeling,' Yokogawa continued 'must be respected on the basis that they are independent of others.' It cannot be allowed that these individual characteristics be 'buried' (*maibotsu*) in the whole such that defendants are unable to say what they wish to. Hence, it was not the Bengodan but the courts who would, through adherence to the criminal code, drawing on their long experience, and by maintaining the correct affective atmosphere in the courtroom, maintain the rights of the students.

Thus, the courts would hear the students' cases in small groups, proceeding on a foundational concern for the defendants 'character and responsibility' and considering the historical and social context while acknowledging the concrete restrictions imposed by the reality of the case. Ultimately, Yokogawa claimed the court's plan was designed to secure the future of these youths (*seinen*). 'We desire a speedy trial,' he stated, 'so that these promising young men and women [*seinen*] are not kept under prosecution proceedings for unnecessarily long periods of time'. Youthful exuberance should not be allowed to destroy the futures of the best of Japanese society. And if the defence acknowledged the sincerity of this position and the necessity of the proposed trial process in securing this outcome, the courts were willing to negotiate over procedure. But in a final turning of the tables on the defence, Yokogawa raised doubts that such a small team of lawyers could adequately represent the students and liaise with their families. 'We hope,' he concluded, 'that the defence will take appropriate measures to ensure that human rights are not compromised, such as calling on a wider range of lawyers or entrusting a certain number of defendants to state-appointed lawyers.' The subtext was obvious: it was the defence, not the courts, who due to their single-minded and monopolistic focus on a group trial, would be responsible for any perversion of justice.[31]

The final document, alluded to in the Basic Policy, was the *Proposal on the Policy for the hearing of the Tokyo University case* (Proposal). This document filled in some of the detail on just how the courts proposed to hear evidence in a way that balanced the need for a speedy trial with the demands of hearing evidence across so many different courtrooms. This issue, the document claimed at its outset, had significant bearing on the question of unified vs. small group trials, and necessitated cooperation by both the prosecution and defence to develop practical (*gutaiteki*) solutions to meet the imperative of a speedy trial as emphasised in the Basic Policy. In keeping with the focus on individuals and their circumstances, the Proposal called upon the prosecution to limit their questioning and evidence to the specifics of each individual case. Witnesses were to be kept to a minimum and photographs should be used if and when prosecutors wished to paint a picture of events. The defence, however, would likely wish to place actions within their broader context, and settling on a proper method for doing this was a significant challenge. Thankfully, the courts noted, the Tokyo University Incident had produced a large amount of primary evidence, such as personal accounts, photographs, and recordings, which could be relied upon as more objective than the secondary evidence of witnesses: a fact the courts 'experience and are acutely aware of in many daily incidents.'[32] As a result the courts requested the Bengodan use this material as the basis for their defence, only using witness testimony for clarification of specific points. To further streamline the process, when testimony was heard, the transcript should be made available to other courtrooms if applicable. Should several witnesses be called upon to testify, the work of hearing the witnesses should be split between different courtrooms and the transcripts shared. Of course, doing so relied on close and careful cooperation between the courts and the defence, especially given that the defence team were spread so thinly across courtrooms. But in the end, realising a 'rational' (*gōriteki*) approach to the trial could only be in the best interest of the prosecution and defence as:

> ... Dividing the hearing of evidence relevant to the case as a whole would avoid impracticality and waste by allowing the presentation of evidence to be focused and effective within the practical constraints of the case. This [approach] would also make it possible to conduct the proceedings in a truly comprehensive and expeditious manner.[33]

Thus, what emerged is the story of a battle between the diligent judiciary toiling under the practical demands of the law, and an intractable legal team whose ideology hampered them in arriving at the best outcome for the defendants. The judiciary, in asserting the necessity of individual trials, underlined firmly the value of acknowledging each defendant's distinct actions and characteristics—a stand against what they saw as indiscriminate treatment and as a testament to respect for individuality. The courts were also keen on maintaining a solemn atmosphere, effectively regulating emotions, and balancing reason and emotion. The pursuit of truth, while acknowledging the historical and social context of the students' actions, was confined within the bounds of the Code of Criminal Procedure, focusing on the defendants' culpability. Furthermore, there was a constant tension between the need for speedy trials and the mandate for fair representation of defendants, necessitating procedural adjustments and cooperation from all parties involved. In this regard the courts asserted themselves as champions of practical judgement, upholding independent character and rights. Thus, the narrative unfolded as a struggle between the experienced judiciary and the ideological Bengodan, with the former framing itself as rational grownups and the latter portrayed as idealistic children.

Making Groups and Impeaching Judges

The final piece in the puzzle was just how to divide the students into groups suitable for trial. In the event, the courts decided to split the student defendants into groups informed by the buildings the students were arrested in, the universities they attended, and when relevant their sect affiliations. While the first two categories were relatively easy to work with, the question of sect affiliation troubled the courts. On the one hand, grouping the students by factional affiliation could potentially give them an advantage by enabling them to cooperate closely. On the other hand, distributing rival faction members across different groups would, in the court's estimation, likely lead to tensions within the groups, outbursts from their supporters and in general 'cause unnecessary disruption'.[34] In the end the courts decided that the smooth running of the trial took precedent, and proceeded to construct, where appropriate, groups by sect. To do so the courts conducted their own investigation into affiliations of students and allocated accordingly. The decision to investigate the students and group by sect, however, now raised another issue: the spectre of judicial prejudice. Article 37 of the Constitution, along with guaranteeing speediness and public transparency, states that in all cases the accused has the right to an 'impartial trial'.[35] This broad guarantee is then governed under Article 256 of the Code of Criminal Procedure, which states 'No documents or other articles which may cause the judge to be prejudiced are to be attached or referred to in the charging sheet.'[36] In practical terms Article 256 had become enshrined in the doctrine of 'one indictment sheet' (*kiso ipponshugi*) and was part of the enactment of Japan's new postwar adversarial system in response to the inquisitorial role played by judges in the prewar legal system. The question now was whether the court's investigation had broken the 'one indictment sheet' doctrine and would prejudice judges against the students.

Of course, the court's response was an emphatic no. This answer rested on a category distinction between two aspects of the work of the courts: legal administration (*hōgyōsei*) and the work of the court as a judicial body (*saihantai toshite no saibansho*). The investigation, the courts argued, was instigated by the Court's Arbitration Committee (*saitei gōgi i'inkai*) as part of the administration of the case and as such had no bearing on the actual trials. Furthermore, citing a previous ruling that concluded such affiliations were nothing more than indicative of 'social position', the courts argued that simply knowing the sect affiliation of any given student would not influence a judge's assessment of the case. This situation was far removed, the court reasoned, from an indictment for fraud stating at the top of the page that the defendant was a serial fraudster. In the case of the fraudster the information was clearly relevant to the substance of the case (*jiken no jitai*) and it would be reasonable to assume the judge could be influenced by the knowledge of the defendant's previous exploits. The same could not be held, the court argued, for sect affiliation and the substance of the crimes for which the students were indicted.[37]

This investigation into factional affiliation by the courts worried the Bengodan, not only for the impact that knowledge might have on the trials, but also for precisely its administrative function. As one of the lawyers recounted in an article for the Japan Civil Liberties Union newspaper, during a bail discussion the judge asked a range of questions about the various sects including their level of violence and their relationship to the labour movement.[38] But those worries paled in comparison to their concerns over documents handed to them by Yokogawa and Judge Toda during discussions of the arraignment of students arrested at Sophia (Jōchi) University and at Chichibunomiya Rugby ground. These documents appeared to show that the court's information gathering went beyond sect affiliation to include whether defendants had confessed or were staying silent, their position within the movement (for example whether they were in a leadership position), and for the Rugby ground students their prior arrest record.[39] In justifying these investigations, the Courts again fell back on the division between administration and the work of the court as a judicial body. Knowing this information, they argued, would help them make good decisions about how to approach each individual defendant: for example, if a student had confessed then unnecessary interrogation of the evidence could be avoided. Furthermore, the courts were adamant that an adequate firewall was in place between the administrative and judicial activities of the court. The investigations had been carried out at the behest of Yokogawa by a fellow judge in the Traffic Department and judges involved in the student cases were never shown the documents (as evidenced by the character for 'secret' appearing in the top left of the Jōchi document, although this stamp was not on the subsequent document).[40] Judge Toda added his own justifications, noting that these practices had in fact been in place since the 1967 Haneda Incident, and would almost certainly continue in cases of large scale arrest and prosecution.[41]

It is clear there was no conspiracy here: if the courts were intent on using secret surveys to somehow pervert the course of justice, they would not have shared the results with the Bengodan. But when taken in the context of the political rhetoric discussed earlier, it is unsurprising that identifying faction leaders and detailing their arrest record, in both cases information with no substantive bearing on the crimes they were charged with, smacked to the Bengodan as a return of inquisitorial practices aligned with state interest: albeit now clothed in the beige of legal administration.[42] It was also, it turned out, untrue that judges presiding over the cases had not seen the documents—members of the committee that commissioned the report were actively presiding over related cases, and in fact Toda was himself acting as judge for one of the Chichibunomiya trials. When Toda's knowledge of the document came to light, Yokogawa maintained at a press conference in June that it was not an issue, arguing that although Toda had seen the reports 'he didn't remember their content' (Toda said the same thing in court a few days later).[43] This was of course hardly convincing for the defence, and for the broader left-wing press following the trial.

The Bengodan seized on these documents, which they publicly labelled 'prejudice tables' (*yodanhyō*), as evidence of their contention that the Japanese courts were now firmly part of Japan's postwar security apparatus. As well as denouncing the tables in the press, on 17 June 1969 the Bengodan filed an official written petition with the Judge Indictment Committee (*Saibankan sotsui i'inkai*) demanding Yokogawa be impeached under the terms of the 1947 Impeachment of Judges Act (*Saibankan dangai hō*).[44] In the petition, lead lawyer Yamane Jirō argued that the tables had two implications. First Yamane asserted that the tables represented a breach of the students' right to be tried based solely on materials made publicly available during the trial and was thus in contravention of Article 37 of the Constitution. Second was the aforementioned issue of prejudice. Notably, however, the complaint argued that the question of prejudice was less about individual judges' opinions and more related to the structure of the trial itself. That the basis of the 'separate trial approach' was information the courts had no right to collect delegitimised the entire process. By allowing these circumstances to come to pass Yokogawa had, in the Bengodan' estimation, committed a 'significant breach of professional duty' as governed by Article 2 Section 1 of the Impeachment of Judges Act and should under that same law be impeached.[45]

In a performative flourish the complaint was co-signed by Yamane, the rest of the legal team, and roughly 100 intellectuals (*bunkajin*) drawn from the worlds of academia, journalism, literature, and politics including Japanese Socialist Party (JSP) grandees Hozumi Shichirō, Okuda Haruo and Kuroda Hisao. It was also accompanied by a statement written by historian and former member of the House of Councillors Hani Goro, whose book *Theory of the City* (*Toshi no ronri*) was widely read by students in the movement, and who had himself served as a juror on the Impeachment Court. In his statement Hani argued that the normalisation of the 'prejudice tables' and Yokogawa's determination to push forward with separate group trials demonstrated that the courts were in danger of privileging technical questions of process over their role as the last bastion of human rights, as well as risking being seen by the people as acting on behalf of the executive branch. In this regard, argued Hani, the Impeachment Committee, which is comprised of members of both houses and in requiring a two thirds majority decision was non-partisan, had a special role to play in enabling democratic oversight of the bureaucratic judiciary.[46] The inclusion in the petition of this raft of intellectuals and politicians likely had in mind two audiences: the general public following the case via the newspapers and weeklies, and the Diet sponsored panel, itself constituted of politicians, who would rule on whether to escalate the complaint to trial. Much as with the Kim Hiro case, with the petition Yamane was not only challenging process, but also challenging the court's hegemony over that process by ushering in voices from different discourse communities.

On 11th July, just three days after a similar petition had been submitted for impeachment of Yokogawa's colleague Monma Yoshio, the Indictment Committee issued a statement to the effect that neither case would be passed onto the Indictment Court, effectively quashing them both.[47] With this victory in hand the judges went on the offensive. At a press conference held the same day, Yokogawa claimed that the so called 'prejudice tables' had in fact been produced to help the defence lawyers at their request. According to Yokogawa the previous lawyers for students arrested at Jōchi and Chichibunomiya (who were arrested before the formation of the Bengodan) had wanted to know which defendants were in leadership positions because their trials would likely drag on and would be better heard together under the panel system (*gōgitai*). Therefore, rather than force the defence to rely on information gleaned from the prosecution, which would be one-sided, the courts decided to gather the information themselves—via the colleagues in the Detention Section (***kōryūbu***) and shared it with the defence in the process of settling the method of trial.[48] Yokogawa framed this process in normative terms as the 'customary' (***kanshuteki***) functioning of the court based on a relationship of 'trust with the lawyers'. Once Yamane and the Bengodan became involved, however, communication had broken down, leading to the petition and the day's ruling. Yokogawa was adamant similar surveys (beyond those related to sect affiliation) had not been conducted for students arrested at Yasuda Auditorium.[49]

We will probably never know whether in fact further surveys were conducted—it was now clearly not in the court's interest to share them even if they were. There are also many inconsistencies in the court's account of events that could easily be seized upon as evidence of conspiracy. But again, given that the documents were voluntarily handed to Yamane's team, such a view is probably unwarranted. More instructive is the fact the courts, as evidenced by sharing the documents voluntarily, by classifying them as administrative did not see how they could be viewed as anything other than helpful in securing an expedient trial. Yokogawa's appeals to the 'relationship of trust' with the defence can best be understood as referring to the tacit assumption that the prosecution, defence, and the courts work together to secure an outcome amenable to all parties as quickly as possible. For the courts the tables were a matter of process. But for the Bengodan—and their supporters outside the legal world—the outcome was conclusive proof that the legal system had been co-opted by Japan's security apparatus. The game was rigged. With legal process now unavailable to them, Yamane and his team vowed to take the battle to the people via the organs of public opinion. With the court system in peril, they argued, it was now up to Japan's sovereign citizens to come to its rescue.[50]

There was, however, an undeniable contradiction at the heart of the legal team's case for impeachment of Yokogawa. As Chief Prosecutor for the Supreme Court Hirade Hiizu, who had himself been a prosecutor before and during the war, argued, the defence's relentless assertion that the 'why' of the incident could not survive separate group trials tacitly admitted that the crimes did in fact happen. Indeed, as was demonstrated in both the legal team's 13 February declaration of intent and subsequent Opinion the legal team showed they had no interest in contesting the crimes the students were charged with. Was it not the Bengodan then, who were prejudicing the trial?[51] What Hirade did not see was that the Bengodan saw the legal process as fundamentally antagonistic to the students' position. The moment the incident became contested as 'crime' was the moment the movement relinquished its ability to define its own meaning. The indictments were part of the double dismemberment of the movement: fragmentation of the incident into a legal truth via the doctrine of constitutive requirements and fragmentation of the Zenkyōtō community via the process of individual group trials.

A Battle of Two Logics

The tensions discussed above were generated by profound differences in worldview manifesting in procedure. Borrowing Sartre's terminology, the Bengodans' conceptualisation of practical freedom and its relationship to their organised 'group in fusion', their view of the indivisibility of that group and the actions they took, and their views on the inseparability of thought and action stood in stark contrast to the court's position on individual responsibility, guaranteeing rights through rational expedient processing, and ascertaining truth only insofar as it related to the actions of the students in the context of the constitutive elements of the crimes for which they were indicted.

A sprawling roundtable in the June edition of leftwing publication *Gendai no me*, which featured Yamane Jirō and his colleague Hayama Takeo alongside constitutional scholars Ōsuka Akira and Kageyama Hideya, gives us an opportunity to investigate further the ideological underpinnings of the conflict, as well as the tensions that existed within Zenkyōtō thought as it manifested in this court case.[52] To summarise broadly, the discussion was framed in terms of a conflict between the logic of the courts as a place of 'bourgeois law' (within the framework of Japan's 'bourgeois democracy') and Zenkyōtō thought, which while more nebulous in its conceptualisation was nevertheless presented as a distinct worldview. As the discussion progressed it morphed into an excavation of the foundations of Japanese Law and a real-time experiment in how far the discussants were willing to go in questioning the assumptions that underpinned postwar Japanese democracy.

In the opening of the discussion Yamane and Hayama made the case that the Tokyo University trial was revealing how the law, in violation of Constitutional guarantees to the contrary, was now being used to police forms of anti-state thought. Yamane's argument was that this happened in two different ways. The first was overt actions by the courts and the prosecution that violated particular rights, such as the right to bail, the relationship between extended detention and confession, and the 'prejudice tables' which the Bengodan argued violated the students' right to an impartial trial. The second issue raised by Yamane was that the courts were applying the legal principle of constitutive facts in a way that suppressed student thought. In one sense this was already the case with prolonged detention and the more lenient treatment given to those students who opted for a quick trial and renounced the movement. But Yamane made the further claim that the principle of constitutive facts, which finds it foundations in Article 31 of the Constitution, was now being used as a weapon against Zenkyōtō thought. Application of the principle of constitutive elements to actions of the students stripped them of their meaning and as such their legitimacy. Thus, for Yamane there was a fundamental need to 'overcome' the principles of the bourgeois court, and with it Japan's 'bourgeois postwar democracy.'[53]

Yamane's argument regarding the need to overcome bourgeois democracy was pushed further by legal scholar Ōsuka Akira in a way that probed further the limits of Yamane's radical project. Ōsuka posited two possible interpretations of Yamane's claim that the goal of the trial was to 'overcome bourgeois democracy'. The first interpretation would be to argue that the courts, by failing to prevent the intrusion of prejudice in the trial, are operating in bad faith. In this interpretation the defence's role was to hold the courts to account using the letter and the spirit of the postwar Constitution. Ōsuka's second reading, was the idea of overcoming the bourgeois court itself. In this second scenario the Constitution transformed from a source of legal and moral authority for holding the court to account into being the fundamental obstacle to the fair and proper treatment of the students. Thus overcoming bourgeois democracy would be to jettison the Constitution itself.[54]

Ōsuka's reframing of the problem provoked a strong reaction from the other discussants. Yamane and Hayama were both clear they wanted to use the Constitution to hold the courts to account, and as such it was beyond the bounds of critique. The conversation then morphed into one about the hierarchy of obligations to the individual inherent in the Constitution. Ōsuka suggested that the yardstick for a proper critique of the trial should be the extent to which the criminal procedure safeguards the human rights of the defendants. For Ōsuka this then became the criteria for assessing the suitability of either the unified or small group trial structure. Yamane however did not see much mileage in this shift of emphasis as it was unclear whether his chief goal of enabling the students to assert their legitimacy fell under the umbrella of human rights. Moreover, it was in the language of human rights that the courts were able legitimise their approach to the trial. The courts could argue that safeguarding human rights necessitated an approach that focused on individual actions and individual responsibilities. Indeed, Yamane argued that the principles of individual responsibility and disaggregation of events into their constituent parts were mobilised at the very moment that the students were removed from their groups, with whom they acted and only through whom could they assert the legitimacy of their actions. Therefore he argued:

> ... I think that the logic of the bourgeois courts is such that they are blind to reality, and that they do not even guarantee real human rights. The bourgeois court logic does not guarantee anything, whether through the theory of constitutive requirements [*kōseiyōhinron*], the adversarial principle [*tōjisha shugi*] or a precise interpretation of the Constitution. In this case, I think we need a different kind of comprehensive thought and epistemology to deal with what is distorting even the very logic of the bourgeois courts.[55]

This question of rights within the context of the Constitution was a core tension in Yamane's thought. The Constitution, which Yamane did not wish to reject, guaranteed individual human rights, including freedom of thought and the right to be tried in accordance with already stipulated laws. The courts spoke in the name of the Constitution of safeguarding the rights of individuals, and the courts could maintain they cannot include the question of legitimacy of the actions in the trial because, as Kagayama argued in the roundtable, the law restricts exploration of legitimacy to the question of legality (and there was no contest that the actions were illegal). Thus, without the extreme step of calling into question the postwar Constitution itself, Yamane was unable to move forward with his argument. The only logical conclusion would be to argue that given the courts were, through the application of the principles of the Constitution, already engaged in a trial of political ideology, it was only right that students be able assert the legitimacy of their own thought. But to do so would be to lose the Constitution as a bulwark against the oppression Yamane and the other members of the roundtable saw occurring.

The conclusions drawn from this impasse by the lawyers and scholars were very different. For Ōsuka and Kageyama, who had clearly nailed their colours to the postwar Constitution, the current juncture necessitated a new 'social scientific' form of constitutional scholarship, which in contrast to traditional interpretive scholarship, was capable of examining the manifestation of the Constitution in the field and by doing so collate empirical evidence that demonstrated the working of state power within the legal system. In this regard, Ōsuka and Kageyama saw not the courts but social movements as the guarantors of Constitutional freedoms and saw the role of scholars as examining interactions between the movements and the law in order to rebuild the legal system on an empirical basis. For Hamaya this point was critical as it acted as a strong argument for unified trials. This was because if movements were unable to present themselves as a collective with their own logics, they would simply have the hegemonic interpretation for the law imposed upon them—and at that point they would have already lost.

For Yamane, however, the outlook was far bleaker. Although agreeing that it was only social movements that could act as a bulwark against the state Yamane concluded that the people should not look to the legal system (lawyers included) to safeguard them. In a conclusion that seemed to acknowledge the impossibility of maintaining group solidarity in the face of state power, and indeed seemed to represent the contradictions his own thought, Yamane concluded that:

> As a lawyer to say this might be irresponsible self-abandonment, but what I want to say is don't expect anything from jurists and lawyers. There might be not-guilty verdicts happening in the courts, but I feel like they are not acting as a break [on state power]. The only thing left is for everyone to stand in court with their own logic. Don't count on legal professionals: they are no more than components of the "logic of the courts"[56]

Yet, despite the fatalism of this statement the battle continued as in May the small group trials got underway, and the trial moved into a new and even more antagonistic phase.

Notes

1. Kitamura Tetsuo, "Shūdanteki kōan soshō no mondaiten–gakusei jiken wo chūshin ni," *Jurisuto*, no. 424 (June 1969): 62–77.
2. Kosugi Ryōko, "zenkyōtō to wa nandatta no ka: tōdaitōsō ni okeru sankasha no kaishaku to imizuke ni chakumoku shite," *Ōhara Shakaimondai Kenkyūjo Zasshi* 697 (2016): 33–48.
3. The statement was written by nine lawyers and published in "tōdai tōsō bengodan: kessei shuisho," *Kyūtai Nyūsu*, March 19, 1969.
4. Kumagai Hiroshi and Kotabe Yonehiko, "Tōdaitōsō bengo-dan no sekken jōkyō," *Juristo*, no. 438 (November 1969): 56.
5. Tōdaitōsō bengo-dan, *Tōdai saiban: towareteiru mono wa nani ka* (Tokyo: Tabata shoten, 1969), 13–15.

6. Ibid., 12–15.
7. Robert Burns et al., "Analyzing the Trial: Interdisciplinary Methods," *PoLAR: Political and Legal Anthropology Review* 31, no. 2 (2008): 303–29.
8. Shigehide Kōbe, "Tōdai zenkyōtō kyūtai no undō keika," *Kyowakoku* 3 (1970): 211.
9. Hiroshi Watanabe, "Tōdai saiban tōsō wo furikaette – kyūtaibu no tachiba kara," in *Shiryō: Tōdai Saiban Tōsō*, ed. Tōdaitōsō tōitsu hikoku-dan (jiritsu-sha) shiryō henshū iinkai (Tokyo: Tōdaitōsō tōitsu hikoku-dan (jiritsu-sha) shiryō henshū iinkai, 1978), 251.
10. "Saiban tetsudzuki keiji jiken," accessed March 22, 2023, https://tinyurl.com/5y329eww.
11. "Tōdai kankei jiken no gurūpu-betsu heigō-an no sakusei keika ni tsuite (Shōwa 44. 7. 10 Tōkyō chihōsaibansho)," *Jurisuto*, no. 438 (November 1969): 70., p. 70.
12. Toda would later become a Supreme Court Justice in 1978. Details of these meetings can be found in Ibid. and *Tōdai saiban: towareteiru mono wa nani ka*, 108–10.
13. Tōdaitōsō bengodan, "Ikensho (Shōwa 44-Nen 3-Gatsu 6-Nichi)," *Jurisuto*, no. 424 (June 1969): 78.
14. For a discussion of Precise Justice see I. Fukushima, "Three Models on Criminal Prosecution," *Journal of Criminal Law* 45, no. 3 (April 2006): 468.
15. "Ikensho (Shōwa 44-Nen 3-Gatsu 6-Nichi)," 78.
16. Ibid., 79.
17. Jean-Paul Sartre, *Critique of Dialectical Reason*, New edition. (London: Verso, 2004).
18. As Manuel Yang notes, as well as the work of Japanese thinkers such as Yoshimoto Taka'aki, it was virtually de jure for student radicals to carry and read the work of Sartre and Herbert Marcuse. See: Manuel Yang, "Yoshimoto Taka'aki's Karl Marx: Translation and Commentary" (The University of Toledo, 2008), 126.
19. Gavin Rae, *Realizing Freedom: Hegel, Sartre and the Alienation of Human Being* (Basingstoke: Palgrave Macmillan, 2011), 97, https://doi.org/10.1057/9780230348899.0012.
20. Gavin Rae, "Sartre, Group Formations, and Practical Freedom: The Other in the Critique of Dialectical Reason," *Comparative and Continental Philosophy* 3, no. 2 (2011): 185.

21. Gavin Rae, *Realizing Freedom: Hegel, Sartre, and the Alienation of Human Being* (Palgrave Macmillan, 2011), 102.
22. Rae, "Sartre, Group Formations, and Practical Freedom: The Other in the Critique of Dialectical Reason," 203.
23. This key document can be found across several sources. For consistency with the *ikensho,* however, I quote from the version found in Toshio Yokogawa, "Tōdai kankei jiken no toriatsukai ni kansuru kihon hōshin (Shōwa 44-nen 4-gatsu 3-nichi)," *Juristo,* no. 424 (June 1969): 79–81.
24. Ibid., pp. 79.
25. This is a reference to article one of the Code of Criminal Procedure (1948) which states in full: 'The purpose of this Code is to clarify the factual background of criminal cases and to adopt and implement criminal laws and regulations quickly and appropriately, while maintaining public welfare and guaranteeing the fundamental human rights of individuals.' "Code of Criminal Procedure (Part I and Part II)," 10, 1948, https://www.japaneselawtranslation.go.jp/en/laws/view/2056/en.
26. Yokogawa, "Tōdai kankei jiken no toriatsukai ni kansuru kihon hōshin (Shōwa 44-nen 4-gatsu 3-nichi)," 80.
27. Ibid.
28. Leif Dahlberg, "Emotional Tropes in the Courtroom: On Representation of Affect and Emotion in Legal Court Proceedings," *Law and Humanities* 3, no. 2 (2015): 176.
29. Yokogawa, "Tōdai kankei jiken no toriatsukai ni kansuru kihon hōshin (shōwa 44-nen 4-gatsu 3-nichi)," 80.
30. Ibid., 81.
31. Ibid.
32. Tōkyō chihōsaiban-sho keiji dai 15-bu saibankan, "Tōdai jiken no shinri hōshin ni kansuru ichi teian," *Jurisuto,* no. 424 (June 1969): 82. It is not overly clear here whether the courts are talking about themselves or making a more general point. As the sentence starts with 'wareware' (we) I have translated this as referring to the experience of the judges.
33. Ibid.
34. "Tōdai kankei jiken no gurūpu-betsu heigō-an no sakusei keika ni tsuite (shiryō)," *Hanrei Jihō,* no. 562 (August 1969): 20–22.

35. "The Constitution of Japan," November 3, 1946, https://japan.kantei.go.jp/constitution_and_government_of_japan/constitution_e.html.
36. "Code of Criminal Procedure (Part I and Part II)" (1948), https://www.japaneselawtranslation.go.jp/ja/laws/view/3364#je_pt2ch3sc1at23.
37. "Tōdai kankei jiken no gurūpu-betsu heigō-an no sakusei keika ni tsuite (Shōwa 44. 7. 10 Tōkyō Chihōsaibansho)," 72.
38. Ishikawa Hiromitsu, "Saibansho kenkai ni tai suru hanron: tōitsu kōhan wo megutte," *Jinken Shinbun*, April 1, 1969, 3.
39. Reproduced in " < 9-Gatsu13-Nichi > Tōdai jiken ni okeru 'bunkatsu hōshin' sakusei keika to tōkyō chisai no sekinin," *Jurisuto*, no. 438 (November 1969): 83.
40. Watanabe Hiroshi, "Gakusei-tachi wa naze shuttei shinai ka – saibansho no yodan o kokuhatsu suru," *Asahi Jānaru* 11, no. 28 (July 1969): 116.
41. Ibid.
42. Ishikawa Hiromitsu, "Saibansho ni taisuru hanron: tōitsukōhan o megutte," *Jinken Shinbun*, April 1, 1969.
43. See "Tōdai jiken ni okeru 'bunwari hōshin' sakuseikeika to tōkyō chisai no sekinin," *Jurisuto*, no. 438 (1969): 82.
44. "Tōdai bunri sainban de sotsui seikyū," *Yomiuri Shimbun*, June 18, 1969. A similar petition regarding Yokogawa's colleague fellow Judge (Monma Yoshio) was submitted on 7th July 1969.
45. The complaint is reproduced in Watanabe, "Gakusei-tachi wa naze shuttei shinai ka – saibansho no yodan o kokuhatsu suru,": 114–116.
46. Hani's statement was reproduced in *Tōdai saiban: towareteiru mono wa nani ka*, 353–59.
47. The short statement was reproduced in "Bunwari, ihō dewanai," *Yomiuri Shinbun*, July 11, 1969.
48. These justifications are reconstructed from the original press conference as discussed in Ibid., 14. and a latter published document "Tōdai kankei jiken no gurūpu-betsu heigō-an no sakusei keika ni tsuite (shiryō)," 71.
49. "Bunwari, ihō dewanai," 14.
50. Tōdaitōsō bengo-dan, *Tōdai saiban: towareteiru mono wa nani ka*, 151.

51. Hirade Hiizu, “Areru tōdai saiban,” *Jiji Hyōron* 1, no. 14 (August 15, 1969): 20.
52. Ōsuka Akira et. al., “Kyōtō kaigi no ronri to hōtei no ronri,” *Gendai No Me* 10, no. 6 (June 1969): 94–107.
53. Ibid., 100.
54. Ibid., 101.
55. Ibid., 102–3.
56. Ibid., 107.

References

“< 9-Gatsu13-Nichi > Tōdai jiken ni okeru ‘bunkatsu hōshin’ sakusei keika to tōkyō chisai no sekinin.” *Jurisuto*, no. 438 (November 1969): 79–83.

Burns, Robert, Marianne Constable, Justin Richland, and Winnifred Sullivan. “Analyzing the Trial: Interdisciplinary Methods.” PoLAR: Political and Legal Anthropology Review 31, no. 2 (2008): 303–29.

“Code of Criminal Procedure (Part I and Part II),” 10, 1948. https://www.japaneselawtranslation.go.jp/en/laws/view/2056/en.

Dahlberg, Leif. “Emotional Tropes in the Courtroom: On Representation of Affect and Emotion in Legal Court Proceedings.” *Law and Humanities* 3, no. 2 (2015): 175–205.

Fukushima, I. “Three Models on Criminal Prosecution.” *Journal of Criminal Law* 45, no. 3 (April 2006): 463–73.

Hirade, Hiizu. “Areru tōdai saiban.” *Jiji Hyōron* 1, no. 14 (August 15, 1969).

Ishikawa, Hiromitsu. “Saibansho ni taisuru hanron: tōitsukōhan o megutte.” *Jinken Shinbun*, April 1, 1969.

Ishikawa, Hiroyasu. “Saibansho kenkai ni tai suru hanron: tōitsu kōhan wo megutte.” *Jinken Shinbun*, April 1, 1969.

Kitamura, Tetsuo. “Shūdanteki kōan soshō no mondaiten--gakusei jiken wo chūshin ni.” *Jurisuto*, no. 424 (June 1969): 62–77.

Kōbe, Shigehide. “Tōdai zenkyōtō kyūtai no undō keika.” *Kyowakoku* 3 (1970): 207–8.

Kosugi, Ryōko. “Zenkyōtō to wa nandatta no ka: tōdaitōsō ni okeru sankasha no kaishaku to imizuke ni chakumoku shite.” *Ōhara Shakaimondai Kenkyūjo Zasshi* 697 (2016): 33–48.

Kumagai, Hiroshi, and Yonehiko Kotabe. “Tōdaitōsō bengo-dan no sekken jōkyō.” *Juristo*, no. 438 (November 1969): 56.

Kyūtai nyūsu. “Tōdai tōsō bengodan: kessei shuisho.” March 19, 1969.

Ōsuka, Akira. “Kyōtō kaigi no ronri to hōtei no ronri.” *Gendai No Me* 10, no. 6 (June 1969): 94–107.

Rae, Gavin. *Realizing Freedom: Hegel, Sartre, and the Alienation of Human Being*. Palgrave Macmillan, 2011.
———. "Sartre, Group Formations, and Practical Freedom: The Other in the Critique of Dialectical Reason." *Comparative and Continental Philosophy* 3, no. 2 (2011): 183–206.
"Saiban tetsudzuki keiji jiken." Accessed March 22, 2023. https://tinyurl.com/5y329eww.
Sartre, Jean-Paul. *Critique of Dialectical Reason*. New edition. London: Verso, 2004.
"The Constitution of Japan," November 3, 1946. https://japan.kantei.go.jp/constitution_and_government_of_japan/constitution_e.html.
"Tōdai jiken ni okeru 'bunwari hōshin' sakuseikeika to tōkyō chisai no sekinin." *Jurisuto*, no. 438 (1969): 79–82.
"Tōdai kankei jiken no gurūpu-betsu heigō-an no sakusei keika ni tsuite (shiryō)." *Hanrei Jihō*, no. 562 (August 1969): 20–22.
"Tōdai kankei jiken no gurūpu-betsu heigō-an no sakusei keika ni tsuite (shōwa 44. 7. 10 tōkyō chihōsaibansho)." *Jurisuto*, no. 438 (November 1969): 70–72.
Tōdaitōsō bengodan. "Ikensho (Shōwa 44-Nen 3-Gatsu 6-Nichi)." *Jurisuto*, no. 424 (June 1969): 78–79.
Tōdaitōsō bengo-dan. *tōdai saiban: towareteiru mono wa nani ka*. Tokyo: Tabata shoten, 1969.
Tōkyō chihōsaiban-sho keiji dai 15-bu saibankan. "Tōdai jiken no shinri hōshin ni kansuru ichi teian." *Jurisuto*, no. 424 (June 1969): 81–82.
Watanabe, Hiroshi. "Gakusei-tachi wa naze shuttei shinai ka -- saibansho no yodan o kokuhatsu suru." *Asahi Jānaru* 11, no. 28 (July 1969): 113–18.
———. "tōdai saiban tōsō wo furikaette -- kyūtaibu no tachiba kara." In *Shiryō: Tōdai Saiban Tōsō*, edited by Tōdaitōsō tōitsu hikoku-dan (jiritsu-sha) shiryō henshū iinkai, 251–53. Tokyo: Tōdaitōsō tōitsu hikoku-dan (jiritsu-sha) shiryō henshū iinkai, 1978.
Yang, Manuel. "Yoshimoto Taka'aki's Karl Marx: Translation and Commentary." The University of Toledo, 2008.
Yokogawa, Toshio. "Tōdai kankei jiken no toriatsukai ni kansuru kihon hōshin (shōwa 44-nen 4-gatsu 3-nichi)." *Juristo*, no. 424 (June 1969): 79–81.
Yomiuri Shimbun. "Tōdai bunri sainban de sotsui seikyū." June 18, 1969.
Yomiuri Shinbun. "Bunwari, ihō dewanai." July 11, 1969.

CHAPTER 6

Court Room Battles Along Parallel Lines

By April the battle over the shape of the trial was coming to an end. Despite the Bengodan's various appeals, protestations, and attempts at impeachment the student defendants were split into groups of around 10 and assigned to their respective courtrooms. The atmosphere both inside and outside the courts was by now febrile. Japan's domestic security apparatus was dealt a blow on 11 April when a student arrested for obstruction of official business (*kōmu shikkō bōshi*) at Hakata Station in the southern city of Fukuoka was found not guilty in the Fukuoka District Court. The presiding Judge Maniwa Haruo, in a statement that had the protentional to set limits on preventative police action in the name of public security, admonished the police for interfering with the helmet wearing students on the suspicion of a later disturbance of the peace, and in so doing placed blame for the subsequent violence solely on the authorities. With this verdict the constitutionality of preventative policing was called into question: 'If there is no specificity' read the verdict 'as to what crimes *will* be committed, rather than what crimes *may* be committed, enforcement under the law is meaningless.'[1] Nevertheless, police action continued apace. On 26 April, riot police broke the student occupation of Waseda University and the following day key members of Chūkaku and Kyōsandō factions were arrested under the Anti-Subversive Activities Prevention Act (Habōhō). Then on April 28, Okinawa Day, 965 people

C. Perkins, *The Tokyo University Trial and the Struggle Against Order in Postwar Japan*, New Directions in East Asian History,
https://doi.org/10.1007/978-981-99-7043-8_6

were arrested during demonstrations that brought Tokyo's rail network to a standstill. Of those 965 arrested, 187 were indicted the following month, bringing the number of students being processed by the courts to over 1200.[2] Renewal of the Anpo Security Treaty in 1970, and along with it the inevitable nationwide mass protest, loomed ever larger on the horizon.

In May, students, their lawyers, and their supporters embarked on a series of rallies to draw attention to the enforced small group trials, which were set to begin later that month. On 10 May, 5000 students and workers gathered at the Hibiya Open-Air Concert Hall in solidarity for those awaiting trial and in protest at the use of the Habōhō in the policing of student demonstrations. At the rally, the previous month's Okinawa Day actions were heralded as the next step towards a decisive battle over renewal of Anpo in 1970, but one that also strengthened the state's resolve in use of the Habōhō. In this context the Tokyo University trial took on even more significance, for if the defendants failed to secure a unified trial the prospects for subsequent trials of student activists—including those arrested on Okinawa Day—would be bleak.[3] The radical action of students had broken through the order in universities to reveal hidden mechanisms of oppression. It was now up to the students to dismantle the legal order, which was for them one and the same as the dominant governing order.[4] As Yamamoto Yoshitaka wrote in the rally publication, the risk now was that the breach in order achieved by Zenkyōtō would be all too soon sutured up through continued rationalisation of university structures and the return to dominance over the student movement of the JCP and Minsei.[5] The risk was also ever present for the movement itself: the words it used and the forms it took. As Yamamoto put it, 'we speak of the Tokyo University struggle now only as a "declaration of struggle" or "declaration of march", but when "rebellion" runs the risk of being replaced by "institutional rationalisation and modernisation", we must recall once more its human elements such as anger, pain, and joy.' In other words, it was only raw human emotion that could keep the struggle from petrifying into a parody of the very process of normalisation it sought to defeat. 'Order [*chitsujo*],' Yamamoto argued in the closing words of his statement, 'has formidable resilience. If we act within the realm of order, our thought—even our 'anti-establishment' thought—will become part of the pseudo-establishment.'[6]

The rally publication also contained an assessment of comparisons made between the Tokyo University trial and the trial that followed the 1952 May Day incident. In response to an Asahi Shimbun article exhorting all involved to avoid repeating the 'stupidity' of the May Day trial, the students argued that while on the surface there were similarities between the two trials, those similarities masked a fundamental difference in orientation. In the students' evaluation, the May Day trial was a contest between popular mass movements and the authority of the police, or in other words a clash between fundamental human rights and state power. In this sense they argued that the meaning of the May Day trial was in locating human rights with the Japanese people (*nihon minzoku*), and in so doing situating the courts on the side of the people against the state. The main issue for Zenkyōtō, however, was that this contest took place under the assumption that the postwar Constitution was a 'wonderful thing' (*subarashii mono toshite*), which the courts should protect. It was here that Zenkyōtō saw the main difference between themselves and the protagonists of the May Day trial:

> [Reflecting on the struggle] If we see the emergence of a fascist mass movement that capitalized on the failure of Minsei's democratization front and the execution of Katō's modernization front in the Tokyo University struggle, our trial fight is not based on the bourgeois law represented by the Japanese Constitution, but is clearly posed as an unyielding fight against the entire bourgeois system of legal order.[7]

Thus, while the May Day trials had resulted in a number of victories for the defendants, Zenkyōtō rejected any direct comparison as a fundamental misreading of the current juncture.

This rejection of the May Day trial paradigm was partly related to a spat that was developing between the Bengodan and the Japan Lawyers Association for Freedom (JLAF), the organisation which had been key to the May Day courtroom battle. In an article entitled 'Do "violent students" have rights?' in the April edition of the major left-leaning intellectual magazine *Sekai*, Bengodan lawyer Ishikawa Hiromitsu had accused Japan's established left-wing legal associations of closing ranks on the students. In response to calls to protect the rights of student radicals in the face of police violence by lawyers who would later join the Tokyo University case, Ishikawa claimed, the JCP dominated Labour Lawyers Association of Japan (*Sōhyō bengodan*, LLAJ) had stated publicly that 'the students' tactics were designed to break apart the forces of democracy [*minshu seiryoku*] in Japan and as such were wrong.' Ishikawa argued that one lawyer associated with the LLAJ went one step further, arguing that 'Sanpa zengakuren students are the enemy of democratic forces in Japan. Class enemies have no rights. The police should crack down on them vigorously.' Similarly, the Japan Lawyers Association for Freedom (*Jiyūhōsōdan*, JLAF), the organisation which had been key to the May Day courtroom battle, came out in strong opposition to defending student radicals. For Ishikawa this opposition had manifested in the JLAF proposing a revision to their constitution which replaced 'human rights' (*jinken*) with 'the rights of the citizen' (***kokumin no kenri***) and insert into its wording, using the same phraseology as the LLAJ, the importance of 'forging alliances with the forces of democracy' in its approach to legal representation.[8]

The JLAF rejoinder to these accusations, penned by the organisation's executive secretary and veteran lawyer of the May Day Trials Ishijima Yutaka, appeared in *Sekai* in July 1969.[9] As well as calling Hiromitsu's article slanderous, the Ishijima accused the students' legal team of making a fundamental mistake in their analysis of the students and human rights. For Ishijima, the issue was not about the human rights of the students per se but should be construed in terms of the students' relationship with the concept of human rights more broadly. While it might appear that the students were engaged in a battle against state power, he argued, the reality was that student provocations gave the state all the reason it needed to extend its coercive power into the realm of human rights. The outcome was that student radicals were complicit in the destruction of the 'democratic movement of ordinary citizens.' The use of repressive weapons—physical and legal—levelled at the students by the state had now been legitimised by their successful usage.[10] With that precedent now set, Ishijima argued, the same weapons could be used against Japan's broader labour movement and indeed all Japanese citizens. As such the correct evaluation of the students was as themselves violators of human rights; in a sense complicit with the state. Defending the very same students would exacerbate this threat:

> Objectively, justifying and defending the actions of such groups [student radicals] would constitute a betrayal of the real democratic movement and the real struggle for human rights in this country. And it would also harm the movement for the protection of 'human rights' in the true sense of the term.[11]

It was in this spirit that the JLAF had debated revising its constitution. For Ishijima, inserting 'democratic forces' into the wording made clear the JLAF's mission of protecting the rights of ordinary Japanese citizens and was designed to nip in the bud any confusion amongst the organisation's ranks as to that fundamental mission.

As well as restating their resolve to battle on in the courts, the demonstrators marched on the Sankei Shinbun company headquarters to register their outrage at what they viewed as press complicity with state security. In March, the tabloid Yūkan Fuji, a publication of the right-wing Sankei Shinbun company, had printed an article entitled 'The Battle for Tokyo University—The Mystery Woman' about a female student awaiting trial who named herself, after the room in which she was initially detained, 'Kikuyabashi Number 101'. After arrest Kikuyabashi had maintained complete silence such that the authorities were unable to ascertain even her true name for the indictment; Kikuyabashi herself maintained that 'as long as I am in this prison I have no name.'[12] The Yūkan Fuji article in question, however, contained an image which appeared to be a montage of a shot of a student wearing a helmet and wearing a towel across their face, and a picture of Kikuyabashi taken at the detention centre. The Bengodan argued in a statement that such a publication violated Kikuyabashi's fundamental rights, including her right to silence and the rights she exercised over the use of her own image. The montage, they argued, seemed a crude tactic by the editorial board of Yūkan Fuji to circumvent the latter right by making the image appear to have been taken in the field and thus a piece of legitimate reportage.[13]

Yūkan Fuji responded typically pugnaciously by publishing Kikuyabashi's real name, her background, information about her family and friends, and images of her in a police paddy wagon. Clearly unmoved by accusations of alignment with the police, Yūkan Fuji simply stated that publication of said details was an editorial decision and there was no need to apologise. In a leaflet distributed during the rally against the publisher Sankei, the students accused the mass media of being in the vanguard of the ruling classes 'actively attempting to overwhelm the [Japanese] citizenry in the name of '"freedom of the press"'. When the demonstrators arrived at Sankei headquarters in Ōtemachi on the evening of the 10th they found the building shutters down, surrounded by riot police and plainclothes policemen, and ready for a siege.[14] After shouting their collective 'non' towards the police and the right-wing press the students dispersed into the night.

All the while the courts were processing students who had opted for separate group trials. While initially it was postulated in the press that around 10 percent of the students constituted this group, by May 150 students, around 25%, had been processed by the courts. Suspended sentences of one to three years imprisonment were the norm, with judges both admonishing students for their violent acts and noting their repentance in their verdicts. Such students were assigned counsel by either their parents or the courts. Courtroom reporters noted that in cases of the former, the defence would simply call upon the defendant's mother to make an emotional statement to the court in what the journalists dubbed a 'tears please' style (***namida chōdai shiki***) defence. At the other extreme it became difficult to tell the difference between the prosecutor and counsel. In one example a journalist reported the following exchange:

> The defence lawyer turned to the defendant and asked whether he will 'wash his hands of the movement', much like you would ask a member of the yakuza. The defendant stayed silent so the lawyer asked, 'you have no intention of washing your hands of them?' [To that the defendant replied] 'Well, I will do it'. [And the lawyer said to the judge] 'Well, as you can see, the defendant is sorry...'"[15]

The courtroom demanded the defendant show remorse, and the defence played its proper role in facilitating this demand. The expression of remorse was internally connected to the act of 'splitting of the self' from activist to general member of society. The student's hesitation a marker of the difficulty entailed in condemning the prior self and the values of the community that helped constitute it.

The Courtroom as Fortress

The group trials started on 27 May. Cases were heard daily, with hearings often running in parallel across several courtrooms at once. Every morning spectators lined up outside the Tokyo District Court building for a chance to be admitted to one of the courtrooms. Due to the significant interest in the trials, spectatorship was ticketed with around 50 people allowed into larger rooms and between 20 and 30 allowed into the smaller courtrooms. Furthermore, the rules for managing spectators introduced in 1952 with the Act on Maintenance of Order in Courtrooms were in force. The long queues were monitored by plainclothes police carrying batons concealed in cloth. One eyewitness courtroom spectator, writing under the pseudonym Muchaku Toki recalled seeing one police officer with communications equipment also wrapped in cloth. Reflecting on the apparent subterfuge she pondered: 'Who were they reporting on us to? Why did he need to hide his radio? I was getting angrier and angrier towards this as yet indistinct person.'[16] Later, while still in the queue, officers of the court approached the line carrying a cardboard box. 'We will look after your umbrellas' he said as he took custody from the spectators of anything rod-shaped that could be construed as a weapon. The hearings took place on the 5th and 7th floors of the court building. The elevator took spectators only as far as the 5th floor; to reach the 7th floor they had to use a narrow central staircase. According to one account the floors used for the trial were 'separated from the other courtrooms and fortified like a citadel.'[17] Another courtroom attendee, 26-year-old teacher Yoshizawa Mieko, also recounted the atmosphere generated by the police presence. 'Even as the tickets were being handed out,' Yoshizawa wrote in a letter to the Asahi Newspaper, 'we were under the gaze of around ten guards. Under this surveillance I felt like perhaps I was a criminal. I felt uncomfortable as I took my seat in the gallery.'[18]

The hearings themselves quickly fell into a pattern. In attendance were the judges, prosecution, defence and students and a small number of students belonging to the group that had been released on bail. Invariably, the remaining students in the group—who were still in detention—refused to appear in court. The first order of business was for the court stenographer or one of the security staff present to note the situation of the students not present: 'Defendant xx at Tokyo Detention Centre stripped naked, clung to the lid of the sink, and shouted "down with separate group trials." All the while his face was rigid [*ganmen kōchoku*], and the situation was extremely difficult.' The journalist who recounted these statements noted to himself that the language used to describe the 'rigid faces' had medical connotations. 'To begin with,' he observed, 'I thought they were referring to some sort of illness of the facial nerves. But all the defendants were described in this way. This was a courtroom-style or detention centre-style rendering of tense student expressions.'[19] In a sense the emotional regulation of the courtroom extended even to those students not in attendance: the raw anger of the moment of student resistance—precisely that which Yamamoto Yoshitaka had urged the movement to maintain—was here translated into the rational formality of a quasi-medical diagnosis.

Next the students present would refuse to sit down when ordered to by the judge and make statements against the enforced group trials. As discussed in the introduction, some would appear with slogans painted across their white shirts or on their bodies.[20] Spectators who voiced their agreement with the students were often ordered out of the courtroom by the judge at which point they would be whisked away by courtroom security acting in pairs. Arguments from the legal team as to the unlawfulness of the proceedings were dismissed by judges as belonging to appeals in higher courts and the judge would declare the opening of proceedings. Muchaku Toki recalled this course of events leading to unrest in the gallery and amongst the students and lawyers. In response the presiding judge stood up ordered the courtroom cleared. As her first experience in a courtroom Muchaku found these events profoundly shocking. According to her account she sat in a daze as the courtroom was cleared, wondering what sort of trial this was and why the judge could not answer the lawyer's questions. When she became aware of her surroundings once more the legal team was gone, as were the two student defendants and all but five of the spectators in the gallery. At this point the trial continued with the defendants and the defence in absentia. Muchaku left the courtroom with the remaining spectators and made her way outside. There she found demonstrating students, including those who had been ejected from the court, being confronted by riot police in body armour. Before she knew it the riot police had bundled the spectators and students to Hibiya Park.[21]

Yoshizawa, who had also witnessed the courtroom being cleared recalled her own experience of security in the court. On returning to the courtroom from the toilet:

> The eyes of the guards in the corridor all sparkled at once, and then I heard one of them say "she's one of them from before [*mae kara ita yatsu*], you can let her through." It is doubtful that the words were not imbued with one-sided hostility. At the same time, this makes me uneasy about the court attitude towards the accused.[22]

Another spectator, 51-year-old philosopher Mononobe Nagaoki, did not get off so lightly. When proceedings were opened and Mononobe saw that neither the defendants nor their lawyers were present he called out 'Judge, can this be a trial?' to which the judge responded, 'Spectators are prohibited from speaking' and continued with the hearing. Mononobe then asked whether this was a 'secret trial' (*ankoku saiban*) and whether the judge was aware of the Constitution. At this point the judge ordered 'the man in the blue shirt' (Mononobe) removed from the courtroom. On leaving however, Mononobe was greeted at the exit by a police officer who escorted him to another courtroom where, by his account, over fifty riot police were stationed. Echoing the concerns raised by lawyers during the Diet discussions on the Act on Maintenance of Order in Courtrooms, who were worried about convictions under the law without due process (see Chapter 2), Mononobe reported being put in handcuffs and escorted to a custodial hearing where a preprepared indictment was read out against him. 'I was not allowed to defend myself,' Mononobe recounted. 'In the end I had the rare pleasure of spending seven days in the Tokyo Detention House. I wonder why my utterances were seen as "abusive language" [*bōgen*].'[23] There were also accounts of violence meted out against students. Lawyer and Director the of the Japan Civil Liberties Union Uchida Takehiro, for example, reported witnessing a female spectator being thrown out into the corridor and her head 'vigorously hit against the wall.' After he spoke out about the incident in the press, however, such overt acts against spectators appear to have been kept to a minimum.[24]

The strategy of the defence in the courtroom was to continue to question the distinction between norms, customs, and the law, with the goal of demonstrating to the assembled journalists the shifting foundations for the courts' claim to legitimacy. Another example recounted by Muchaku helps illustrate this. As Judge Iguchi entered the courtroom for the trial of Yasuda Group 5 on 29th July those in attendance were ordered to stand. Apart from two people the room stayed seated. After those who remained seated did not respond to orders from courtroom security, Judge Iguchi ordered them ejected from the courtroom. In the scrum that followed students were knocked over and one female student, who refused to let go of her seat, was dragged away by three guards. When the defence demanded the reasoning behind ejecting the spectators Muchaku recounted the following exchange:

> -Judge! Why have you ejected the spectators? A public trial is guaranteed by the Constitution. Call back the spectators.
>
> -Those who don't stand when asked were ejected from the court. That uproar just now...
>
> -Where is it written in law that those who don't stand when asked must be ejected from the court?

-It isn't written in law. But in this courtroom, it is a long-established custom that you must stand.

-Judge, which carries more weight, custom or the Constitution?

-It is not a question of which carries more weight. Customs are customs, and those who disobey the Judge's orders are ejected from the court.

-Judge! There are journalists in this room. The fact you have trampled over the constitution to enforce custom will be reported in the newspapers. And this is okay with you?

-You [*kimi*], be careful with your words. What are you thinking, talking to a judge like that? Sit down. You people [*kimi tachi*] have come here to defend your clients. If you are lawyers, then how about behaving like lawyers?[25]

-Judge, you just referred to us as *kimi*. I will also refer to you as *kimi*.

-Ah, go ahead.

-You, *kimi*, said that if we are lawyers we should behave as such. But I have put my career as a lawyer on the line to defend the rights of my clients. It is precisely because I am a lawyer that I will not comply with these illegitimate group trials.

-We have already given our opinion on the legitimacy of group trials. There is no use in arguing with you. Remove these three [lawyers] from the courtroom.[26]

Events such as those witnessed by Muchaku resulted in many indictments of the lawyer in question—Yamane Jirō—under the Act on Maintenance of Order in Courtrooms. An indictment for a similar situation described a testy exchange with Judge Kiyomizu over cross-examination of a witness during which Yamane accused Kiyomizu of not answering his questions. Kiyomizu ordered the legal team removed from the court, but Yamane and his team refused to leave and resisted the efforts of court security to bundle them away. As this was going on, Yamane was noted as shouting: 'Judge Kiyomizu, you see lawyers as nothing more than a court ornament. We are all lawyers. And we won't acknowledge a court that doesn't acknowledge us as such!' The indictment, which called for a 20,000 yen fine, concluded that Yamane's 'failure to take his seat, his disregard for orders to stay silent and to leave the courtroom, his abusive language, and his obstruction of the trial had profoundly damaged the dignity of the court'. This fine was not the first, nor would it be the last. Indeed, the fines escalated until in October, after another exchange with Judge Iguchi, Yamane faced his first custodial sentence of 5 days.[27]

As will be discussed later in this book, this exchange with Iguchi would come back to haunt Yamane years later.

Once the courtroom was cleared the prosecutor and judge would proceed to an investigation of the evidence. Despite earlier claims by the prosecution that long detention was necessary for their investigations, as in previous trials of students witness testimony from riot police involved in the arrest of the defendants was the central plank of their case. The prosecutor went through the motions of asking the background, rank, police section, and where they were deployed at the university. After these preliminaries were finished the prosecutor would show the witness a photograph of the defendant and ask whether this was the student they had arrested. Once confirmed the prosecutor would rest their case. As was stipulated in the *Proposal on the Policy for the hearing of the Tokyo University case* discussed in the previous chapter, the judge would then use Zenkyōtō literature and any statements from the defendants' family to defend and contextualising the defendants' actions.[28]

There were of course differences in how various judges handled their courtrooms. As the press observed, judges fell into two camps. On the one hand, the 'doves' tended to be tolerant of courtroom noise and were keen to explain process and decision making, resisting as much as possible calling upon the guards or the riot police to clear the courtroom and even then, being targeted in who was asked to leave. On the other hand, 'hawks' were more provocative in their approach—being quick to ban people from speaking and then making liberal use of that pretext to expel spectators, defendants, and their lawyers. One judge seen by the press as a prime example of a dove was Urabe Mamoru. Urabe had attracted some interest in the press due to a letter he wrote to students asking them to exercise their rights to a trial, and for seemingly drinking tea with student defendants, which while taken out of context certainly provoked the anger of the right-wing press. But Urabe's conduct demonstrated clearly that there was an alternative to hard-line policing of the courtroom. At one hearing, for example, Urabe noted that a spectator was taking notes. This, Urabe stated, was against procedure. The student protested that he was not obstructing the trial and given that the press was allowed to take notes so should he. At this point, the exchange could easily have taken the path of those seen earlier—ejection of the student from the court. But instead, the conversation proceeded as follows:

-Journalists have an obligation to report on events impartially. You do not.

-They [the press] don't report impartially. And do you have a basis for stopping me?
-I do. But I don't have time to go into the details now.
-If I come to your chambers after the trial, will you explain it to me?
-If I have time, yes I will.[29]

After this exchange the hearing continued. Urabe was also an important counterfactual to the Bengodan argument that the courts had in this case simply aligned themselves with the prosecution. One such example was a heated argument in his courtroom over the prosecution's obligation to disclose evidence. This issue, on which the law was fuzzy, was a significant point of contention across the trials, and as observers noted a prime cause of courtroom strife. After the prosecution had questioned a witness, the defence argued that the prosecution had not disclosed the content of the witness' statement prior to the trial, which contravened the Code of Criminal Procedure. The prosecutor countered, citing a High Court decision, that as the witness had been called to the courtroom to be questioned, there was no obligation to disclose prior evidence to the defence. Urabe, however, remained unconvinced and suggested to the prosecutor that they should share the statement. The prosecutor's argument then shifted to worries over destruction of evidence and the potential that student activists would attack the witness outside the courtroom. Urabe's move was to ask the defendants for their opinion. The reply Urabe received was that the students were only interested in continuing their courtroom battle and making that battle known to the public. They therefore had no intention of doing something as 'trivial' (*tsumaranai*) as intimidating witnesses. Urabe allowed the debate, which the spectators in the gallery followed with great interest, to continue into the next session of the court. In the end Urabe ordered the defence be allowed to view the statement, which was to be placed in his chambers, reasoning that not having prior sight of the documents impeded the students' lawyers in mounting an adequate defence, and that there was no threat of destruction of evidence or witness intimidation.[30]

That being said, even Urabe found himself in the firing line. In an attempt to meet some of the demands of the defence Urabe had decided to amalgamate two groups of defendants belonging to Chūkaku and Gakusei Intā factions, who had been arrested at Yasuda Auditorium on 19 January. On the day, however, of the 22 students only the 6 already on bail appeared in court. Urabe was subject to a strong appeal from the prosecution that his decision was contra to the Basic policy, that the trial of such a large group was dangerious, and that it would be impossible to adequately crossexamine the witnesses. The Bengodan lawyers were also dismissive of the move, arguing that it had only been done to expedite the trial further, and was simply a continuation of Basic Policy. Urabe responded to the unlikely alliance before him that amalgamation was allowed within the framework of the Basic Policy, and he had done so because he believed it would be beneficial for the students' defence. The Bengodan ignored Urabe's reasoning and as a back and forth between the lawyers and Urabe continued the room descended into chaos. In the end Urabe too turned to the riot police to have the defendants removed.[31]

Not withstanding incidents such as this, Urabe's conduct made a significant impact on the press, who were starting voice doubts as to the desirability, and indeed legitimacy, of the liberal use of the Act on Main tenance of Order in Courtrooms. As one journalist, on observing Urabe in the courtroom, put it:

> [The courts] should proceed with substantive authority rather than formal authority. The point is that you can have good hearings and good verdicts. It is of course desirable to have a quiet courtroom, but I don't think that is good if there are no observers [in the courtroom].[32]

The two authors of the report in which these events were recounted speculated in their conclusion as to who the 'dignity' of the courts was really for. 'A trial,' they concluded, 'has no physical power. It is unarmed. As such with only a small application of force a hearing can be obstructed.' At the very least, such force would prevent a fine-grained hearing. However, the very visible presence of the state in the courtroom was perhaps even more of a cause for worry. As the authors of the report concluded:

> With riot police flooding in and out of the building, an 'armed court' makes us question the independence of the judiciary. The courts have no physical strength, they are only protected by public trust, which is intangible. Isn't it right that the dignity of the courts is predicated on whether that public trust exists?[33]

Indeed, magazine headlines wrote of the unusualness of courtrooms where, at the wave of a judge's hand, permanently stationed riot police would spring into action.[34] Moreover this creeping concern over the basis of the legitimacy of the courts was being voiced within the judiciary itself. Yokohama District Court Judge Nose Takao, for example, penned an article for a special edition of the magazine *Hōritsu Jihō* on the trial, arguing that in its single-minded focus on maintaining 'dignity', the courts were in danger of destroying the relationship of trust with the public that was the foundation of its authority. In a pointed criticism of the hawks among the judiciary who were quick to clear their courtrooms, Nose argued such measures must always be the option of last resort and those who turned to them early 'were like a poor warrior who all too quickly drew his sword.' Rather than focus on dignity, for Nose, it was right to recognise the courtroom as a place of battle: a place where defendants who believed in their innocence should be expected to fight for that innocence to be recognised. The ultimate irony, Nose observed in his conclusion, was that the very same riot police who threatened the dignity of the university, who were for the defendants a sworn enemy, were charged with policing the dignity of the courts.[35]

As the trials continued members of the Tokyo District Court, in a break with convention, turned to the media to counter this growing narrative that, due to invocation of Article 286 Section 2 and the ejection of all spectators, the Tokyo University trials were a legal aberration in danger of losing their legitimacy. The most high-profile of these media interventions came from Yokogawa himself in leading monthly magazine *Bungei shunjū* in an article entitled *Let the Judge Speak: is the Tokyo University Trial a Secret Trial?* His article was framed in urgent terms. While the choice to try the students in absentia was from a legal perspective only natural, he argued, the media narrative was raising doubts about the foundations of Japan as a constitutional democracy that in turn threatened the rule of law. As well as restating the arguments made in the documents discussed in the previous chapter, Yokogawa spent considerable time setting out his interpretation of the students' situation. With reference to one hearing involving students who travelled from Kansai to join the occupation of Yasuda, Yokogawa argued that many of the defendants had no idea of the purpose behind the struggle. Instead, he argued they were simply instructed by the leadership to defend the buildings. When the police arrived the students 'got excited and threw stones at the police'. 'Other than the fellow students they arrived with they didn't know the names or faces of the other students,' Yokogawa reflected. 'They didn't know who was defending where… to evaluate these students in the same way as those who gave the orders would be a pity.' The real issue in the court's eyes was the student support organisations themselves. 'On a one-to-one basis many [students] were good, obedient young people [*sunao na ii seinen*]' noted Yokogawa. As such 'the judges felt strongly [the students] must not sacrifice their individuality for the sake of the group'.[36]

In making his case for the court's approach Yokogawa drew heavily on comparisons with the UK and the US to argue the discourse around the trial indicated that Japan's appreciation of the law, the proper place of the courts, and indeed the concept of human rights, was still lacking. In the US, he opined, lawyers and their clients would jump at the chance to be tried on an individual basis. This demonstrated that Americans had an intrinsic understanding of what is meant by human rights. Sadly, the same could not be said of the Japanese. 'Only Japanese lawyers,' with their implied lack of understanding of rights, he lamented, 'would ask for everyone to be lumped together.' Yokogawa cited approvingly Oliver Wendell Holmes Jr.'s statement that the 'life of the law has not been logic; it has been experience,' and exhorted 'talented young lawyers in Japan to expand their horizons and study more diligently.' In sum, Yokogawa argued that judges should be seen as the 'umpires of society', making final decisions about the rules that enable the 'game' of collective life to continue. This, he argued, was what was meant when he stated that the judiciary had their own form of *government*: they make distinctions that enable any sort of social life possible. Should the lawyers fail to come out onto the pitch and abide by those decisions then the game could not continue: 'as long as the lawyers and the clients do not revise their thinking, trial in absentia is unavoidable.'[37]

Yokogawa was also adamant that although invited by the media to debate Yamane he would not do so: the umpire's decision was final. So, it was a surprise when, on 31 July, as the courts entered their summer break, Yokogawa made the decision to appear on NHK's flagship early morning television news programme *Studio 102* alongside lead lawyer for the defence Yamane. But as the presenters noted in their opening statement, NHK had only secured Yokogawa's involvement in the programme because the questions had been agreed in advance and would be asked of each participant in turn. In the end, however, the broadcast did little more than confirm the gulf between the two sides. Yokogawa reiterated that he did not want to try the students in absentia but given the responsibility to society bestowed on the courts he had no other option. Yamane countered that he would not allow the trials to continue on the basis of

Tokyo District Court's 'unconstitutional' process. After listening to Yokogawa and Yamane talk past each other, a clearly exasperated presenter summed up the exchange with a bleak prognosis for the reopening of proceedings in October. 'As we can see,' he concluded, 'the two sides are completely out of synch with each other. At this rate it is impossible to imagine compromise.'[38]

While Yokogawa was appealing to the public for their understanding of the proper role of the courts, another judge—Kumagai Hiroshi—was busy writing letters, both to students' parents and the students in detention. In contrast to Yokogawa's procedural approach to reasoning Kumagai's style was significantly more forceful; his publications and letters were a mixture of legal reasoning, moral suasion and at times aggressive statements of frustration directed at the students. Kumagai's views on reasons for detention became prominent in the discourse surrounding the case when his court published an opinion (*kenkai*) justifying the necessity for invocation of Article 286 Section 2 should the student defendants continue with their refusal to appear in court. Although penned by three judges, the document became known as the Kumagai Opinion, and came to stand with Yokogawa's *Basic Policy* as a key component of the court's view of the case.[39] The Kumagai Opinion built on Yokogawa's original plan for the trial to argue that the arguments of the Bengodan were, from the perspective of legal reasoning, nothing more than 'rhetoric' without the precise use of language necessary to pass muster. While noting that the tone of his Opinion was 'on the strong side', Kumagai argued such a firm hand was necessary due to the fact that the students' lawyers' arguments had strayed so far from the proper academic understanding of key legal terms and their postulates. Indeed, in contrast to the mild appeals of Yokogawa, Kumagai saved the last few paragraphs of his Opinion for an excoriating criticism of the Bengodan, whose failure to appear in court when requested constituted a dereliction duty that demanded the 'lawyers become aware of their own professional responsibilities.'[40]

Kumagai's letters to the parents of detainees were equally direct in their criticism of the legal team. In a 23rd July letter to parents who had requested the release on bail of their sons and daughters, Kumagai rehashed the argument that releasing students risked them tampering with evidence before lambasting the students' legal team for allowing the courtrooms to descend into chaos. From the perspective of the courts, he argued, the legal team had with their actions thrown away their right to call themselves lawyers and had made the trial in absentia an inevitability.

He further appealed to the parents' sense of moral right as Japanese citizens by collapsing any distinction between the students and criminals: 'if a violent criminal decided they did not want to be tried, would it be okay to let that rest? The overwhelming majority of Japanese citizens would see that as a problem.' And while it would be possible in that case to force the criminal into the courtroom, to do so would have little meaning; presumably because only a volitional trial would contain the component of moral performance required. The letter ended with an appeal to the parents for them to persuade the students to attend the trials. For once indicted, to attend court 'was the obligation of all Japanese citizens,' as well as being the 'manly' (*otokorashii*) thing to do. Otherwise, the students risked going down in history as nothing more than youngsters who committed 'savage acts' (*yaban na kōi*).[41]

In his letters to students in detention, entitled ***kari no tayori*** after a Kabuki play of the same name, Kumagai in equal parts set out the legal reasoning of the courts and challenged the students to attend the hearings. A dialogue of sorts formed around these letters, with students writing back disputing aspects of the trial as it progressed. In his fifth letter to the students, Kumagai argued that much of the misunderstanding in the trial stemmed from the problem of youth itself. 'You are young,' he told them, 'which is why you strive for logical thoroughness… [h]owever in actual society, rather than consistency we strive towards practical compromise.' Kumagai's defence of the theory of constitutive elements was equally robust: to do otherwise had echoes of German justice under the Nazis and would bring Japan perilously close to totalitarian dictatorship. And much as with the letter to parents, Kumagai finished with a bold challenge: 'It won't be your lawyers who look stupid when a verdict is read out without the court understanding the position you want to take. It will be you. It is still not too late. Be brave, come to court, and quietly state your case. That is the most correct course of action.'[42] Kumagai was also keen to appeal to an abstract understanding of humanity in his letters, something he clearly felt the students lacked. In his final correspondence, Kumagai addressed students' accusations that his letters, though polite, were coercive and intimidating. These accusations were evidence, according to an intellectual in Kumagai's acquaintance, that his letters were effective and as such were threatening the students' word view. Although ideologically worlds apart, Kumgai continued, he and the students shared the same human sentiment (*ningen toshite no kanjō*). And it was this humanity that was at stake:

> Wasn't the root cause of the Tokyo University Incident concern about the alienation of people at the university? If you, who raised this issue, were to think of future reforms only with dry theories and mechanical attitudes, I believe you would bring about a horrifying society.[43]

Part of Kumagai's critique of the students, their lawyers and the support groups was their use of language within their community. The students' method of communication, 'mass negotiation' (***taishū dankō***), had been developed as a technique during the university struggles. For Kumagai this technique did not rely on a process of listening to an interlocuter and then attempting to convince them of one's position, but instead was 'a method by which many people speak simultaneously to impose their side's arguments on the other side.' But while acknowledging this approach might work against individuals, Kumagai argued that in the broader realm of public discourse it was the main barrier preventing the students from asserting their claims effectively. Indeed, their use of words amounted to a form of violence that must be abandoned:

> At the very least, students must end this form of mass group discussion if they are to justify their actions with logic. [This method of communication] is a kind of violence of words. Compared to the 'violence of silence' or 'violence of disregard' discussed by commentators, this violence of words is much closer to the original meaning of violence and must be rejected.[44]

This issue of verbal violence Kumagai connected to youth. In his reckoning a key issue in the case was that many of the lawyers representing the students were of a very similar age and as such had been swept up in the students' methods of communicating. Consequently, the lawyers had abandoned the 'manners of legal discourse' leading to the disintegration of trial.[45]

Resisting Administrative Bail

While this had been going on the Courts were beginning to change their approach to bail. In contrast to the policy of monthly renewal of detention on the basis that students might destroy evidence material to their cases, in early July Judge Mukai decided to grant bail for the five students still in detention belonging to the Yasuda Auditorium Occupation Group.

Given that bail was made conditional on the students attending the courtroom, this decision was likely Mukai's attempt to deal with the problem of absentee trial.[46] Mukai's tactic, however, met with resistance from the Tokyo District Prosecutors Office who filed an injunction with the district court and then, when that injunction was dismissed, appealed to the Tokyo High Court, arguing that while the conditions of bail placed limitations on the students' movements, there was still the danger that they would interfere with witnesses and tamper with evidence.[47] On 7 July the Tokyo High Court upheld the injunction and revoked bail.[48] This did not stop another attempt at bail at the end of the month, this time with a group of 10 students (Group 19). True to form the Prosecutors Office once again filed an injunction. But it was clear the mood had now shifted. Although the Tokyo Hight Court did not discount the possibility that the students might collude and/or tamper with persons related other cases, the fact they had been in detention for more than six months, that some of the students were suffering from illness, and oddly the observation that 'many of them have not lost their enthusiasm for returning to study' all weighed now in the students' favour. 'When considering that the maximum sentence for obstruction of justice or illegal occupation of a building is three years,' the High Court concluded, 'it is correct that we grant bail at this juncture.'[49]

If the Courts had hoped that the granting bail would ameliorate tensions in the courtroom, however, they were to be sorely disappointed. Students and their support groups condemned the change in policy, which they dubbed 'administrative bail' (*shokken hoshaku*), as a ploy to break their solidarity and force them to engage with the group trials.[50] As such courtroom refusal was now to be supplemented with the policy of 'bail refusal' (*hoshaku kyohi*). 'The fight to return you to us,' declared Tōitsu kyūtai, 'is not predicated on our swallowing the policy of group trial. It should be taken via the power of the masses in our battle against prolonged detention and the inflated price of bail.'[51] This decision, however, had not been easy to settle—indeed, cracks were starting to deepen along factional lines within Tōitsu kyūtai. Factions including Chūkaku, Gakusei Intā and Kaihō were all in favour of bail refusal as a logical continuation of the current position of non-compliance with the courts. But an increasingly vocal group that included ML-faction and Tokyo Zenkyōtō argued that more than anything the battle against extended detention and the return of their comrades to the fold was paramount.[52]

This debate continued for two weeks until an uneasy collective decision saw the policy of bail refusal ratified by Tōitsu kyūtai on 1 August followed by the Defendants Organisation on the 3rd.[53] These resolutions were bolstered at a national meeting of the Family Association (*Kazokukai*) on 4 August at which a motion was passed stating that families would not apply for bail against the wishes of their detained family member.[54] It was clear that some students on the inside agreed with this sentiment: 'My meaningless detention is illegitimate', wrote one detainee to the Tokyo District Court, 'therefore, I will not comply with this new policy of granting bail. As long as the court does not fully revoke my custody, I will not leave the detention centre'.[55] By mid-August, of the 32 students granted bail only four took up the opportunity: the remainder refused (or failed) to pay the 150, 000-yen bond.[56] It is difficult to ascertain exactly what settled the debate on the side of bail refusal. For their part, prison authorities, who without direction from the courts had no choice but to keep the students in custody, speculated that the real reason students were refusing bail was that they could not afford the 150, 000-yen bond. Indeed, it was strange that the courts would allow bail to be granted but did nothing to address the bail bond itself, rendering the gesture somewhat empty. And there was some evidence to suggest that the price of the bond, rather than solely ideological consistency, was part of the decision. As Watanabe Hiroshi, the postgradute member of Zenkyōtō kyūtai, recalled: 'at the July meeting of the top factions (Chūkaku, Bund, ML) Yamamoto summarised our position as we cannot get the money together for bail so we should go for bail refusal, and by doing sent the unified trial in a strange direction.'[57]

While Judges Yokogawa and Kumagai continued to engage in the public discourse on the trial, the Tokyo District court also applied pressure on the Tokyo Bar Association to intervene in the conduct on the students' legal defence. On 19 July, Tokyo District Court Chief Justice Niizeki (Shinzeki) Katsuyoshi sent an official notice to the Tokyo Bar Association entitled 'On actions constituting a lawyers' dereliction of duty' (*bengoshi no shokumu getai no kōi ni tsuite*) accusing the Bengodan of not only preventing an appropriately expedient trial as guaranteed by the constitution, but of also violating the ethical standards of Japan's legal world (*hōsō rinri*). Niizeki requested the lawyers be subject to 'independent and appropriate measures' (*jishuteki ni tekisetsu na sochi*) by the Bar for their behaviour.[58] This notice was followed by a similar request for censure in August. The Tokyo Bar Association was cautious in its response, with the incoming head of the association Futoshi Igarashi telling the press that while they would of course cooperate in helping progress the trial, 'should we find issue with how the courts have managed the trial, we will request the court reflects [on the situation]'.[59]

In fact, the Japan Federation of Bar Associations (JFBA) had since the end of July instigated an investigation into the Tokyo University trial via its Central Court Committee (*Chūō hōtei i'in kai*), which over a series of five meetings had gathered and examined reports on the trial in the hopes of de-escalating the unfolding courtroom conflict.[60] On 6th September, with no resolution in sight, the JFBA issued its official statement on the trial entitled 'A comment on the maintenance of legal order in student cases (University of Tokyo Incident)'. While the JFBA had been following the trial with the hopes that the 'good sense' of those involved would resolve the chaos in the courtroom, the notice explained, it was now clear that the situation was if anything intensifying to the point of becoming an existential threat to the Japanese criminal justice system itself. As such, it was vital lawyers abide by the rules of the court, even when they believe those rules to be themselves in violation of the law. 'Under the current law,' stated the JFBA 'all complaints about proceedings should be made by way of a formal objection, challenge, or appeal, and even if the court's opinion is illegal or unjust, it is not permissible to enforce the claim by force or similar acts. That is the ethics of lawyers and their legal duty'. The notice finished with an appeal:

> Counsel, your actions also affect the credibility of the entire legal profession. You should follow the good sense of the legal profession and take immediate steps to guide the accused to normalise proceedings [*soshō seijōka*]. I sincerely hope that you will take immediate and voluntary action.[61]

The notice was compiled by the head of the JFBA's Central Court Committee (*Chūō hōtei i'in kai*) Ōtaka Michitsuke, a 70-year-old veteran lawyer with 50 years of experience. Although the tone of the notice hinted at the possibility some sort of punishment in the future, Ōtaka was adamant sanctions were not as yet on the table. Indeed, he preferred to see the relationship between the JFBA and the Bengodan as similar to that of parents and children. 'For me, the lawyers at issue are like my children' he told journalists for a profile piece at the time the notice was issued. 'Sanctions are out of the question. We must guide them with an eye to the future. This is how new possibilities will be realised.' The core of his message was to reinforce a framework of legal ethics. When challenged that some may see his approach to the Bengodan as overly accommodating, Ōtaka again referred to the nature of the relationship between generations. 'Well, they are our juniors [*kōhai*]. They will listen to their elders when the time comes.'[62] The Tokyo Bar Association followed with their own message to affiliated members of the Bengodan on 13 September. 'It is not the job of a lawyer to take the same actions as the defendant,' they concluded. Even if the will of the defendant conflicts with the system, one should 'protect the fundamental rights of the defendant as an independent lawyer.'[63]

Of course, this appeal to legal ethics was never likely to convince the legal team to change tact, as it was precisely the ethical norms of Japan's legal system and the assumptions that constituted Japanese legal 'good sense' that was their primary point of contention in the trial. Such good sense, they argued, would see them working against the express wishes of their clients in order to secure an expedient trial. It would also mean working, as they saw it, against the very principles of protecting the rights of their clients and striving for social justice as espoused by the JFBA itself. In a sense the lawyers were arguing that representing their clients meant viewing their clients' wishes as determining the framework for evaluation of the correctness of their actions rather than the ethical norms safeguarding the system itself. In late November the Bar Association wrote to the Bengodan once more. 'To avoid an absentee verdict, which would be the worst possible outcome, will you not consider arguing for the defence?' The lawyers' response was unwavering: 'There is no room for discussion as long as the courts do not completely revoke these illegal group trials.' Three days later the first trial ended in Japan's first ever convictions in absentia.[64]

The Okagaki Ruling

On 28 November, after the proceedings resumed following the summer break, Judge Okagaki reached the first verdict in the trials for his group of students (Yasuda Auditorium Group 3). Okagaki, who was seen by the media as a 'hawk', made it clear to the assembled lawyers that he would not give them time to speak and stated that he was simply there to do 'the obvious thing' in reading out his verdict. When the defendants who had made an appearance accused Okagaki of acting like a dictator, and spectators shouted 'Nonsense!' from the gallery, Okagaki had the legal team and all but one of the defendants removed from the courtroom.[65] To the families of the accused assembled in the courtroom he expressed a sense of moral frustration at the defendants in surprisingly graphic terms:

> The defendants are colour-blind, unable to see whether the world is red or white. We have the option to remove and wash their eyes for them, but if they are weak-willed, that could make things worse. I don't know which is better, so I don't ask you to advocate they comply with the trial.[66]

The barely concealed antipathy for the defendants extended to sentencing. Finding all defendants guilty of the charges, sentences ranged from 14 to 20 months imprisonment. These sentences were all significantly more severe than those handed out to the 'repentant group' even though they were mitigated by the number of days each had spent in detention. In fact, one of the defendants received a sentence heavier than that requested by the prosecutors.[67]

After reading a statement of the students' actions, which in effect mirrored the indictment sheet, Okagaki presented a narrative account of the events leading to the 18th-19th January incident which emphasised the violence between Zenkyōtō and Minsei within the context of an increasingly despondent general student body. The crimes committed by the students were, adopting language from Zenkyōtō publications, summarised as motivated by a will to 'resist inhumane state power.' In the courts view, however, consistent with the 1963 Poporo ruling this motivation and the actions that followed went beyond the purview of university autonomy. In coming to this conclusion, the verdict emphasised that the courts did not take the students' political motivations into account when determining their sentences. After noting a spectrum of opinion on the student movement—from a view of students struggling against alienation as part of a humanistic response to modern city culture, to student unrest as a 'pathological phenomenon' in which students were 'puppets under the mistaken control and exploitation of political sects engaging blindly in energetic resistance'—Okagaki argued that under the Constitution of Japan there was no place for assessment of the students' political motivations.

As discussed in the introduction to this book, the way society is regulated in the courtroom does not rest solely with how members act with regard to established social rules, but also how members 'express their feelings about their actions'.[68] By demonstrating remorse the offender rejects the part of themselves that transgressed against the community—splitting the self into two and condemning, in concert with the hegemonic national community, the former self.[69] It is in this regard, under the subheading of 'attitude post arrest', that Okagaki's verdict was at its harshest. 'The current Constitutional order is designed to guarantee individual liberty to the fullest extent possible,' Okagaki stated. But the verdict deemed the actions of the students to have transgressed the boundaries of individual liberty (emphasis added):

> The defendants have made a misguided demand that the legitimacy of their political beliefs be subject to trial, which is completely unfounded in light of the current Constitution, and when they realised that this demand, made in the name of a "unified trial", would not be effective in court, they refused to appear before the court. This behaviour not only shows the defendants *have no remorse*, but also that since their arguments were denied in court, they have been determined to carry out *by force* what they *subjectively believe to be justice*, regardless of the other party or place. These acts must be given a severe negative legal evaluation as a direct challenge to the rule of law and ideological tolerance as set out in the Constitution.[70]

The final comment was an assessment of the social impact of the crimes. While allowing for the fact that the students actions had been intended to draw attention to societal issues, and may well have been successful in doing so, the verdict assessed the social impact of the students' actions as striking at the heart of Japan's postwar legal order (emphasis added):

> [The students] sought to realise their subjective vision *hastily and violently*. They did this by direct action without *regard for others who should be as free as them*. They carelessly destroyed property built only after *long years of human endeavour*. It is undeniable that these actions brought about a trend that is extremely detrimental to the legal stability of society.[71]

As defiant offenders—refusing to show remorse and arguing the crimes were morally justified—the students called into question the legitimacy of the trial and the moral authority of the state to pass judgement.[72] Okagaki's verdict can be read in this context as a reaffirmation of the legitimacy of the trial. This was done through a series of implied contrasts between the students and the court. By labelling the students views of justice subjective the courts affirmed their objectivity; by drawing attention to student force the courts affirmed themselves as a place of reason; by drawing attention to the freedoms of others in society they affirmed themselves as guardians of individual liberty; and by referencing the work of human endeavour the courts placed themselves on the side of civilisation.

Two of the defendants, however, received suspended sentences and here the moral function of the court was once again at work. The narrative of justifying suspension of the first student was one of naivety and guidance. The court recognised that student O had become caught up in events at Yasuda Auditorium but had not participated in any violent action. More importantly the verdict noted that a letter from the defendant's father to the court had affirmed that after the trial student O was now in the mental state (*shinkyō*) of wishing to return to his hometown, find a job, and 'work diligently.' The letter also pledged to accept O back into the family warmly (*atatakai kimochi de ukeire*). It was thus the assessment of the court 'that the accused will continue to build a legitimate life for himself under the warm advice and guidance of his family'. Family was also key for student K. According to testimony from the students' father, student K's wife had given birth to their first child shortly after the events at Tokyo University and K was now coming to understand his position and responsibility within the family as a father. Thus, although K had thrown his fair share of stones at the police, the court deemed that given K's new circumstances, and under the guidance of this father, it was unlikely that K would reoffend. For the other students there was no evidence of remorse and no evidence they would not reoffend. Unlike defendants O and K, there was no intimation that their families would take responsibility for their reintegration into society. Therefore, they were to serve their sentences in full.[73]

In the distinction made between those students who could be rehabilitated via the 'warmth of the family' and the prospect of suitably productive hard work the verdict was clearly performative. It constructed a narrative of redemption via the embrace of national community values and enacted the damnation of those who continue to reject those values. For those inching towards jail the reaction was mixed. 'This verdict in absentia is no victory,' stated one student as they prepared for their sentence, 'but I don't think it means defeat. A forced end to the struggle delimited by the powers that be. It's like a manga… No, perhaps that's an exaggeration.' But even K, who had received a suspended sentence, appeared far less repentant than the verdict made him out to be. Speaking to journalists after the verdict K seemed unmoved by the benevolence of the court: 'we cannot acknowledge the outcome of this trial. The trial has been structured so we have been forced to accept the outcome, but judicial power is just a decoration. We've fought against this delusion.' K's father was also somewhat sceptical of the rosy outlook Okagaki's verdict painted of K's future. 'I'll do my best to watch out for him,' he told Okagaki during sentencing, 'but his chances of employment will likely be limited.'[74]

Although the absentee conviction came with a sense of the inevitable, the reality of judges passing judgement over defendants who had, along with their lawyers, been removed from the room came as a shock to the media and other commentators. Much like the joint statement issued by newspapers calling for a return to parliamentary democracy after the death of Kamba Michiko during the 1960 Anpo protests a decade earlier, papers now called for a return to established legal practices. The general sense was that the outcome was an aberration that cast a pall over the Japanese justice system which should never be normalised as a legitimate legal outcome. As the Asahi Shimbun wrote in its editorial on the Okagaki verdict: 'so that this unhappy outcome is not repeated we must consider seriously what needs to be done.'[75] The consensus in the national newspapers was that ultimately responsibility for this outcome fell heavily on the Bengodan. Indeed, both the Asahi and Yomiuri in their editorials on the verdict to renormalise the position of the defence within the tripartite Japanese legal world. The job of the lawyer, argued the Asahi, was to utilise their specialised knowledge to lead their client through the legal process while securing their rights from state interference. In the case of recalcitrant defendants, it was 'common sense' that the lawyer's duty was to 'convince them [the client] of the circumstances sufficiently enough to make the hearing proceed as favourably as possible.' In fact, in the Asahi's formulation an abstract concept of 'rights' trumped the will of the defendant: 'even if defence activities go against the will of the defendant, should those activities be the best option with regard to a lawyer's responsibility to safeguard their client's rights, they should be taken.'[76] For the Yomiuri the evidence of this failure, and the need for defence lawyers to defer to the courts over the wishes of their clients, could be seen in the difference in outcomes for the 'repentant group' and those student who fought for a collective trial. 'Instead of having their arguments made for them,' the Yomiuri bemoaned, 'isn't it the case that they simply made their sentencing more severe?'[77] On this point, however, there was a clear contradiction running through both editorials. As the Yomiuri argued, 'criminal trials are there to determine guilt or innocence, and the severity of punishment… they are always about judging the act itself, not motive or thought'.[78] Yet the difference in sentencing had nothing to do with the acts of the students at the time they were arrested; the sole differentiating factor was their post-arrest behaviour in not complying with the courts. In this sense thought, as manifest in behaviour that rejected the court's need for a performance of splitting through apology, had indeed been on trial.

The Japan Federation of Bar Association's (JFBA) opinion on the absentee verdict was published in November. On the outcome of the trials, Chair for the federation Itoh Toshio wrote of a deep sense of shame in the breakdown of the judicial process:

> Such a large number of trials in absentia are unprecedented in the history of the judiciary in Japan and will become a major stain on our judicial history. Future historians will undoubtedly criticize not only the courts and lawyers but also all legal professionals who lived in the present era. More importantly, this is disadvantageous for the hundreds of young student defendants. If trials in absentia are forced through, it will result in closing the door for the defendants to directly reflect their claims and defences in the trial. Even if the court exercises its authority to collect evidence favourable to the defendant, it is by no means a normal litigation procedure. It is impossible to fully secure the rights and interests of the defendant guaranteed by the Constitution and the Code of Criminal Procedure.[79]

The JFBA opinion took the courts to task for being too wedded to the small group trial approach from the outset and as such lacking in a spirit of cooperation and compromise, but as with the national newspapers placed the lion's share of the blame on the actions of the Bengodan. The issue, Itoh argued, stemmed from the logic of the Bengodan's anti-establishment thought which viewed the courts as playing a role as an 'institution of systemic violence' that legitimised the current legal order even when that order was harmful. As a result, the lawyers were both of the system and opposed to it, placing them in a position of contradiction. 'Consequently,' argued the opinion, 'it is natural for the anti-establishment movement to confront this with "force," which is where the tactical significance of courtroom struggle lies. Defendants and others argue that the courtroom struggle becomes a battle to judge the authorities, the University of Tokyo, and the class trial itself. Thus, the courtroom struggle inevitably becomes a power struggle.' Within this framework of struggle the courts are provoked into judicial overreach, making decision about procedure that the Bengodan could seize upon as illegal exercises of power. While the JFBA remained agnostic as to whether these acts—pushing through the small group trials and gathering data to support those trials—were illegal, the opinion was adamant that the only correct way to contest them was in adherence to the Criminal Code of Procedure and the Code of Ethics for Lawyers. And while the Bengodan might claim a natural right to resist an unjust law:

> ... recognizing the right to self-defense or resistance against the actions of courts would be tantamount to negating the judicial system and the rule of law. It is not limited to confrontations with individual governments. There is a risk that it may lead to total disorder and human rights violations. Consequently, even if there are inherent flaws in the judicial system within the establishment, it is the rule of law to accept and follow the rules to rectify the situation.

The Bengodan, argued the JFBA, had violated these ethical obligations and brought about hazardous conditions for rule of law in Japan. The opinion ended with a sense of regret that the JFBA had allowed the Bengodan to go so far:

> ...when considering the historical significance of the Tokyo University incident, it seems that the court authorities and the JFBA should have discussed and considered the path to normalizing the trial in a dimension separate from parties in charge of the case [*jiken tantōsha*], and then proceeded accordingly. If possible, it is still desirable to do so even now.[80]

While national newspapers and the JFBA were keen to shore up Japan's legal order by disciplining the Bengodan other voices located the significance of the convictions elsewhere. In his critique of the Okagaki verdict that prefaced the verdict's publication in the legal journal *Hōgaku seminā*, law professor Yokoyama Kōichiro reflected on the significance of the response of a journalist in the courtroom who wrote that 'unlike at Yasuda Auditorium, we cannot see what has been destroyed here. But it is a fact that something has been lost.' In trying to ascertain what drove the journalist to this statement Yokoyama felt it was the courts, not the lawyers, who had inflicted upon themselves the most damage. The question to be answered for Yokoyama was why, even though the courts had stated an absentee trial and conviction was 'as far as possible from how a trial should look,' and indeed that 'judges themselves felt this most painfully,' those same judges had rushed to hold a trial that 'could not be called a trial.' Yokoyama's main interlocutor in his discussion was Judge Kumagai, who had penned an article for the journal *Juristo* in which he argued that the Tokyo University trial presented a real threat to Japan's system of criminal justice.[81] As Kumagai had argued 'can a state's legal system allow people to refuse to be tried based on their own views?… Should [such behaviour] be allowed, in that moment the state and the law would be on the verge of death.'[82] For Yokoyama, statements such as these demonstrated that the courts had staked the continued existence of court authority in Japan on the outcome of the trial and viewed divergence from the Basic Policy as a direct threat to that authority and thus the law itself.

In Yokoyama's analysis, however, this approach was backwards. While the courts proclaimed that the Basic Policy was the only practical approach to the trial, and also the only approach that would secure the defendants' human rights, in the end it did neither. And while such failure could be blamed on the students and their lawyers, the courts knew from the outset that it was highly unlikely the legal team would comply with the Basic Policy and that such an outcome was all but inevitable. While the papers argued that lawyers who do not champion the law were a self-contradiction, Yokoyama called out what he saw as the hypocrisy of a court system that put authority and process above all else:

> Court process does not determine judicial purpose; judicial purpose determines suitable judicial process. When process and outcome come into contradiction with each other it should be process, not purpose, that is discarded. In supporting judicial process (and the authority of the court that decided upon that process) the Okagaki verdict and those arguments supporting absentee trials have discarded judicial purpose, which is to protect fundamental human rights while discovering the factual truth. More than anything else, democratic nations expect the primary responsibility of the courts to be the protection of fundamental human rights. The court has replaced and left behind this responsibility and replaced it with protection of its own "authority".

It was thus this apparent abdication of responsibility towards the rights of accused, that Yokoyama saw as provoking the journalist's reaction that with the absentee convictions 'something had been lost.'[83]

Yokoyama's criticism of the courts was met with a stinging rejoinder from Kumagai himself in the following issue of *Hōgaku seminā*. Yokoyama, argued Kumagai, had missed out two significant factors in his criticism of the courts and their process. Leaning heavily on Japan's status as a democratic nation, Kumagai agreed the legal system had a responsibility to guarantee the human rights of defendants, but in contrast to Yokoyama, he argued that should defendants decide not to comply with the system (by for example refusing to appear in court), then by their actions they were relinquishing their right to be heard. This was the meaning behind Article 286 Section 2 and as long as that Article was deemed constitutional, and the defendants had been given every chance to defend themselves at trial, there was no wrongdoing on the part of the courts. In response to the accusation that the courts failed to adequately account for the clearly foreseeable resistance to the trial, Kumagai argued that while resistance was considered, the sheer abnormality (*ijōsa*) of the defendants' actions, their 'childish selfishness' (*wagamama*) was simply beyond all prediction. In overlooking the responsibility of the defendants to comply with the process, and in failing to adequately interrogate the validity of the students' reasons for refusing to appear in court Kumagai argued that as an article written by a professor of criminal law 'there was something clearly missing in what seemed like a piece of reportage written by a social psychologist.'[84]

Kumagai's criticism went beyond the logic of Yokoyama's argument, however: not only was Yokoyama wrong, but he was irresponsibly so. While it was right to accept the criticism of students when warranted, Kumagai also saw it as the responsibility of those in positions of authority to push back and correct students when they were mistaken. In the realm of the law such didactic function fell to judges, in the universities to professors. But for Kumagai Yokogawa's lack of criticism of the students and their lawyers suggested the existence of a taboo against such opinions amongst progressive intellectuals. It was clear that Kumagai saw this as a failure of university education that pandered too freely to student whim. In the same vein Kumagai went as far as to rebuke Yokoyama for misleading *Hōgaku seminā's* young readers. 'As an article written for people entering into law,' noted Kumagai bitterly, 'this piece will have a large influence.' While it was clear Kumagai saw this (negative) influence as affecting readings of the journal, he also saw the impact in broader terms. As the trials continued into early 1970, he argued, arguments that pamper (*amayakasu*) the students and their lawyers would only lead to more absentee verdicts, which would do only harm to those involved.[85] The overall tone of Kumagai's argument was littered with terms that framed the students and their legal team as children: they were childishly selfish (*wagamama*), their requests were arbitrary (*katte*), they were not to be spoiled (*amayakasu*). They were in need of strong correction to ensure they would not look like idiots (*baka wo miru*).[86]

As the absentee convictions continued there was a sense that the tone of the courtroom battle was beginning to change. Yamane Jirō continued to maintain that the Okagaki verdict was designed to prompt tenkō in the students and was nothing more than a 'verdict of retribution'. And while students did continue to resist the trial, some were starting to break ranks. On 3 December one student in Judge Kumagai's court proclaimed that 'in the context of absentee verdicts, I personally think that I have to reconsider my actions', while on the following day in Judge Iguchi's courtroom another student told the courtroom that 'I think that, as the Court has said, assembling over 300 defendants in one room for a trial is impossible.' Granted both students went on to criticise other aspects of the trial, but these statements would have been unthinkable before the verdicts began. In both cases the media reported the judges looking on in satisfaction, with Kumagai quoted as saying approvingly 'now you will comply with the trial.'[87]

The question facing the students and their support groups was now whether to fight on or to simply support the students through their sentences. Over this question a rift was now developing between two broad camps within the students and their support groups. Already the alliance of sects under the Tōitsu kyūtai banner was starting to lose its coherence. Despite the July declaration of 'bail refusal', by October of the 100 students granted bail only 40 were continuing with their refusal. The evident difficulty of convincing students to stay in detention, and the competing demands of the various factions hoping to bolster their numbers in preparation for the coming 1970 Anpo demonstrations led to Tōitsu kyūtai abandoning the refusal policy and facilitating bond payments.[88] But the real pressure came with interpretation of the significance of the Okagaki ruling. In fact, the Okagaki verdict presaged a fissure in the defendants' organisation that would see it split irrevocably within the next few months.

The catalyst for this disintegration was a missive distributed by the Marxist-Leninist League (ML-faction) on 13th January 1970. The ML-faction document acknowledged what they saw as important gains of the Tokyo University struggle in solidifying revolutionary subjectivity, broadening the struggle via the support groups, and through the strategy of courtroom refusal disrupting the rationalisation of state power. They argued, however, that with the Okagaki ruling the struggle for a single trial no longer held any meaning for the movement. For ML, who had opposed the bail refusal policy, continuation of the struggle was now driven purely by ideology without any practical consideration for those in detention, or for the needs of the movement more generally. In a thorough criticism of the strategy to date, ML argued that the aim of provoking trials 'in which defendants do not show their faces' had come to dominate all other considerations, but all this had achieved was to harden the resolve of the courts. That strategy had now become an end in itself: a form of egotism that that had taken on a life of its own. But with the Okagaki verdict, ML argued, it was now impossible to imagine a how a unified trial could come about. Even appeal to the High Court would be a waste of time given that (in ML's analysis) the High Court was far more conservative than the district courts. As such, rather than be governed by an ideology of resistance, ML argued for the need to 'return our people' to the movement, and once on the outside develop practical strategies for forwarding the cause on a case-by-case basis both inside and outside the courtroom.[89]

Although ML came under some level of criticism from all the other factions for being so quick to change tack, their analysis of a need to 'change of direction' (*hōshin tenkan*) was shared by a large number of organisations including Tokyo University Zentōren, Red Army Faction, Gakusei International, and the Front, who all saw the Okagaki verdict as necessitating a re-evaluation of tactics beyond holding out for a unified trial.[90] This group was soon dubbed the 'change of direction' faction (tenkan-ha). At the opposite end of the spectrum were the Chūkaku faction, who were firmly wedded to the strategy of non-cooperation. Holders of this position, which included the Proletarian Army (*Puroretaria gundan*), became known as the 'see it through' faction (*kantesu-ha*).[91] The showdown between these two blocks within the Defendant's Organisation came the 21 February 1970 National Meeting of the Defendant's Organisations (*Hikokudan zenkoku sōkai*).

In fact, this meeting had been planned for 7th February, but had been pushed back by the Kantetsu-faction, seemingly as a tactic to force a quick decision that would see their position vindicated. In their proposal to the conference, Chūkaku denounced vociferously ML as cowards who had 'crumbled completely in the face of judicial power'.[92] For the Kantetsu faction, the power of the Tokyo University trial was in making clear the complicity of the courts with state power and had forced an escalation of repression that revealed to the masses the violent nature of the state apparatus. To comply with that power would therefore undo these gains. As such, Chūkaku argued that, despite 200 members of their own organisation facing stiff custodial sentences, the Defendant's Organisation should hold the line in demanding for a unified trial, even into the appeals process and even if this meant students faced prison. To change tactics now would, they argued, undermine the 'heroic' efforts of the detainees in turning their incarceration into a strength and would undermine the work done by the student's legal team in challenging the legal process.

But what of those detainees? Where were their voices in this debate and how had their incarceration impacted them? It is to those voices that we now turn.

Notes

1. My emphasis. See 'Chian Tōkyoku Shokku', *Yomiuri Shimbun*, 11 April 1969. and Yomiuri Shimbun 1969. 'Toki No Hito: Maniwa Haruo', *Yomiuri Shimbun*, 12 April 1969. The case later raised the question of press complicity with the state when, after the Maniwa verdict was quashed by the Fukuoka High Court, a retrial was ordered. As part of evidence gathering for the new trial four television companies including NHK Fukuoka were ordered to hand over their footage of the incident. The TV companies refused, arguing that to do so would break their relationship of trust with the public. The Supreme Court, however, disagreed and the film was ordered into evidence.
2. Gokuchū shokan hakkan iinkai, ed., *Tōdai tōsō gokuchū shokanshū 1* (Tokyo: Mitani Shobo, 1970), Memorandum, 3.
3. Tōdaitōsō zengakukyōtōkaigi and Tōdaitōsō zengaku kyōtōkaigi kyūen taisaku honbu, *tōdaitōsō: tōitsukōhan shōri no tame ni* (Tokyo: Tōdaitōsō zengakukyōtōkaigi kyūen taisaku honbu jōsenbu, 1969), 36.

4. Ibid., 9.
5. In terms of rationalisation of the universities, the Nikkeiren had made clear they saw the issue as one of university management. High up on their list of their proposed reforms was a radical revisioning of the university self-governance via the professorial senate with the aim of developing new systems of management modelled on private industry. This would include concentration of decision-making power in university vice-presidents, and training of specialised staff who could lead in the rationalisation of university processes. See Nikkeiren, 'Chokumen suru daigakumondai ni kansuru kihonteki kenkai,' in *Shiryō: Nihonkenpōhō 3*, ed. Kenichi Nagai (Tokyo: Sanseidō, 1986), 507–10.
6. Tōdaitōsō zengakukyōtōkaigi and Tōdaitōsō zengaku kyōtōkaigi kyūen taisaku honbu, *Tōdaitōsō: tōitsukōhan shōri no tame ni*, 14.
7. Ibid., 13.
8. Ishikawa Hiromitsu, 'Bōryoku gakusei ni jinken ga nai no ka - bengonin kara no repōto,' *Sekai*, no. 281 (April 1969): 180.
9. Ishijima Yutaka, "Bōryoku' gakusei to 'jinken'– kotoware naki jiyū hōsō-dan hibou ni kotaeru 〔sekai 281-gō keisai ishikawa hiromitsu 'bōryoku gakusei ni jinken wa nai no ka' ni taisuru hanron〕,' *Sekai*, no. 284 (July 1969): 207–10.
10. Ibid., 210.
11. Ibid.
12. Sunami Shunsuke, 'Hōdō no jiyū to mokuhiken, shōjōken: kikuyabashi 101-gō o meguru shomondai,' *Hōgaku Seminā* 41, no. 7 (1969): 96.
13. The statement is reproduced in Ibid., 94.
14. Muraki Yoshihiko, 'Kikuyabashi 101 gō' mondai wo kyūdan suru,' *Eiga Hyōron* 26, no. 7 (1969): 93–95.
15. Aoki Hisa et. al., 'Shihōkisha zadankai: tōdai saiban,' *Hōgaku Seminā*, no. 163 (September 1969): 145.
16. Tōdaitōsō bengo-dan, *Tōdai saiban: towareteiru mono wa nani ka* (Tokyo: Tabata shoten, 1969), 392.
17. 'Jikkyo rupo: hikoku nuki, kidōtai tsuki, todaisaiban,' *Shūkan Yomiuri*, 27 August 1969.
18. 'Tōdai jiken kōhan no fuan,' *Asahi Shimbun*, 30 June 1969.
19. Nomura Akira, "Repōto tōdaisaiban: tōitsukōhan yōkyū o meguru hikoku, bengodan, saibankan,' Tenbō, no. 11 (1969): 134.
20. 'Rupo tōdai saiban,' *Shūkan Asahi*, no. 2637 (8 August 1969): 17.

21. Muchaku Toki, 'Tōdaisaiban bōchōki,' in *Tōdai saiban: towareteiru mono wa nani Ka*, ed. Tōdaitōsō bengo-dan (Tokyo: Tabata shoten, 1969), 396. This account was published in the Bengo-dan's collection of materials about the case, and it is therefore not surprising that the perspective in sympathetic to the students. However, that these events took place is corroborated by a timeline of courtroom events published in Aoki, 'Shihōkisha Zadankai: Tōdai Saiban,' 139.
22. 'Tōdai jiken kōhan no fuan.'
23. 'Rupo tōdai saiban,' 18.
24. Uchida Takahiro, 'Tōdai jiken saiban to shihō no byōri genshō,' *Jinken Shinbun*, 1 August 1969.
25. Kimi is an informal word for 'you' in Japanese that in this context would be rude.
26. Muchaku, 'Tōdaisaiban bōchōki,' 397–98.
27. 'Hōtei nado no chitsujo iji ni kansuru hōristu ga tekiyō sareta jirei,' *Jurisuto*, no. 438 (1969): 72–73.
28. 'Tōdai saiban' o miru me – tsuzuki,' *Jiyū to Seigi* 21, no. 2 (1970): 36.
29. Ibid., 45.
30. 'Tōdai saiban' o miru me – tsuzuki.'
31. 'Tōdai kōhan-hatsu no 'heigō' shinri sore mo ōare, kidōtai/ tōkyō chisai,' *Yomiuri Shimbun*, 26 August 1969.
32. 'Tōdai saiban' o miru me – tsuzuki,' 43.
33. Ibid., 46.
34. 'Jikkyō rupo: hikokunuki, kidōtai tsuki, tōdaisaiban,' *Shūkun Yomiuri*, 27 August 1969.
35. Nose Takao, 'Saiban no dokuritsu to hōtei no ken'I,' *Hōritsu Jihō* 41, no. 8 (1969): 62–68.
36. Yokogawa Toshio, 'Saibankan ni mo iwasete hoshii – tōdai saiban wa ankoku saiban ka?,' *Bungeishunjū* 47, no. 11 (October 1969): 121–23.
37. Ibid., 128.
38. Tōdaitōsō bengo-dan, *Tōdai saiban: towareteiru mono wa nani ka*, 240–46.
39. For example, both documents are discussed in the Chief Prosecutor for the Supreme Court of Japan Hirade Hiizu's summary of the case for the magazine Jiji hyōron. See Hirade Hiizu, 'Arareru tōdai saiban,' *Jiji Hyōron* 14, no. 1 (1969): 10–22.

40. Kumagai Hiroshi, 'Tōsaiban no kenkai,' *Hōgaku Seminā* 161 (1969): 90–93.
41. Tōdaitōsō bengo-dan, *Tōdai saiban: towareteiru mono wa nani ka*, 223–26.
42. Ibid., 231.
43. Ibid., 232.
44. Kumagai Hiroshi, 'Tōdaisaiban ni okeru hikokunin no jitsujō,' *Hōritsu No Hiroba* 23, no. 2 (1970): 20.
45. Ibid.
46. 'Go hikoku no hoshaku torikesu chiken no kōkoku mitomeru tōkyō kōsai _ tōdai jiken kōhan,' *Asahi Shimbun*, 8 July 1969.
47. 'Chisai, go-ri no hoshaku kettei chiken wa teishi mōshitatete _ tōdai jiken kōhan,' *Asahi Shimbun*, 5 July 1969.
48. 'Go hikoku no hoshaku torikesu chiken no kōkoku shitatameru tōkyō kōsai _ tōdai jiken kōhan,' *Asahi Shimbun*, 8 July 1969.
49. 'Tōdai jiken no kōchi gakusei 10-ri o ikkatsu hoshaku tōkyō kōsai chiken no kōkoku o kikyaku,' *Asahi Shimbun*, 29 July 1969.
50. See for example 'Zenhikoku wo sokuji zenin hoshaku seyo,' *Zenshin*, 4 August 1969.
51. 'Gokuchū shokan' hakkan i'inkai, ed., 'Tōdaitōsō gokuchū shokanshū 13' (Gokuchū shokan hakkan i'inkai, 11 July 1969), 15.
52. Nihon marukusu-rēnin shugisha dōmei kyūtai-bu and Zenkoku gakusei kaihōsensen kyūtai-bu, 'Tōdaisaiban tōsō sōkatsu to 70-nen saiban tōsō hōshin,' in *Tōdaisaiban tōsō ronshū: chūkan sōkatsu to kongo no hōshin*, ed. Tōdai tōsō tōitsu kūtai jimukyoku (Tokyo: Tōdaitōsō tōitsu kūentaisaku honbu, 1970), 16.
53. 'Gokuchū shokan' hakkan i'inkai, ed., 'Tōdaitōsō Gokuchū Shokanshū 20' (Gokuchū shokan hakkan i'inkai, 6 September 1969), 15–16.
54. 'Tōdai bunrisaiban tsuitachi ni saikai,' *Zenshin*, 18 August 1969.
55. 'Hoshaku kyohi suru hikoku-tachi tōdai saiban kara _ tōdai jiken kōhan,' *Asahi Shimbun*, 19 August 1969.
56. Ibid.
57. Tōdaitōsō tōitsu hikoku-dan (jiritsu-sha) shiryō henshū iinkai, ed., *Shiryō: Tōdai Saiban Tōsō* (Tokyo: Tōdaitōsō tōitsu hikoku-dan (jiritsu-sha) shiryō henshū iinkai, 1978), 251. It is unclear, however, who Watanabe is referring to here.

58. Takasaka Hajime, 'Tōdaisaiban dakai no kage: rinshi ikensho no katsuyō to bengoshikai no hantai,' *Keizai Ōrai* 22, no. 11 (1969): 83.
59. Ibid., 84.
60. 'Bengodan, Rūru Wo Mamore: Tōdaisaiban, Bengoren, Irei No Shiji,' *Yomiuri Shimbun*, 7 September 1969.
61. Jinkichi Abe, 'Gakusei jiken (tōdai jiken) ni kansuru hōtei chitsujo iji ni kansuru danwa,' 6 September 1969, https://www.nichibenren.or.jp/document/statement/year/1969/1969_3.html. See also 'Hōritsuka Dokuji No Handan de Saiban Seijōka Hakare,' *Asahi Shimbun*, 14 November 1969.
62. 'Toki no hito: Ōtaka Michitsuke,' *Yomiuri Shimbun*, 13 September 1969.
63. 'Tōdaisaiban seijōka: dai-2 Tōkyō bengoshikaichō mo yōkyū,' *Yomiuri Shimbun*, 14 September 1969.
64. 'Bengoren to no hanashiai kyohi,' *Yomiuri Shimbun*, 26 November 1969.
65. The students not ejected accepted the legitimacy of the verdict. 'Tōdai Bunri Kōhan. Shijō Hatsu No Kesseki Hanketsu,' *Yomiuri Shimbun*, 28 November 1969.
66. 'Hikoku-tachi wa shikimō jōtai: tsuyoki ittenbari no okagaki saiban-chō,' *Yomiuri Shimbun*, 28 November 1969.
67. 'Tōdai bunri kōhan. shijō hatsu no kesseki hanketsu.'
68. Richard Weisman, *Showing Remorse: Law and the Social Control of Emotion* (London: Routledge, 2014), 19.
69. Ibid., 27.
70. Okagaki, 'Shiryō/ tōdai yasuda kōdō jiken okagaki hanketsu zenbun,' *Hōgaku Seminā*, no. 168 (1970).
71. Ibid., 7–10.
72. Weisman, *Showing Remorse: Law and the Social Control of Emotion*, 76.
73. Okagaki, 'Shiryō/ tōdai yasuda kōdō jiken okagaki hanketsu zenbun,' 10.
74. 'Manga chikku danaa. higezura gakusei hikoku usuwarai,' *Yomirui Shimbun*, 28 November 1969.
75. 'Shasetsu: irei no kesseki hanketsu to bengonin no sekimu,' *Asahi Shimbun*, 29 November 1969.
76. Ibid.

77. 'Todaijiken hanketsu to bengodan no sekinin,' *Yomiuri Shimbun*, 30 November 1969.
78. Ibid.
79. Itō Toshio, 'Tōdai saiban o meguru nichibenren no kenkai,' *Jurisuto*, no. 438 (1969): 45–51.
80. Ibid.
81. Yokoyama Koichirō, 'Tōdai kesseki hanketsu no kowashita mono,' *Hōgaku Seminā*, no. 168 (1969).
82. Ibid.
83. Ibid., 6.
84. Kumagai Hiroshi, 'Kesseki hanketsu wo dō kangaeru beki ka yokoyama ronbun wa jūyō na ten wo miotoshiteiru,' *Hōgaku Seminā*, no. 169 (1969): 62–69.
85. Ibid.
86. Ibid.
87. 'Kyūsaika tōsōka: jikkei ni yuragu hikoku,' *Asahi Shimbun*, 5 November 1969.
88. 'Tōdai saiban hikoku ga senjutsu tenkan hoshaku kyohi yame, asu shussho,' *Yomiuri Shimbun*, 5 October 1969.
89. Nihon marukusu-rēnin shugisha dōmei kyūtai-bu and Zenkoku gakusei kaihōsensen kyūtai-bu, 'Tōdaisaiban Tōsō Sōkatsu to 70-Nen Saiban Tōsō Hōshin.'
90. Tōdai zentōren hikokudan 16-mei naka 14-mei, 'Tōdaisaiban Tōsō Wo Tatakainuku Tame Ni (an): 70.1.13,' in *Tōdaisaiban Tōsō Ronshū: Chūkan Sōkatsu to Kongo No Hōshin*, ed. Tōdai tōsō tōitsu kūtai jimukyoku (Tokyo: Tōdaitōsō tōitsu kūentaisaku honbu, 1970), 50–57.
91. Tōdai tōsō sengakuren tōitsu hikokudan chūkaku-ha, 'Jikkei-hanketsu o Uchikaeshi Tōdaisaiban Tōso No Saranaru Shingeki o: Tōdai Tōsō Hikokudan Sengaku Sōgōkai e No Teian,' in *Tōdaisaiban Tōsō Ronshū: Chūkan Sōkatsu to Kongo No Hōshin*, ed. Tōdai tōsō tōitsu kūtai jimukyoku (Tokyo: Tōdaitōsō tōitsu kūentaisaku honbu, 1970), 36–49.
92. Ibid., 36.

References

Aoki, Hisa et al. 'Shihōkisha zadankai: tōdai saiban.' *Hōgaku Seminā*, no. 163 (September 1969): 136–51.

Asahi Shimbun. 'Chisai, go-ri no hoshaku kettei chiken wa teishi mōshitatete _ tōdai jiken kōhan.' 5 July 1969.

Asahi Shimbun. 'Go hikoku no hoshaku torikesu chiken no kōkoku mitomeru tōkyō kōsai _ tōdai jiken kōhan.' 8 July 1969.

Asahi Shimbun. 'Go hikoku no hoshaku torikesu chiken no kōkoku shitatameru tōkyō kōsai _ tōdai jiken kōhan.' 8 July 1969.

Asahi Shimbun. 'Hōritsuka dokuji no handan de saiban seijōka hakare.' 14 November 1969.

Asahi Shimbun. 'Hoshaku kyohi suru hikoku-tachi tōdai saiban kara _ tōdai jiken kōhan.' 19 August 1969.

Asahi Shimbun. 'Kyūsaika tōsōka: jikkei ni yuragu hikoku.' 5 November 1969.

Asahi Shimbun. 'Shasetsu: irei no kesseki hanketsu to bengonin no sekimu.' 29 November 1969.

Asahi Shimbun. 'Tōdai jiken kōhan no fuan.' 30 June 1969.

Asahi Shimbun. 'Tōdai jiken no kōchi gakusei 10-ri o ikkatsu hoshaku tōkyō kōsai chiken no kōkoku o kikyaku.' 29 July 1969.

Gokuchū shokan hakkan iinkai, ed. *Tōdai tōsō gokuchū shokanshū 1*. Tokyo: Mitani Shobo, 1970.

———, ed. 'Tōdaitōsō gokuchū shokanshū 13.' Gokuchū shokan hakkan i'inkai, 11 July 1969.

———, ed. 'Tōdaitōsō Gokuchū Shokanshū 20.' Gokuchū shokan hakkan i'inkai, 6 September 1969.

Hirade, Hiizu. 'Arareru tōdai saiban.' *Jiji Hyōron* 14, no. 1 (1969): 10–22.

'Hōtei nado no chitsujo iji ni kansuru hōristu ga tekiyō sareta jirei.' *Jurisuto*, no. 438 (1969): 72–73.

Ishijima, Yutaka. "Bōryoku' gakusei to 'jinken'-- kotoware naki jiyū hōsō-dan hibou ni kotaeru [sekai 281-gō keisai ishikawa hiromitsu 'bōryoku gakusei ni jinken wa nai no ka' ni taisuru hanron] '. *Sekai*, no. 284 (July 1969): 207–10.

Ishikawa, Hiromitsu. 'Bōryoku gakusei ni jinken ga nai no ka - bengonin kara no repōto.' *Sekai*, no. 281 (April 1969).

Itō, Toshio. 'Tōdai saiban o meguru nichibenren no kenkai.' *Jurisuto*, no. 438 (1969): 45–51.

Jinkichi, Abe. 'Gakusei jiken (tōdai jiken) ni kansuru hōtei chitsujo iji ni kansuru danwa.' 6 September 1969. https://www.nichibenren.or.jp/document/statement/year/1969/1969_3.html.

Kumagai, Hiroshi. 'Kesseki Hanketsu wo dō kangaeru beki ka yokoyama ronbun wa jūyō na ten wo miotoshiteiru.' *Hōgaku Seminā*, no. 169 (1969): 62–69.

———. 'Tōdaisaiban ni okeru hikokunin no jitsujō.' *Hōritsu No Hiroba* 23, no. 2 (1970): 20.

———. 'Tōsaiban no kenkai.' *Hōgaku Seminā* 161 (1969): 90–93.

Muchaku, Toki. 'Tōdaisaiban bōchōki.' In *Tōdai saiban: towareteiru mono wa nani ka*, edited by Tōdaitōsō bengo-dan, 392–402. Tokyo: Tabata shoten, 1969.

Muraki, Yoshihiko. 'Kikuyabashi 101 gō' mondai wo kyūdan suru.' *Eiga Hyōron* 26, no. 7 (1969): 93–95.

Nihon marukusu-rēnin shugisha dōmei kyūtai-bu, and Zenkoku gakusei kaihōsensen kyūtai-bu. 'Tōdaisaiban Tōsō Sōkatsu to 70-Nen Saiban Tōsō Hōshin.' In *Tōdaisaiban tōsō ronshū: chūkan sōkatsu to kongo no hōshin*, edited by Tōdai tōsō tōitsu kūtai jimukyoku, 6–35. Tokyo: Tōdaitōsō tōitsu kūentaisaku honbu, 1970.

Nikkeiren. 'Chokumen suru daigakumondai ni kansuru kihonteki kenkai.' In *Shiryō: Nihonkenpōhō 3*, edited by Kenichi Nagai, 507–10. Tokyo: Sanseidō, 1986.

Nomura, Akira. 'Repōto tōdaisaiban: tōitsukōhan yōkyū o meguru hikoku, bengodan, saibankan.' Tenbō, no. 11 (1969): 134.

Nose, Takao. 'Saiban no dokuritsu to hōtei no ken'i.' *Hōritsu Jihō* 41, no. 8 (1969): 62–68.

Okagaki. 'Shiryō/ tōdai yasuda kōdō jiken okagaki hanketsu zenbun.' *Hōgaku Seminā*, no. 168 (1970).

'Rupo Tōdai Saiban'. *Shūkan Asahi*, no. 2637 (8 August 1969): 16–23.

Shūkan Yomiuri. 'Jikkyō Rupo: Hikokunuki, Kidōtai Tsuki, Tōdaisaiban.' 27 August 1969.

Sunami, Shunsuke. 'hōdō no jiyū to mokuhiken, shōjōken: kikuyabashi 101-gō o meguru shomondai.' *Hōgaku Seminā* 41, no. 7 (1969): 96.

Takahiro, Uchida. 'Tōdai jiken saiban to shihō no byōri genshō.' *Jinken Shinbun*, 1 August 1969.

Takasaka, Hajime. 'Tōdaisaiban dakai no kage: rinshi ikensho no katsuyō to bengoshikai no hantai.' *Keizai Ōrai* 22, no. 11 (1969).

'Tōdai saiban' o miru me - tsuzuki.' *Jiyū to Seigi* 21, no. 2 (1970): 36–40.

Tōdai tōsō sengakuren tōitsu hikokudan chūkaku-ha. 'Jikkeihanketsu o uchikaeshi tōdaisaiban tōso no saranaru shingeki o: tōdai tōsō hikokudan sengaku sōgōkai e no teian.' In *Tōdaisaiban tōsō ronshū: chūkan sōkatsu to kongo no hōshin*, edited by Tōdai tōsō tōitsu kūtai jimukyoku, 36–49. Tokyo: Tōdaitōsō tōitsu kūentaisaku honbu, 1970.

Tōdai zentōren hikokudan 16-mei naka 14-mei. 'Tōdaisaiban tōsō wo tatakainuku tame ni (an): 70.1.13.' In *Tōdaisaiban tōsō ronshū: chūkan sōkatsu to kongo no hōshin*, edited by Tōdai tōsō tōitsu kūtai jimukyoku, 50–57. Tokyo: Tōdaitōsō tōitsu kūentaisaku honbu, 1970.

Tōdaitōsō bengo-dan. *Tōdai saiban: towareteiru mono wa nani ka*. Tokyo: Tabata shoten, 1969.

Tōdaitōsō tōitsu hikoku-dan (jiritsu-sha) shiryō henshū iinkai, ed. *Shiryō: Tōdai Saiban Tōsō*. Tokyo: Tōdaitōsō tōitsu hikoku-dan (jiritsu-sha) shiryō henshū iinkai, 1978.

Tōdaitōsō zengakukyōtōkaigi, and Tōdaitōsō zengaku kyōtōkaigi kyūen taisaku honbu. *Tōdaitōsō: Tōitsukōhan Shōri No Tame Ni*. Tokyo: Tōdaitōsō zengakukyōtōkaigi kyūen taisaku honbu jōsen-bu, 1969.

Weisman, Richard. *Showing Remorse: Law and the Social Control of Emotion*. London: Routledge, 2014.

Yokogawa, Toshio. 'Saibankan ni mo iwasete hoshii -- tōdai saiban wa ankoku saiban ka?' *Bungeishunjū* 47, no. 11 (October 1969): 120–28.

Yokoyama, Koichirō. 'Tōdai kesseki hanketsu no kowashita mono.' *Hōgaku Seminā*, no. 168 (1969).

Yomirui Shimbun. 'Manga chikku danaa. higezura gakusei hikoku usuwarai.' 28 November 1969.

Yomiuri Shimbun. 'Bengodan, rūru wo mamore: tōdaisaiban, bengoren, irei no shiji.' 7 September 1969.

Yomiuri Shimbun. 'Bengoren to no hanashiai kyohi.' 26 November 1969.

Yomiuri Shimbun. 'Chian tōkyoku shokku.' 11 April 1969.

Yomiuri Shimbun. 'Hikoku-tachi wa shikimō jōtai: tsuyoki ittenbari no okagaki saiban-chō.' 28 November 1969.

Yomiuri Shimbun. 'Tōdai bunri kōhan. shijō hatsu no kesseki hanketsu.' 28 November 1969.

Yomiuri Shimbun. 'Tōdai kōhan-hatsu no 'heigō' shinri sore mo ōare, kidōtai/ tōkyō chisai.' 26 August 1969.

Yomiuri Shimbun. 'Tōdai saiban hikoku ga senjutsu tenkan hoshaku kyohi yame, asu shussho.' 5 October 1969.

Yomiuri Shimbun. 'Todaijiken hanketsu to bengodan no sekinin.' 30 November 1969.

Yomiuri Shimbun. 'Tōdaisaiban seijōka: dai-2 tōkyō bengoshikaichō mo Yōkyū.' 14 September 1969.

Yomiuri Shimbun. 'Toki no hito: maniwa haruo.' 12 April 1969.

Yomiuri Shimbun. 'Toki no hito: ōtaka michitsuke.' 13 September 1969.

Zenshin. 'Tōdai bunrisaiban tsuitachi ni saikai.' 18 August 1969.

Zenshin. 'Zenhikoku wo sokuji zenin hoshaku seyo.' 4 August 1969.

CHAPTER 7

Words, Emotions, and Life in the State's Perpetual Present

Speaking to a journalist for the magazine Shūkan Asahi, the administrative head of the Tokyo Detention House Furuda Minoru painted a rosy picture of the lives of the student detainees. 'I'm impressed by how well the students study,' he remarked. 'When they are on the outside, they are probably too busy with the movement. Indeed, because they are now living a life with good routines, it seems that many of them are putting on weight.'[1] Furuda's characterisation of the students' experience awaiting trial is in one sense quite accurate. As one detainee interviewed for the same magazine article reported, by August he had put on 12 kilograms and had met his reading target of 10,000 pages.[2] But as Wada Eiji noted in a recent account of awaiting trial, there was a powerful contradiction within the experience.[3] On one hand Wada recounted that, in accordance with Furuda's assessment, his time in prison was generally peaceful, affording him much free time to read widely and to reflect. Life passed by with mechanical regularity in tiny rooms that contained a covered sink and toilet.[4] Pop music floated down from the ceiling, and meals appeared through a slot in the door with fastidious punctuality. On the other hand, Wada recounted the sustained efforts taken by the prison guards to erode his sense of connection to his community of students, both inside and outside the prison walls. Students were almost entirely isolated from each other 24 hours a day, and prison guards went to great

C. Perkins, *The Tokyo University Trial and the Struggle Against Order in Postwar Japan*, New Directions in East Asian History,
https://doi.org/10.1007/978-981-99-7043-8_7

lengths to maintain this separation. Students were forbidden from looking through the covered slot on the outside of their door, rollcall was by prisoner number rather than name to maintain the anonymity of those being held, and movement in corridors was choreographed such that students would never see each other being transported around the facility. Exercise took place in a spoked building purpose built for the student detainees which was configured such that students could run along thin, walled off 20 m strips of land while being observed by the guards. Finally, this peaceful, regular, isolated monotony seemingly had no end.[5]

As discussed in the Chapter 3, Zenkyōtō functioned as a collective cognitive framework or discourse community, through which members developed new ways of relating to themselves and others in a perpetual process of becoming. In Wada‘s recollections we see a counter process of ‘mortification of the self’, a process first discussed by Erving Goffman and characterised by Richard Wiseman as one in which ‘the self is stripped of its social and psychological supports in order that a new identity might replace the identity that has been lost.’[6] Goffman observed that in total institutions such as prisons and asylums the mortification of self takes place through a number of different processes. Inmates are often inducted into the institution through a process of cataloguing. Weight, height, and other bodily characteristics are measured and noted as the inmate becomes an object to be carefully monitored. Induction also necessitates removal from inmates of identifiers of their previous lifeworld on ‘the outside’, to be replaced with possessions belonging to the institution itself that can be revoked at any time. Once on the inside, inmates are forced to engage in activities whose symbolic implications are incompatible with their sense of self: daily routines that are ‘alien’ to the rhythms of the life word the inmate has left behind. And as this continues the inmate is subject to what Goffman calls ‘contaminative exposure’ by which ‘the territories of the self are violated; the boundary that the individual places between his being and the environment is invaded and the embodiments of the self profaned.’[7] When the subject reacts to maintain this sense of distinction, that defence itself becomes subject to intervention. Combined, these mechanisms work to erode in the inmate a sense of themselves as an autonomous subject, prompting shifts in the inmate's ‘moral career’.[8]

Wada's description of life in detention contains many characteristics of this process of mortification. Roll call by number, isolation from fellow inmates, routinisation of life into alien rhythms stripped from the students their social and psychological support structures. But this picture does not give us a sense of the methods through which students on the inside attempted to resist these processes. Of course, the work of the student support groups was a crucial, and well documented, part of this resistance.[9] In this chapter, however, I focus on an as yet neglected method students used to maintain their community in the face of state pressure: a student run publication circulated both inside and outside prison called *The Prison Letters* (*Gokuchū shokanshū*).[10]

The first collection of the Prison Letters was published on 20 April 1969, almost three months to the day of the fall of Yasuda Auditorium. It contained ten pages of manually typeset letters from students detained in the Tokyo Detention Centre at Kosuge and Toyotama Prison in Nakano. Publication of the Prison Letters was attributed to the Prison Letters Publication Committee, and the head of the committee, in a play on the name of Acting Principal Katō Ichirō, Katō Jirō. A contact address at the Tokyo University Oiwake dormitory was listed, and the contact name was Mazaki Mōtetsu. Both names, as well as most of the students' names in the publication, were pseudonyms. Distribution was through a few small book shops near to Tokyo University's Komaba campus and by hand in Shinjuku. Each edition cost 50-yen plus any donations the purchaser wanted to make.[11]

Despite its humble origins, the Prison Letters proved incredibly popular, with the first volume selling over 5000 units. It went on to 25 volumes and became an important source of income for the students support groups. The editors defined the publication's mission in volume one as follows:

> If you have ever attended those hearings for disclosing reasons for detention, you would recognize the following: the irrationality, the extreme irrationality of the legal system, and the unsettling absurdity of it being conducted openly in the name of logic. Amid this farce, only the "accused" possesses a human face. If you have ever experienced a "visit" in a "detention facility," you would become aware of the following: the disturbing truth of humans held in cages by humanoid beings, and that torture is executed by isolating humans from one another.
>
> Revealing these truths on a societal level is among the essential tactics in the struggle for just trials. This approach inevitably necessitates another key tactic: fostering human solidarity between those inside prison and those outside, and through this, reinstating human communication among inmates.

> Why "Prison Letters"? There isn't any other method to communicate the vivid human emotions across the impenetrable barrier of authority. As a result, in order to establish human solidarity between those in prison and those outside, and to further reinstate human communication among inmates using this medium, there is no other option but to utilize "this."[12]

Most of the work of editing and producing the publication was in fact done by Mazaki, who was a fourth-year humanities student at the Tokyo University. His motivation for starting the publication came from a mixture of guilt and frustration. In an interview with the Mainichi newspaper, Mazaki recounted that during the struggles he had been injured in an instance of factional infighting (*uchigeba*) and was unable to take part in the defence of Yasuda Auditorium, which saw many of his friends arrested. This sense of guilt combined with his feeling of impotence and frustration as the student struggles wound down at the university. When one of his imprisoned friends, known as Suijō No. 26 in the Prison Letters,[13] wrote him a letter from prison Mazaki saw an opportunity to continue the struggle through the press. In this regard he was also keen to redress what he saw as an imbalance in reporting on the student movement which, much like the students' view of the trials, he saw as creating a narrative divorced from the lived experience of the students:

> Various books and reports have been written about the Tokyo University struggle up to now. However, all of them have been told by people who were not directly involved in the struggle and are one-sided. The words are dead on the page. That won't do. The struggle itself was far more vibrant and dynamic.[14]

Soon what looked like a short-lived project gained momentum, becoming in the words of the Mainichi newspaper a 'Hidden Best-Seller.'[15] A number of reasons can be attributed to this success. There is no doubt that the detainees had a level of capital within the movement. For example, one female student interviewed in the Mainichi stated that 'those students who fought bravely in the Tokyo University struggle and were arrested were cool to begin with, but now they are sending us letters from prison—they are even cooler!' Students also seemed to like the feel of authenticity about the Prison Letters: 'They have a sense of authenticity about them that goes far beyond the leaflets distributed by Zenkyōtō'. But as one 'veteran' of the movement suggested, the success of the publication lay also in its function in maintaining a sense of community: 'Since the Haneda struggles, the number of students arrested at demonstrations and so forth has risen dramatically. Being arrested is now an everyday experience. People read [the Prison Letters] for the sense of a generation sharing the same experience.'[16]

The Prison Letters were also distributed to the detainees by Tōitsu kyūtai. As an extension of the policy of solitary detention practiced across the prisons, letters were always censored so that students could not see who wrote them or where their comrades were being held. This, however, did not stop conversations developing on various themes and granting a sense of solidarity as students devised ways to work around the censorship. Often pseudonyms were chosen that students could recognise, and even the content of the redacted sentences themselves could be revealed by careful application of water to the blacked-out sections. The content of the Prison Letters ranged from serious theoretical missives to poetry, to wry in-jokes and observations. This is not to pretend that the letters were harmonious. As should be expected given the range of factional affiliations represented in prison, at times they were anything but. Pencils were worn down articulating complex—and often quite blunt—arguments in response to other detainees, mirroring in microcosm the factional infighting that was developing on 'the outside'. That being said, even this linguistic sparring seemed to have given the detainees a sense of pleasure and purpose. In general, it is clear from reading the letters that they were on the whole a great source of emotional support.

In approaching the Prison Letters this chapter asks questions about how students understood and grappled with life in perpetual detention; how they reflected on the trial as it progressed; and how they tried to make sense of their position within the wider movement from within their cells. Contamination in many forms permeates the letters: from the food they ate, the language in which they were surrounded, visits from their families, and the general atmosphere in which they spent their time. In extreme cases, contamination came in the form of forced feeding couched in the terms of medical science. Combined, these mechanisms worked to erode the students' sense of themselves as autonomous subjects in an effort to prompt shifts in their 'moral careers'. I show how the letters offer a window into the ways in which the movement was negotiated as practice in prison by individuals but also through dialogue as the letters were published and circulated across the detention centres. I also show how the function of the letters became a source of controversy for the detainees. As the trial continued, questions about the relationship between the detainees and those on the outside (referred to as *shabu* by the students) became increasingly acute. The Prison Letters, while facilitating forms of communication that transcended prison walls, were simultaneously at risk of fetishizing the detainees, transforming them into a source of revolutionary language for the movement at the expense of understanding the reality of their experiences behind locked doors. Indeed, for some letter writers, the fetishization of the detainees went hand in hand with what they saw as the essentialisation of the trial itself. The determined resistance to any form of cooperation with the courts was seen as losing sight of the human costs of such an approach. And as events on the outside began to show, the human cost was begining to rise.

Life in Perpetual Detention

As discussed in earlier chapters, a key threat for the students was what they called normalisation (*seijōka*). This normalisation referred to the suturing up of the breach in the order of everyday life, its routines and the common-sense bodies of knowledge that supported them. In the letters students reflected on how the configuration of the detention centres seemed geared towards this normalisation, but through methods far divorced from the brute power of the riot police. This was a power that was subtle, defuse, and that turned the subject in on itself. Within this context, many of the letters reflected on the quiet sterility of the prison buildings, and the seemingly never-ending loop of their existence within the cells, corridors, and exercise areas. One engineering student set it out for readers of the letters: 'wake up at 7am, eat breakfast, exercise for 30 mins, eat again at 11:30, again at 4:30, in bed at 5:15, and asleep by 9 pm.'[17] As another put it 'it is a simple life: wake, sleep; eat three meals (barly gruel), chew on chocolate, chew on an orange, use the toilet, pace my two tatami room like a polarbear.'[18] And although students were allowed to read and study, which they did, caught within this loop students talked of a dulling of the senses and general lack of any form of stimulation. The space itself was complicit in enforcing banality: 'white painted doors stretch on forever, the prison smells like a hospital [...] the thought of being here for another year is enough to drive me mad.'[19] In this world even the covers of the Prison Letters brought joy: '...dark blue, light blue, red. The colours of covers of the Prison Letters brings such happiness in a place like this. Much like "red" clothing is forbidden here, prison is a grey word where colour is stolen'.[20]

The effect of this routinisation was to remove students from the people and practices that helped them constitute themselves as activists, both in the physical sense of removing them from the front line, but also by regulating their emotions. In particular, as Yamamoto Yoshitaka had argued at the May rally (see Chapter 6) the danger of loss of anger was at the forefront of many students' minds. Whereas on the outside anger had a clear object of focus in the riot police as manifestation of state power, on the inside that object was removed and replaced by the detainee themselves. As one student put it, 'when I was being interrogated by the police, I felt relatively comfortable because I had real power [*genjitsu no kenryoku*] in front of me. *But as I calmed down* in this small, solitary cell, I realised the enemy was not real power, but it was actually myself—the petit-bourgeois nature of my own mind.'[21] A later account, worth quoting at length, revealed more of the emotional toll wrought on the student detainees by this environment:

> My day. I feel extremely upset by the fact that half of the social pages of the morning paper are blacked out, and the loss of a place to vent my anger has me turn inwards and clatter up and down the toilet flush handle in vain. Daytime. Thirty minutes of exercise. I jump rope and do short sprints in a narrow cage in the exercise yard. I hold my chest out, I stick my sweaty forehead out into the early summer sunlight and look up at the sweltering blue sky, knowing that the nauseating, stale grey air in the cell is settling into my lungs and my organs. The guard's voice, "Finish your exercise!", is infuriatingly that of a powerful, invisible 'authority'.[22]

For this student, however the point of comparison was not the hospital as above—with its connotations of illness and healing—but instead the crematorium:

> Mr Katō, have you ever seen the corpse-burning area of a crematorium? It is like this, rows of small white doors lined up on either side of a long concrete corridor. My cell is at the end, on the right. Every time I see that long row of doors, the devil on my shoulder whispers about the prospect of spending the rest of my life in this place. I enter the cell. A one-and-a-half-mat room with running water and a toilet (as well as a desk and a chair). An extremely abstract living space: design genius (!). The room suppresses the normal functioning of the five senses; it pushes the extinction of our sensibility to the limit. The resistance of those who have been declared 'socially dead' begins in the bosom of colossal 'state power'.[23]

One student described how he found night the most difficult to bear. As the radio died out and the music signalling night-time began to play, he described time taking on the texture of 'hard rubber' and the fear that came with knowing that this 'hard time' (***katai jikan***) would continue until he fell asleep. In the dark a menagerie of things passed his eyes, a mass of people 'floating, sinking, being expelled, falling, piling up, shaking, howling…'.[24]

Within this environment students struggled to maintain their emotional connection to the movement. With the riot police replaced by their own selves as 'the enemy', some battled to find new techniques to resist falling back into an unthinking and unfeeling everydayness:

> The battle against the self [*jiko*] is very hard. The greatest enemy is the loss of sensitivity to "order" [*chitsujo*]. We cannot forget our anger. We have to sharpen our sensitivity. I try to objectify myself constantly in order to maintain a state of tension. Although it is extremely difficult because I am detached from 'actual practice', I try to follow the printed word to extract the humanity between the printed lines. Because when you are 'objectified', you are finished...[25]

This fear of objectification, expressed across many of the letters, is congruent with what Goffman referred to as 'trimming' or 'programming', whereby the subject is coded into an object that can be 'fed into the administrative machinery of the establishment, to be worked on smoothly by routine operations.'[26] In this regard, as a Hōsei University student recounted, the detention centre was both separate from yet seemingly emblematic of society at large. The bureaucratic formality of interactions, the emphasis on maintaining order through authority, and recourse to violence should that order breakdown all seemed a distillation of life on the outside the prison walls. Drawing the comparison explicitly he reflected: '[Inside] we are thoroughly free. As long as we do not break the rules, we are free. The freedom to be allowed to eat. The freedom to be made to exercised. The freedom to be made to work.'[27] To be objectified for the students was to lose their emotional bulwarks against the encroachment of order.

Their Words/Our Words

Although silence was part of routinisation in the prisons, the letters also ruminated on how sounds, words, and vocabularies were also part of the process of mortification. One student, for example, dwelled on the use of radio in prison. He related:

> The radio programmes here are for the enjoyment and edification of the inmates. So they switch off relaxing music programmes and instead present us with programmes like 'The Prison Guard's Notebooks' or 'A Guide to Getting a Job'. It's the bourgeois dog's 'view of life', 'our words' [*watashi tachi no kotoba*] that are needed to build the 'bright society'. Even in news programmes, criminal cases are edited out. As boring as this is, it still happens every day.[28]

The use of 'our words' (*watashi tachi no kotoba*), here referring to the words of Japan's economic order using the term *watashi tachi* in contrast to the movement's preferred term *wareware*, to describe the content of the radio programmes is indicative of the students' sensitivity to the integrity of the community to which they belonged. When seen in this way the dense language of the movement was therefore not just theoretical but also performative and productive. The students' use of language and the recognition of terms, reference points, and grammatical and lexical choices were all part of maintaining a structure of belonging: a boundary that separated 'us' from 'them'.[29] For the students the fear was that words of Japan's 'bright society' economical miracle would begin to contaminate their use of language, and they articulated this fear keenly. For example:

> What we want most in prison is language. Even on the 'outside' our language is stolen by the ruling classes. Their language is imposed on us (for example: the term public negotiation [*taishūdankō*] is taken from us and we are arrested for 'false imprisonment' [*fuhōkankin*]. But here this [deprivation of words] is conspicuous and thorough. Words that burn with human anger are cut out by the censor. To prevent us from talking to our comrades, we are thrown into solitary confinement. And punishment awaits us if we overcome this wall and speak out.[30]

The embodied nature of this need was evident in other letters. A Tokyo University student writing in Volume 8 spoke of his sense of fulfilment when he was allowed visitors for five minutes. However, while he noted he wanted to speak to everyone he could get his hands on, the student made a special case for speaking to 'us' (*bokura*):

> I want to meet and talk to those people who are part of 'us'. By meeting them and talking to them, the gestures, the nuances of the words would give me strength. I want to recognise every single expression. And the truth is that sometimes I cannot tell the difference between this anxiety and physical desire [*nikutaiteki yokyū*].[31]

For one student the experience in prison clarified the nature of the student movement as a whole:

> … the "fight" was not something spectacular, it was not a strike; at the risk of being misunderstood, I don't think it was even political action [*seijiteki kōdō*]… It is about stopping the encroachment of power in a daily life characterised by providing for wife and child (even if this might be the case soon) and providing for myself and holding onto my own "language"[32]

Through these quotes we can see how the prison was for the students a distilled version of the banality of the everyday. A temporally, spatially, and socially isolating routine that could eat away at their words as markers of identity and belonging. But as long as that language was alive, so too was the movement and the potential for new narrative forms of belonging.

Another source of mortification came from the family. As has been shown in earlier chapters, the family was integral to the state's attempts to rehabilitate the student radicals awaiting trial. Prosecutors and judges urged families to intervene in the thinking of their 'children', or relinquish that responsibility to the state, and similarly urged the students to consider the impact their actions had on their families, leveraging emotions of guilt and responsibility in the process. Even during sentencing of students who continued to opt for a unified trial, it was the assurances of family members, and even the birth of children to create new families, that tipped the scales in favour of suspended sentences. The family was a method of intervention, safe hands, and unit of socialisation back into the national fold. Not surprisingly, then, the 'family problem' became a prominent theme in the letters. To begin with contributors conceptualised the family problem as directly linked to the Japanese state and the vestiges of Japanese imperialism. As Suijō 26-gō put it in Volume One, realisation of himself as an independent political actor necessitated severing his bonds with his father (as embodiment of capitalist paternalism) and his 'good' mother, who he saw as inseparable from the institution of motherhood that had raised soldiers for the Japanese Empire. His position on the family problem was stark: 'Let us cause the literal death of "mother" as family and "father" as bourgeois state. Only by doing so can we live.' In a similar vein a Tottori University student proclaimed that families posed a continuous threat of tempting students back into bourgeois society. 'Family is like a woman of the night wearing thick makeup,' he argued in an ugly turn of phrase. 'When the makeup is removed you feel nauseous.'[33]

Suijō's rejection of his family, however, was met with nuanced and ambivalent responses as the discourse of the family problem developed through the letters. While all agreed that the theoretical argument for dissolving the family as a precondition for self-realisation rang true, the reality of the choice and the complex emotions that the choice engendered were quite another matter. Some argued that engagement through careful logical reasoning was more realistic than rejection, but it was clear that letters and visits from family members could become moments of intense frustration. One student, writing under the pseudonym K.K., reflected on how he seemed to be caught in a web of guilt that was eating away at his sense of autonomy. His mother took responsibility for his decision to join the movement, blaming her lack of care for him by not making him lunch; in the same breath, she would accuse K.K. of creating familial guilt, asking 'why would you bother your grandmother by partic ipating in such anti-social activities? His political choice as an independent human being was reduced to the breakdown of reciprocal relationships of 'love' (*aijō*).[34] And even when families were not actively attempting to dissuade detainees from political action, visits were a source of exhaustion and internal conflict as selves were crafted to meet familial expectations. This long reflection is illustrative:

> I don't want to see my mother or my relatives, I get tired every time I see them, I'm so fed up with them. I see clearly that I become limp, flabby and my whole body is grey. But I try not to worry them and try to sound cheerful. Then, lo and behold! They either decide that I am just trying to sound cheerful, or they take me at face value and decide that I am fine. Either way, their attitude is that as long as my body is healthy, they don't care about the rest. How can they not see that the rest is more important to talk about? The untruths build up and may be beyond my reach. Perhaps

> because they cannot understand the "I" that is part of "us", or because they cannot be satisfied without forcibly taking me away [from us] for their visits, in the end, because they cannot understand 'I', they indulge in the most easily accessible emotions. They feel sorry for me. "He is so unlucky!" "He has been caught up in such a terrible series of events!" "He had the wool pulled over his eyes!" This is how they wallow in front of me. If it were up to me, I would pour petrol on it all and watch it burn. But for some reason they cannot be happy without wallowing. Their eyes can't help but pity me. They are eyes against a backdrop of public recognition in newspapers and on television; like the currency that circulates through everyday life. This is what covers my face with a human personality that is somehow different from my own. So when I ask them for this or that, their faces contract into a look of joy and they nod their heads in agreement. For me, this is an infuriating compromise.
>
> I have no need for pity or comfort. In fact, they are terribly harmful. For I am not a criminal, I am not mentally ill, I am not an invalid. I am not covetous of material possessions. When we talk only about our bodies, food, clothes, other possessions, I feel a sense of unbearable barrenness.[35]

The construction of a character by external viewpoints and the subsequent incongruity with the student's self-perception, cultivated through their involvement in the movement, caused considerable distress. The discourse, limited to daily life elements such as food and clothing, appeared to them as a futile attempt to conceal systemic fissures through trivial language. This predicament was visibly embodied, resulting in their physique turning 'limp, flabby, and grey'. Interestingly, a significant focus on the physical form is observable in these correspondences, a topic to which we now turn.

Bodies as Sites of the Struggle Against Order

For many of the students their bodies became an index of the effect the detention centres were having on them. Their meals mostly consisted of tasteless barley gruel, which was a fitting gastronomic extension of the monotone banality of the students' surroundings. When they had access to meat it was in the form of whale, pork fat, or chicken skin.[36] As one student noted in a letter to the Agricultural and Industrial Students' Association Newsletter *Expose,* the food was so tasteless that when he received care parcels from friends containing chocolate or oranges he experienced 'a deliciousness that was impossible to experience in civilian life'.[37] Yet despite its lack of flavour, prison food was dense in calories and portions were generous. Many students referred to the shock of weight gain in prison. As one put it: 'would you understand the pattern of life here if I said, magazine in my right hand, Marx in my left hand, revolution in the heart, subcutaneous fat across the whole body?' For this student his weight gain prompted him to consider what it meant to maintain a revolutionary movement in prison. His conclusion was that he had to be ready for whatever tomorrow may bring, which necessitated exercise.[38] In another letter:

> They weigh us before and after we are punished with solitary confinement, a punishment familiar to many comrades. When I saw the needle pointing at 71kg, even considering the sweater I was wearing to protect myself from the cold day, I was shocked. Since then, I have been desperately trying to condition my body and lose weight by putting all my energy into jumping rope. I jump rope 3300 times and do 77 push-ups [a day].[39]

These reflections on weight gain, which were peppered all through the letters, suggest the students' concern with the environment extended to how it was remoulding their physical bodies: making them soft, lethargic, and ultimately unfit as a revolutionary subject. The grey gruel was a contaminant which blurred the boundary between themselves and the environment.[40] In this context exercise was not just a way of using up time, but a method of guarding against this physical contamination of the self in order to reclaim that boundary.

At the opposite end of the spectrum in the battle for bodily autonomy was the decision to go on hunger strike. For those students who decided to do so, hunger-strike was the final method left to continue contesting for a group trial. Of course, the decision to go on hunger strike would have been made in isolation and came with much fear that one was embarking on this course of action alone. However, the letters played a role in making such a decision a shared experience, as later letters engaged with the reflections of letters published earlier on. The letters also provide insight on the process of hunger strike within the detention centres, how it was managed by the authorities, and the difficult decisions students made as they struggled with their decisions to refuse food. Hunger strike, unlike overt forms of resistance such as breaking silence by shouting slogans or singing the Internationale, occupied an ambiguous position within the prisons. Although there were no specific rules against it, hunger strike was treated as a form of self-harm that violated institutional regulations. As such students who declared hunger strike were subject to a range of privations: reading matter was taken away, newspapers were removed, and access to the radio was revoked.[41] In some cases students were moved from their cells into a spartan, windowless 'cooler' for an indeterminate amount of time. A student subject to this punishment noted that, in contrast to penalties resulting from clear rule violations, he was not given any warnings, explanations or written notifications as to the reasons for his punishment and was given no opportunity to explain his choice.[42]

But the experience of hunger strike was not simply one of resistance and punishment: it was also a process of rationalising the institution's interventions into the bodies of the students. One Waseda University student calling himself Yūshima Kōji submitted a lengthy account of his hunger strike. On a previous occasion in April when Yūshima had refused breakfast he had been sent to a punishment cell. This time however, after submitting a document detailing their intention to go on hunger strike, Yūshima was visited by a guard who suggested that one or two days of refusing food would be tolerated, but any more than that would be 'difficult' (*komaru*) and Yūshima should stop. After four days of hunger strike the food delivered to Yūshima's cell was switched from the barely gruel that came as standard to a marginally more palatable rice porridge (*okayu*) made with white rice. In the meantime, however, Yūshima started making regular visits to the prison physician, who recorded his weight and took his blood pressure. Ironically although he had dropped from 65 to 61 kg since beginning his hunger strike, Yūshima noted in his letter that he was still 6 kg heavier than he was when he entered detention, a fact he put down to a singular lack of food during his initial three-week custody and interrogation by the police.

On the fifth day it was clear the prison authorities had lost patience: the institution had decided Yūshima was no longer a competent social actor and that intervention into his body was required in the form of forced feeding. Yet there was a strange disconnect between this intervention and the atmosphere in which it occurred. It was not a violent scene, and Yūshima did not report his resistance to the process. Instead, he described in his letter being lectured by the doctor at length and in detail on the dangerous effects of starvation while the doctor inserted a drip containing a litre of 'yellow liquid' into both thighs. The effects of this contamination were visibly evident: Yūshima reported 'my legs were swollen. It was hard to get my trousers back on. Apparently, that litre [of liquid] contained a day's worth of nutrition.' The doctor's calm rationalisation in the language of biology made it difficult for Yūshima to maintain his resistance, as to do so would have marked him as irrational, unconcerned with his body, and thus in even greater need of medical intervention. This process was repeated the next day, during which a further mortification came when the guard commanded Yūshima to thank the doctor. 'You must be kidding!' reflected Yūshima. 'How can I say thank you after being deprived of even my own freedom of existence? I am the one who should be thanked for allowing them to carry out their duties.'[43]

As Goffman argues, when an individual in civil society must accept circumstances that go against their sense of self they still have recourse to defiance as a method of 'face-saving'.[44] In contrast, the guard's demand for thanks was also a demand that Yūshima collapse himself into the process, accept the scientific objectification of his body as a site of intervention, and acknowledge the moral superiority of that rational approach. As his hunger strike continued, Yūshima observed two further okayu adorned with pickled plums (*umeboshi*) being delivered, leading him to speculate that two more students were currently on hunger strike. Yūshima's resistance, however, was coming to an end. With his trial date looming, he put chopsticks to rice, which tasted 'watery and disgusting'. Now it was he himself facilitating the transgression of the body by the state's contaminant, the okayu with its pungent umeboshi imbued with nostalgic symbolism as staple of the Japanese family. This one volitional transgression—self contamination—appeared enough for the institution. The following day the watery okayu was gone, replaced once more by barley gruel.[45]

Another student, referring to himself as Itaya Motoaki, also related the moment his hunger-strike was broken, and his account adds a further dimension to how words and violence came together in the policing of student resistance within the detention centres. Like Yūshima, after five-days he was taken for a medical examination and told if he continued he would risk permanent physical damage. Undeterred he resisted, only to be tied down to a bed with a belt and injected with what he described as '1000 cc of liquid'. As with Yūshima, Itaya described hunger strike as his final freedom. It was his 'last weapon of resistance and protest,' and when looking at his thighs 'now swollen up like an elephant's' he felt a great sense of loss. Yet more than the actual violence of this experience, it was the words that accompanied the injection that came to haunt him:

> The words of the guard as he stared down at me while I was being forcibly hydrated, his gaze cold as if he were observing an experiment on a guinea pig, left a deep mark on my soul. 'This is great, isn't it?' he said. 'It's the sort of thing the laziest of us would do. You can get nutrition without moving your mouth, without making your stomach work. If I get tired of eating, I could ask them to do it for me.'[46]

Why was there emphasis on words rather than the violent act of forced injection? Again it was an instance of normalization, but this time accompanied with trivialization of the experience of the student. The guard's straightforward remarks, the casual jest, and the intimate language all collapsed the student into the process. It was an assertion that normalized the intrusion of power into the body, against the (sovereign) volition of the body's possessor. It depicted the act of usurping the students' 'final freedom' as 'something great'. These utterances also carried a demeaning, infantilizing tone. Notably, when the account of the guard's words was printed and circulated back within the prison, including the student's name and place of detention, it was entirely redacted.

Controversy and Fetishization of Language

As has been shown in previous chapters, Tōitsu kyūtai was an uncomfortable alliance of a range of actors with differing priorities regarding the Tokyo University Trial. Conflict over the proper relationship between the detainees and activists on the outside existed from the initial formation of the alliance, with fault lines developing between those who prioritised the students' quick release and those saw them as totemic in the larger battle with the state. These divisions played out too in the letters, both on the side of the editorial team and with the letter writers themselves.

While the publication had got off to a good start, as the trial continued self-doubt began to set in. During the editorial meeting for the 6th volume of the Letters the editorial team found themselves questioning their endeavours. At the outset their goal had been threefold: to create a publication for imprisoned comrades; to spread the word of their conditions; and to raise money for their activities. However, far fewer letters were arriving than they had hoped. Indeed, after a peak of 13 letters in issue two, the editors were only publishing four letters per issue, representing a tiny proportion of the over 400 students holding out for unified trial. 'More than anything we counted on letters arriving. We are making this thing so why aren't we receiving letters?' they questioned. This led to a crisis of confidence in the value of the publication: 'For those in detention does our work amount to nothing? Is it having a negative impact?' If that were the case, they concluded, the only option was to give up and move on. A public debate with readers of the letters held in May cured them of their sense of despair, however, and resulted in a reformulation of the goals of the publication.[47]

The outcome was a new vision of the purpose of the Letters. Whereas previously the aim was on the detainees as a special category of student activist, this new direction subsumed those in prison into a broader category of *wareware*, or "us".[48] Rather than in service of the detainees, then, this new direction reconceptualised the detainees as a source of language (*kotoba*) as resources for the movement. This shift in emphasis now saw the Letters as a mechanism for 'taking language' (*kotoba o pakuru*). 'Even if they don't like it,' stated the editors, 'we must take the words we need from them.' And even if an edition of the Letters contained nothing but the editorial afterword it would still be meaningful if 'filled with rich language from prison.' According to the editors this language would function as 'true agitation' with the power to co-opt into the movement the sort of people on the outside who say they understand all the reasons for the struggle, but still will not fight. Transforming the language of this reasoning into a form of universal rhetoric of agitation was now the goal of the letters. Such language was to come from an ever moving present and from detainees involved in all forms of struggle produced by living at the extremes of the movement. Doing so necessitated moving past the Tokyo University Struggle as point of reference fixed in the past.[49]

So why was it the language of inmates in particular that was necessary? 'We on the outside run away from the question of why we must fight', the editors reasoned. 'We sway. But those on the inside live wrapped in "the struggle and its results".'[50] The detainees were therefore seen as occupying a position of authentic struggle. In an article published in the Zenkyōtō newspaper *Shingeki*, the editors outlined this logic further:

> The way they [the detainees] battle against stark reality in this extreme situation - a reality that entails a direct confrontation with power - is revealed only in fleeting 'visits' and letters penned during a few painstaking hours each day. This is grossly inadequate, but it is exactly for this reason they surpass the shortcomings of linguistic expression, speaking to us with their whole beings, from the deepest recesses of their hearts.

> We've grown overly accustomed to empty agitation. However, shouldn't genuine agitation be the words of those living at their 'limit' in the confines of their prison cells?[51]

This reframing of the letters met with a mixed response from the detainees. For some the lack of letters was simply a reflection of the conditions in prison. 'Even though there are over 400 people inside I was surprised that such a dumb thing could happen,' wrote one student on reading in the editorial of the lack of correspondence. 'But when I think about it,' he continued, 'I am one of them. I wanted to send a letter straightaway, but I was going through my second round of [solitary] punishment, so it was impossible.' Even so, this did not mean the letters had no meaning for they helped detainees 'understand the thoughts and worries of their comrades in the most vivid terms.'[52] But for others this new direction was evidence of the true challenges of bridging the gap between inside and outside. Although language was clearly important to them, some detainees raised fears over the fetishization of language: particularly the idea that there was a universal key hidden in the experiences of those in prison that could somehow unlock the latent forces of activism in those on the side lines of the struggle. 'Cool language, language that appeals to everyone that can pull people into the struggle. I think that's impossible,' wrote one student soon after the new direction was declared. For them the only reliable method of conversion was to place the individual and their personal circumstances within a political and economic analysis. And even this was in many cases not enough. 'People who are more or less content with life will not fight,' he concluded. 'In response to the question of why I fight, all I can say is that after thinking things through I concluded "there is no alternative"'.[53] Another line of criticism was the editorial team's use of the term *wareware* in its declaration, which in its attempt to bring meaning to the publication seemed to place the detainees outside the collective whole. As a scathing critique put it in volume 10: 'Who was this "us"? What was the relationship between defendants and activists on the outside? Without internalising these questions all the new direction amounted to was the editorial team's simple "statement of self-purpose"'.[54]

A letter from a female detainee, Kashiwazaki Chieko, from volume 12 of the letters developed this criticism of how the editors conceptualised the relationship between those on the inside and the outside.[55] Kashiwazaki's perspective was unique in that, in contrast to the majority of the contributors, she had been arrested in a café in April and had therefore the experience of reading the letters in the real word as well as on the inside awaiting her trial. This also meant she had also only been in detention for two months, in contrast to those arrested at Yasuda Auditorium who were now five months in, and those arrested in October 1968 who were now on their tenth month of incarceration. In response to a call from the editors for 'real agitation, rich words from those in prison, words that will truly move people', Kashiwazaki was indignant:

> I want to respond with questions. Is the reality we are now facing in this prison really something that can be expressed in words? And how much do those on the outside understand that it is the people in prison who are truly in need of words, agitation, and letters?

For Kashiwazaki it was impossible for people on the outside to fully grasp the nature of existence in the detention centres. Reflecting on her own position she noted that:

> Of course, when I was on the outside, I had them [the detainees] in my mind all the time. But I didn't understand their boundless expectations, their hope that I, from the outside, would wreak vengeance on the authorities for them. Even when I visited them in prison, I didn't think about how painful it must have been for them to return to their dark solitary cell, while I, after passing through that long tunnel, would enter an outside world bathed in sunlight...

Indeed, there was a sense for Kashiwazaki that those on the inside were being idealised as heroes and in that process were being forgotten as people. This she saw as the greatest danger to those awaiting trial as what they needed most was reassurance that the fight on the outside was continuing and that only this reassurance would help them continue on the inside. Kashiwazaki's letter was thus a warning against deification of the inmates:

> I send this [letter] as a warning against falling into the trap of reading the Prison Letters and being dazzled by wonderful, admirable language – treating us like heroes – while forgetting the pain behind those words.[56]

These sentiments, concern over fetishisation of the courtroom battle, could also be found in the prisoners' discussions about the aims of the trial itself. An early letter questioning the direction of the trial came from Imai Kiyoshi. Imai had been a leading member of the Tokyo University Medical Struggle Committee and had become the de facto leader of Zenkyōtō during the battle for the university in January after the police issued an arrest warrant for Yamamoto Yoshitaka. He became head of the Tōitsu defendants group in July.[57] In his letter printed in Volume 13, Imai wrote of what he saw as a contradiction within the Tōitsu strategy. Broadening the reach and appeal of the Tokyo University Struggle through engagement with the masses was clearly a crucial component of its strategy. Fostering such engagement with the trial through spectatorship and the media would broaden Zenkyōtō's base of support. For Imai, however, securing the release of the prisoners so that they could return to the struggle was paramount. In his eyes, the battle with the courts was taking on a life of its own at their expense, with little regard for the consequences of prolonged detention and eventual conviction. The strategy of 'refusing bail' was therefore misguided. While acknowledging that the court's change in policy on bail was clearly a strategy to encourage compliance with the process, Imai refused to see the choice in black and white terms. 'It is an unjust bail, but for us it is a step forward, indeed it is progress of real substance,' Imai wrote at the end of his letter. 'We should be happy to be unjustly released on bail.'[58]

As on the outside, the detained students responded to Imai's arguments from a variety of positions. Two quick and direct responses came from Kyoto University students, perhaps reflecting the growing tension within the student movement (and especially the Bund) between the Kyoto and Tokyo factions. The first Kyoto student replied that Imai's position was based on the false assumption that the trial was somehow a secondary battle (*nijiteki tōsō*) that was diverting resources from the main front on the streets of Japan's cities. But for them, such a view was misguided in that it failed to recognise the political significance of the struggle as a site for direct challenge to state power. As long as the students refused to submit to the trial process, the 'hegemony' of the struggle remained with the students. But perhaps there was also a sense of the sunk costs of the struggle so far: '[a]ll comrades in prison, including myself, have reached almost an extreme point mentally and physically, but now that we have reached this point, we must strike the final blow to power.'[59] The second student was keen to point out that they didn't see much point in interacting with the prosecutors in the courtroom, but rather in the aim of using the trial to dismantle the courts. The power of the trial lay in constantly challenging the court's reliance on its authority to legitimise its decision-making. For once the 'courts fail to function, there is nothing left [for them] but violence'. In this sense, the unitary trial was not necessary. In fact, small group trials could still implement this strategy as long as defendants, lawyers and spectators were absent, and the overt power of the state was exposed.[60]

Subsequent letters reflected the growing hostility between the factions over this decision, particularly between the ML and Chūkaku-factions. While Chūkaku letters denounced the ML position as 'harmful to the mental hygiene' of prisoners, ML students pushed back against what they saw as Chūkaku's passive tactic of waiting for the masses to lose faith in the absentee trials and rise up against the political order. As one unpublished ML letter put it, this position allowed the state to consolidate its peace-keeping apparatus by first using and then normalising the use of absentee trials through the media. As this debate continued in the letters, the human cost of these internecine battles was starting to trickle into the prisons. The first such death due to internal faction conflict (*uchigeba*), on 18 September, was that of Saitama University graduate student Takizawa Noriaki, a leading member of Chūkaku, who was killed by a breakaway group from the same faction while resting in an occupied building at Shibaura Institution of Technology. Newspaper coverage of Takizawa's death in the Yomiuri made hay out of the fact that Takizawa's body could only be identified by his fingerprints, of how his peers did not seem to know him when questioned by the police, how according to the reporter students refused to help the authorities because Takizawa was in a different sect, and how Takizawa's parents expressed their grief at a son who they had tried so hard to dissuade from falling further into the movement. The article was dominated by a photo of a mother in a Tokyo hospital looking over another victim of *uchigeba* Mochizuki Jōji.[61]

In a letter not published in the original collection, a student referring to themselves as Kojima, who was close to Takizawa, took it upon himself to redress the balance of this coverage and humanise his friend and mentor. Hearing the news of his friends death on the radio brought the struggle with the emotional dampening effect of prison into stark relief. Kojima wrote that when he heard the news, he suddenly stood up, overwhelmed by feelings that shot through his chest, and then collapsed, 'trembling, my skin covered in goose bumps'. He was compelled to use words as an outlet for his feelings but knew he could not make a sound:

'...I immediately picked up a ballpoint pen and decided to write something. I felt that I couldn't stay quiet if I didn't do that. But I felt an inescapable frustration at the sluggishness of my hands'. Kojima's letter was written in response to coverage of his friend's death in the Yomiuri. 'The man found dead,' the Yomiuri reported, 'wore white shirt and black trousers in the style of a student. He was barefoot. He had no personal identification on him, except for a black leather wallet found next to his body.' He had been, in the newspaper reporting, reduced to an anonymous student without individuality. In response, Kojima's letter focused on the details of Takizawa's life. He painted a picture of a man who regularly tore the knees out of his black trousers, who took off his glasses and socks to sleep (which is why he was found barefoot), who used that black wallet every day. A man whose language was punctuated with 'of course' (*yahari*), and who pushed himself to the brink of physical and mental breakdown in his efforts to organise the movement at Saitama University. When Kojima escaped arrest while receiving medical treatment after the Tokyo University Struggle, it was Takizawa who hired a car, travelled to Tokyo, and cared for Kojima while he recovered. More than anything, in the letter there was a sense of gratitude towards a man who had helped Kojima fully realise himself. 'I will fight,' Kojima concluded. 'I will fight for him. This I promised to my now departed comrade as I paced my two-mat cell.'[62]

Although this chapter has focussed on the Letters as a method of communication internal to the movement and as a window into their experieneces, they were of course read more widely and were subject to a range of criticism. In an article for the magazine *Shūkan Shincho* on the Letters, Liberal Democratic Party (LDP) politician Inaba Osamu, for example, had the following to say:

> [The letters] don't amount to anything. I don't understand what they are saying. But that isn't my fault. Extreme complication of thought is indicative of a lack of critical faculties. Difficult words appear one after another, but I can't see the logical connection between them. Bluntly, it is like schizophrenia. Fixing this way of thinking would take a very long time. There are great teachers in special education to be sure. But I would never be able to civilize these students. We'd better keep them locked up for as long as possible.[63]

As Richard Weisman argues the absence of remorse from an offender can invite not only moral condemnation but also can be viewed 'as a symptom of an underlying pathology that marks the wrongdoer as variously diseased, impaired, or otherwise incapable of feeling what a normal member of the community would feel under similar circumstances.'[64] In this way, the performances and linguistic rituals in the letters, so important to the maintenance of the students' sense of belonging, were evaluated by Inaba as illogical, and analogous to the mentally ill (schizophrenic) or to people with learning disabilities (his reference to special education). Furthermore, Inaba's overall evaluation was that the structures of thought and feeling expressed in the letters were indicative of people who were dangerous to the rest of society. Inaba therefore constructed a social position for the students beyond the realm competent social actors, who were rational, productive, and subscribed to a shared set of social priorities and common-sense principles. The students were placed outside 'Japan' as a political community and put into containment in perpetuity. Inaba denied the position of the students and their ability to speak, incomprehensible to normal people to the extent that they belonged in the same category as those with profound mental illness. Indeed, the word schizophrenia conjured up images of disjuncture, delusion, an irrational fragmentation of the self into unconnected parts; unpredictable and dangerous.

Although not as viscerally offended as Inaba, two university professors interviewed for the same *Shūkan Shincho* article on the letters were also critical. Their approach was also to remove the students from the national community. They did this, however, not by placing the students beyond the realm of competent social actors, but by rendering them non-coterminous with contemporary Japan. Ikeda Kiyoshi, a scholar of British culture at Keio University, for example, argued that the students were, in their embrace of German abstract philosophy, inadvertently reproducing the 'meaningless' academic discussion of the prewar period that he argued had rendered academia impotent against the totalising state. This romanticism he explicitly linked to the students' youth. 'It would be good to wait twenty or thirty years then show these letters to them' Ikeda suggested. A Tokyo University Professor who was described as sympathetic to the movement also commented with the same sense of frustration:

> When someone reads this, they may recall how students from earlier high schools discovered themselves through the works of Nishida Kitarō and

> Kurata Hyakuzō, seeking self-understanding through struggle. However, shouldn't the process be reversed? It seems that self-affirmation should come first, at least to some extent, before engaging in the struggle. Otherwise, one risks playing at revolution without truly comprehending the underlying reasons.[65]

The image of the student movement that develops out of the letters, however, is one that rejects the dichotomy between thought and action that underpins these evaluations. For the students contributing to the Letters the movement was an emergent process rooted in the present—it was not about self-affirmation but, at least in spirit, one of self-transformation in their own perpetual present. As one contributor to the Letters stated: 'We did not stand up because we saw the light of the future. No one can guarantee that there will be light in the future. We have set fire to our struggle because the present is gloomy and empty. There is no vision except the one we create.'[66]

But of course, the students themselves were aware of the dangers of their approach. In a letter entitled 'On Laziness' (*datai to iu koto*), Ozaki Fumiaki highlighted the double-edged nature their emergent politics: the need for continued performance and routine for a structure for their community to continue, but that students ran the risk of falling into unthinking conformity.[67] Ozaki split his ideas about the movement into three categories: humanity (*ninjō*), duty (*giri*), and laziness or inertia (*datai*). Humanity referred to simply having zero tolerance when observing those in pain; the act of observing the pain of others should always be a surprise, it should always arouse genuine anger (*shinjitsu ni okotte*) and should always shock into action. The second point he made was about duty. Ozaki noted wryly that much of what he did as a student radical was not that interesting. Attending conferences and listening to boring speeches, sitting on concrete while the cold winds blew, staying up all night stuffing envelopes with flyers nobody wants. So, why continue? The argument was that these acts have political meaning in that they perform dedication to a political cause, and they also maintained the structural vehicle that created the potential for new emergent outcomes. If the movement turned into nothing but words, wrote Ozaki, engagement became 'nothing more than a game of intellectual and egotistical fulfilment'.[68] Political legitimacy only came from this dedication: 'When you develop a duty towards your thought and your ego, you for the first time have the qualification and the right to criticise those who are called "progressive men of culture"'. Yet Ozaki wrote of the danger of the moment thought stops and people start using off the peg theory and analysis and gave up on the goal of questioning the everyday. He turned his criticism towards the movement, which talked about negating the self (*jikohitei*), while demanding self-criticism (*jikohihan*) from others. This he labelled a nonsensical 'lazy use of words', and that those who would demand self-criticism from others must not hide in the meaningless of self-negation (which would mean the end of everything) and instead engage in a process of reflection, criticism, and development.[69]

Notes

1. "Rupo tōdai saiban," *Shūkan Asahi*, no. 2637 (August 8, 1969): 16–23.
2. Ibid.
3. Wada Eiji, *Tōdai tōsō: 50-nenme no memorandamu* (Tokyo: Weitsu, 2018).
4. Nakano Prison, known until 1957 as Toyotama Prison, has historical significance as a major site of incarceration of 'thought criminals' (*shisōhan*) under the 1925 Peace Preservation Law. The prison was demolished in 1983 and is now the site of a 'Peace Park' (*Heiwa no mori kōen*). Three tatami mats equate to roughly 4.6 Sq. Metres.
5. Ibid., 146–48.
6. Richard Weisman, *Showing Remorse: Law and the Social Control of Emotion* (London: Routledge, 2014).
7. Erving Goffman, "Asylums, Essays on the Social Situation of Mental Patients and Other Inmates," 2007, 23.
8. Ibid., 14.
9. Patricia G. Steinhoff, "Doing the Defendant's Laundry: Support Groups as Social Movement Organizations in Contemporary Japan," *Japanstudien* 11, no. 1 (January 27, 2000): 55–78; Patricia G. Steinhoff, "Emotional Costs of Providing Social Support to Political Prisoners," *Contemporary Japan* 31, no. 2 (2019): 1–18.
10. A note on sources. The Letters were published as separate booklets during the trial and were subsequently published in two collections. In the following I cite the original publications unless otherwise noted. The two edited collections: Gokuchū shokan hakkan iinkai, ed., *Tōdai tōsō gokuchū shokanshū 1* (Tokyo: Mitani Shobo, 1970);

Gokuchū shokan hakkan iinkai, ed., *Tōdai tōsō gokuchū shokanshū 2* (Tokyo: Mitani Shobo, 1970).
11. "Gokuchū Shokanshū," *Mainichi Shimbun*, July 12, 1969.
12. "Gokuchū shokan" hakkan i'inkai, ed., "Tōdaitōsō gokuchū shokanshū 1" (Gokuchū shokan' hakkan i'inkai, April 20, 1969). Preface.
13. The pen name of this student is likely a reference to the police cell he was first held in, Tōkyō suijō keisatsusho, room 26 (now Tokyo wangan keisatsusho).
14. "Tōdaitōsō 'gokuchū Shokan-Shū' Ni Miru Yūki to Hiretsu," *Shūkan Shinchō*, May 24, 1969, 35.
15. "Gokuchū Shokanshū.".
16. Ibid.
17. "Gokuchū shokan" hakkan i'inkai, ed., "Tōdaitōsō gokuchū shokanshū 2" (Gokuchū shokan hakkan i'inkai, April 27, 1969), 3.
18. Ibid., 4. Chocolate and oranges would have been brought to the students by one of the relief organistaions.
19. Ibid., 13.
20. "Gokuchū shokan" hakkan i'inkai, ed., "Tōdaitōsō gokuchū shokanshū 9" (Gokuchū shokan hakkan i'inkai, June 14, 1969), 13.
21. Gokuchū shokan hakkan iinkai, *Tōdai tōsō gokuchū shokanshū 2*, 6. My emphasis.
22. Here the student uses the word *undō,* which literally means movement/exercise but is also the same word used for social movements. Finishing his 'movement' thus took on a double meaning.
23. "Gokuchū shokan" hakkan i'inkai, "Tōdaitōsō gokuchū shokanshū 9," 14–15.
24. "Gokuchū shokan" hakkan i'inkai, ed., "Tōdaitōsō gokuchū shokanshū 8" (Gokuchū shokan hakkan i'inkai, June 8, 1969), 3–4.
25. Gokuchū shokan hakkan iinkai, *Tōdai tōsō gokuchū shokanshū 1,* 130. This letter was not published in the original monthly publication.
26. Goffman, "Asylums, Essays on the Social Situation of Mental Patients and Other Inmates.".

27. "Gokuchū shokan" hakkan i'inkai, ed., "Tōdaitōsō gokuchū shokanshū 11" (Gokuchū shokan' hakkan i'inkai, June 25, 1969), 2.
28. "Gokuchū shokan" hakkan i'inkai, "Tōdaitōsō gokuchū shokanshū 2," 5.
29. Nira Yuval-Davis, "Belonging and the Politics of Belonging," *Patterns of Prejudice* 40, no. 3 (July 2006): 197–214.
30. Gokuchū shokan hakkan iinkai, *Tōdai tōsō gokuchū shokanshū 1*, 308. This letter was not published in the original monthly publication.
31. "Gokuchū shokan" hakkan i'inkai, "Tōdaitōsō gokuchū shokanshū 8," 3.
32. "Gokuchū shokan" hakkan i'inkai, ed., "Tōdaitōsō gokuchū shokanshū 6/7" (Gokuchū shokan hakkan i'inkai, May 28, 1969), 3–4.
33. Gokuchū shokan hakkan iinkai, *Tōdai Tōsō Gokuchū Shokanshū 1*, 213. This letter was not published in the original monthly publication.
34. Gokuchū shokan hakkan iinkai, *Tōdai Tōsō Gokuchū Shokanshū 2*, 116–17. This letter was not published in the original monthly publication.
35. "Gokuchū shokan" hakkan i'inkai, "Tōdaitōsō gokuchū shokanshū 8," 3–4.
36. "Rupo Tōdai Saiban.".
37. "Gokuchū Api-Ru," *EXPOSE*, April 12, 1969, 1.
38. "Gokuchū shokan" hakkan i'inkai, ed., "Tōdaitōsō gokuchū shokanshū 14" (Gokuchū shokan hakkan i'inkai, July 18, 1969), 3.
39. "Gokuchū shokan" hakkan i'inkai, ed., "Tōdaitōsō gokuchū shokanshū 13" (Gokuchū shokan hakkan i'inkai, July 11, 1969), 4.
40. Goffman, "Asylums, Essays on the Social Situation of Mental Patients and Other Inmates," 21.
41. "Gokuchū shokan" hakkan i'inkai, ed., "Tōdaitōsō gokuchū shokanshū 10" (Gokuchū shokan hakkan i'inkai, June 21, 1969), 11.
42. Ibid.
43. Ibid., 7.

44. Goffman, "Asylums, Essays on the Social Situation of Mental Patients and Other Inmates," 32.
45. "Gokuchū shokan" hakkan i'inkai, "Tōdaitōsō gokuchū shokanshū 10," 8.
46. "Gokuchū shokan" hakkan i'inkai, "Tōdaitōsō gokuchū shokanshū 6/7," 5.
47. Gokuchū shokan hakkan iinkai, *Tōdai tōsō gokuchū shokanshū 1*, 162–63.
48. This word is emphasised in the text.
49. Ibid.
50. Ibid.
51. Gokuchū shokan hakkan i'inkai, "Gokuchūshokan to ajitēshon," *Shingeki*, May 22, 1969.
52. "Gokuchū shokan" hakkan i'inkai, ed., "Tōdaitōsō gokuchū shokanshū 15" (Gokuchū shokan hakkan i'inkai, July 25, 1969), 18.
53. "Gokuchū shokan" hakkan i'inkai, ed., "Tōdaitōsō gokuchū shokanshū 12" (Gokuchū shokan' hakkan i'inkai, July 4, 1969), 4.
54. "Gokuchū shokan" hakkan i'inkai, "Tōdaitōsō gokuchū shokanshū 10," 14–15.
55. It is likely this name reflects the students' hometown, Kashiwazaki in Niigata prefecture.
56. Gokuchū shokan hakkan iinkai, *Tōdai tōsō gokuchū shokanshū 1*, 236. This letter was not published in the original monthly publication.
57. Imai would later have a succesful political career with first the Japan Socialist Party, and then the Democractic Party of Japan (DPJ).
58. "Gokuchū shokan" hakkan i'inkai, "Tōdaitōsō gokuchū shokanshū 13," 3.
59. "Gokuchū shokan" hakkan i'inkai, ed., "Tōdaitōsō gokuchū shokanshū 19" (Gokuchū shokan hakkan i'inkai, August 30, 1969), 5–8.
60. Ibid., 8–10.
61. "Uchigeba hijō: shibakōdai jiken," *Yomiuri Shimbun*, September 19, 1969. Mochizuki Jōji was a member of the Kansai Bund Sekigun-faction. Mochizuki had, with other leading members of the Kansai faction of the Bund, been taken prisoner by the Kanto

faction of the same organisation. On July 25th the Kansai prisoners tried to escape from the third floor of Chuo University Law School building. Mochizuki slipped and fell, sustaining serious head injuries. He later died of his injuries on 29th September 1969.

62. Gokuchū shokan hakkan iinkai, *Tōdai tōsō gokuchū shokanshū 2*.
63. "Tōdaitōsō 'gokuchū shokan-shū' ni miru yūki to hiretsu," 37.
64. Weisman, *Showing Remorse: Law and the Social Control of Emotion*, 48.
65. "Tōdaitōsō 'gokuchū shokan-shū' ni miru yūki to hiretsu," 37.
66. "Gokuchū shokan" hakkan i'inkai, "Tōdaitōsō gokuchū shokanshū 1," 4.
67. Ibid., 9.
68. Ibid.
69. Ibid., 10.

References

EXPOSE. "Gokuchū apīru." April 12, 1969.

Goffman, Erving. *Asylums, Essays on the Social Situation of Mental Patients and Other Inmates*. 2007, 321–86.

Gokuchū shokan hakkan i'inkai. "Gokuchūshokan to ajitēshon." *Shingeki*, May 22, 1969.

Gokuchū shokan hakkan iinkai, ed. *Tōdai tōsō gokuchū shokanshū 1*. Tokyo: Mitani Shobo, 1970.

———, ed. *Tōdai tōsō gokuchū shokanshū 2*. Tokyo: Mitani Shobo, 1970.

"Gokuchū shokan" hakkan i'inkai, ed. "Tōdaitōsō gokuchū shokanshū 1." Gokuchū shokan' hakkan i'inkai, April 20, 1969.

———, ed. "Tōdaitōsō gokuchū shokanshū 2." Gokuchū shokan hakkan i'inkai, April 27, 1969.

———, ed. "Tōdaitōsō gokuchū shokanshū 6/7." Gokuchū shokan hakkan i'inkai, May 28, 1969.

———, ed. "Tōdaitōsō gokuchū shokanshū 8." Gokuchū shokan hakkan i'inkai, June 8, 1969.

———, ed. "Tōdaitōsō gokuchū shokanshū 9." Gokuchū shokan hakkan i'inkai, June 14, 1969.

———, ed. "Tōdaitōsō gokuchū shokanshū 10." Gokuchū shokan hakkan i'inkai, June 21, 1969.

———, ed. "Tōdaitōsō gokuchū shokanshū 11." Gokuchū shokan' hakkan i'inkai, June 25, 1969.

———, ed. "Tōdaitōsō gokuchū shokanshū 12." Gokuchū shokan' hakkan i'inkai, July 4, 1969.
———, ed. "Tōdaitōsō gokuchū shokanshū 13." Gokuchū shokan hakkan i'inkai, July 11, 1969.
———, ed. "Tōdaitōsō gokuchū shokanshū 14." Gokuchū shokan hakkan i'inkai, July 18, 1969.
———, ed. "Tōdaitōsō gokuchū shokanshū 15." Gokuchū shokan hakkan i'inkai, July 25, 1969.
———, ed. "Tōdaitōsō gokuchū shokanshū 19." Gokuchū shokan hakkan i'inkai, August 30, 1969.
Mainichi Shimbun. "Gokuchū shokanshū." July 12, 1969.
"Rupo tōdai saiban." *Shūkan Asahi*, no. 2637 (August 8, 1969): 16–23.
Shūkan shinchō. "Tōdaitōsō 'gokuchū shokan-shū' ni miru yūki to hiretsu." May 24, 1969.
Steinhoff, Patricia G. "Doing the Defendant's Laundry: Support Groups as Social Movement Organizations in Contemporary Japan." *Japanstudien* 11, no. 1 (January 27, 2000): 55–78.
———. "Emotional Costs of Providing Social Support to Political Prisoners." *Contemporary Japan* 31, no. 2 (2019): 1–18.
Wada, Eiji. *Tōdai tōsō: 50-nenme no memorandamu*. Tokyo: Weitsu, 2018.
Weisman, Richard. *Showing Remorse: Law and the Social Control of Emotion*. London: Routledge, 2014.
Yomiuri Shimbun. "Uchigeba hijō: shibakōdai jiken." September 19, 1969.
Yuval-Davis, Nira. "Belonging and the Politics of Belonging." *Patterns of Prejudice* 40, no. 3 (July 2006): 197–214.

CHAPTER 8

Epilogue

After the Okagaki verdict the trials continued apace, such that by 17th May 1970 a total of 610 students, a number which included those arrested prior to the 18th and 19th of January 1969, had received their verdicts. Of this number 590 were found guilty, 20 not guilty, and in the case of 5 defendants, proceedings were suspended. 147 of those found guilty received custodial sentences, although some of those sentences were suspended on appeal.[1] The presence of remorse and the nature of the students' home environment continued to be a deciding factor in sentencing. Indeed, in some cases redemption through the family trumped demonstrations of remorse. In Judge Mukai's verdict on his group, which consisted of Chūkaku students from Hōsei university and two Tokyo University students, it was the Tokyo University students that received suspended sentences despite their lack of apology for their actions. The first student was given probation because 'under the enthusiastic guidance of his parents it is believed that he will certainly realise his actions.' For the second it was because if their sex: '[H] is a female and is not thought to have committed violent acts…it is expected that she will soon realise the foolishness of her actions and reflect on them sooner or later.'[2] The communicative function of these verdicts was still clear, however. The family was the proper unit of socialisation for youth

C. Perkins, *The Tokyo University Trial and the Struggle Against Order in Postwar Japan*, New Directions in East Asian History,
https://doi.org/10.1007/978-981-99-7043-8_8

who were apt to be led astray by a politics foreign to them and which they were not equipped to understand.

By 1970 the students and their support groups had split: there were now two groups of 'unified' defendants moving into the appeal phase of the trial. Members of the 'see it through' Kantetsu-faction, which was dominated by Chūkaku students, ejected Imai Kyoshi from his position as head of the Defendants Organisation and prepared to fight for a unfied trial in the Tokyo High Court. The 'change of direction' Tenkan-faction also began planning for the next stage of the trial through their organisational vehicle: the *Tōdai tōsō tōistu hikokdan, jiritsu-sha* (from now Jiritsu-sha). The relationship between the two factions was hostile, with the Kantetsu-faction disparaged Jiritsu-sha for, as they saw it, performing an act of tenkō and betraying the true meaning of the struggle for a unified trial.[3]

With the student groups now split the Bengodan faced a difficult decision. A significant minority saw the fragmentation of the support structure for the students as destroying the communal foundations of reliance and trust that had underpinned the struggle, and as such the idea of a unified legal group was now untenable. When the proposition of dissolution of the Bengodan was put to a vote, however, it was rejected and those lawyers who felt they could not continue in the new conditions left the organisation. Of those remaining, some joined forces with Jiritsu-sha and devised a new direction for the struggle based on what had been pejoratively seen before as the traditional model of courtroom battles. In the analysis of Sugimoto Shōjun, one of the lawyers in the new Bengodan, the 'absolutism' of courtroom denial, which had led to viewing non-attendance at the trial and absentee verdicts as goals in and of themselves, had in fact made it easier for the state to supress the movement. The job of the new Bengodan, then, was to unwind the damage done so that the struggle could continue. 'The so-called shift to courtroom battles' wrote Sugimoto in the founding publication of the new organisation 'is indeed a step back from unified trials in a formal sense. However, by returning to the rationale for demanding unified trials and building upon the accumulated struggles thus far, we believe that we are continuing the fight against oppression and fragmentation.'[4]

In this there was some success as the lawyers were in some cases able to argue for bigger and internally more coherent groups. As student activists continued to be arrested and processed throughout 1970, Jiritsu-sha expanded its remit to include support students beyond those immediately involved in the Tokyo University case. This change in scope was reflected in the renaming of the organisation's newspaper to 'Mogura' in December 1971. But as the courtroom battle progressed the ML-faction assessment of the higher courts—that they were even less likely to side with the students—proved correct. Appeals in the Tokyo High Court, which rested on claims of the illegality of the proceedings were dismissed, and by 1978 the Supreme Court passed its final verdict, in which it found that the trial process, invocation of Article 268–2 of the Code of Criminal Procedure, and the resultant trial and verdicts in absentia were legal.[5]

1975 saw published the last edition of Mogura. In it two students reflected on fact of their impending incarceration. In a sense their letters spoke to fundamental divergence of perspectives on the struggle. Takizawa Masahiro, who in an exception to the standard charges levelled at the students was convicted for 4 years for arson, exhibited a sense of betrayal by his comrades—two thirds of whom had confessed and received suspended sentences—and pride at his continued resistance. His final statement was on the moral implications of splitting:

> Looking back, some individuals cited family issues or "being deceived by those in higher positions" as an excuse for repenting. However, [now that they have done this] by what principles will they live their lives? Even though their lifestyle and outward appearance may not differ significantly to us, we have lived with confidence, staying true to ourselves. This distinction is bound to become a significant dividing line.[6]

In contrast, for former central committee member of the ML-faction Mitobe Takashi, his verdict confirming his prison sentence unleashed a more ambiguous and conflicted mix of emotions. The shock of the verdict, and the fact of prison left him speechless, but he was later taken over by a sense of release from the feeling of been pursued by a nameless threat for the past six years. And although he believed in the actions at Tokyo, his letter demonstrated a splitting of the self, brought about both by the trial and the increasing violence of the movement. 'We have been given an opportunity to reflect on our struggle, on the way in which we see things' he wrote. 'Theory that allows violence is theory without human feeling, it is an impoverished way of thinking.' Indeed, Mitobe's view of the world appeared to embrace the court's view of individual responsibility. 'In general,' Mitobe concluded 'we tended to evaluate ourselves based on the logic of our political factions and to seek organizational alibis of our actions. However, through the Tokyo University trial, which has lasted six years since the indictment, I have come to think that even one instance of intra-group conflict is our personal problem.'[7]

The question of the impact of inter-group conflict was taken up in 1977 by Watanabe Hiroshi, the postgraduate student at the University of Tokyo in 1968/1969 and member of the Zenkyōtō support group whose recollections were discussed in Chapter 5. In a reflection on the trial written for Jiritsu-sha's collection of trial materials published in 1978, Watanabe saw the outcome as a result of the inability of Tōistsu kyūtai to overcome the differences in opinion over the proper focus of the trial between the political factions, the non-aligned (non-sect radical) members of Zenkyōtō, and the different factions within the Bengodan. For Watanabe, had Zenkyōtō been able to better advocate for a focus on securing bail for its members (and especially postgraduate Zentōren members who were able to contribute to strategy), it would have been easier to pursue a more flexible and pragmatic approach to the trial. In Watanabe's estimation the uncompromising approach to the trial had stemmed from a combination of the dominant faction within the Bengodan's desire to engage in self-criticism and self-negation as lawyers, and a lack of interest from the political factions in pursuing in the courts the Tokyo University struggle in any meaningful way. Had the Zenkyōtō support group been able to better voice their concerns, and had effort been put into supporting the defendants with their individual struggles in the small group trials, the outcome may have been different.[8] It is of course impossible to tell if Watanabe was right in his assessment. The time and resources that would have been necessary to coordinate a strategy across so many different groups, and the courts' commitment to fast processing of cases and zero tolerance of any disturbance, raise questions as to whether a more pragmatic stance would have brought the students any closer to their goal of developing the Tokyo University struggle in the courts. Yet examples such as that of Judge Urabe, who was willing to listen to the students, challenge the prosecution, and compromise regarding the constitution of groups suggests that there was still room for co-operation. In this regard Watanabe's reflections are instructive in restating that the outcome of the trial was not inevitable but to an extent born of decisions made by competing parties within the student organisations that were shaped by their own conceptualisations of what the trial, as a vehicle for struggle, was for.

As the trial was working its way through the higher courts, commentators, researchers, and policy makers were beginning to question its significance for the criminal justice system, and in particular policing of radical social unrest. These interrogations came with their own narratives of cause, effect, and solution. For Kawaguchi Kōtaro, a veteran prosecutor who started his career in the early Shōwa period and had overseen prosecution during the Mitaka and May Day incidents, the story was one of societal alienation and social intervention. Japan had seen great economic progress over the past decade with living standards and productivity rising precipitously, wrote Kawaguchi, but with that came modern ills of pollution, traffic chaos, rising prices, university disruption and juvenile delinquency. The contradictions inherent in this process of transformation caused violent ideological schisms amongst the people of Japan, of which the student movement was an example. Rather than see the students as criminals of conviction (***kesshinhan***), and thus impossible to rehabilitate, Kawaguchi argued that as young people whose way of thinking had not yet settled, they should be treated in a similar way to delinquents whose criminal actions stemmed from poverty or a broken home. As such the goal should be their rehabilitation and reintergration. Indeed, observed Kawaguchi, not all the students arrested could be said to have had such conviction: the existence of the repentant group who opted for small group trials, and examples of students condemning their own actions in court, even after displaying resistance in detention, was evidence of this fact.[9]

Yet there was the issue of what to do with the remaining students who continued with their resistance. Should they be sent to general prisons with murders and thieves, or to specialised facilities that were reserved for minor crimes such as traffic offences? Was there a need for probation officers with specialised skills in dealing with student radicals? And finally, even though Kawaguchi acknowledged there was as yet no provision in law, was it really in the best interest of the individual, or society, to simply release a student radical when prosecution was deferred? Should even these students not be subject to some sort of probationary measures? These were all questions in need of answers from experts in probation and rehabilitation. Thus, while acknowledging the legitimate social causes of the student unrest, Kawaguchi saw all intervention focusing on the individual offender. There was no answer to the question of what that intervention would look like. Yet the analogy of delinquents from a broken home demonstrated the underlying thought. The damage had been done; the job was now to pick up the pieces. And this could only happen through consistent education and monitoring with the aim of fixing the psychological damage caused.[10]

While Kawaguchi mused on approaches to rehabilitation, 1969 had witnessed a significant expansion of Japan's domestic security apparatus. The centralised riot police had increased in numbers by 1969 to 10,000 officers, and information gathering activities had expanded to such an extent that it was joked among the movement that the police knew of their plans before the students did. In contrast to the frustrations of 1968, beginning with the intervention at Tokyo University in January police appeared to have hit upon a formula of mass arrest and detention that was consistent in removing students from the streets and in so doing significantly reducing the threat of their organisations to domestic order. Importantly this expansion in state power was coupled with a strategy of Community Relations policing (*CR sakusen*), which recognised the importance of not only communicating with the Japanese public, but proactively coopting them into policing activities. As the legal scholar Ebashi Takashi wrote in a special issue of the journal *Hōritsu jihō* on security and human rights in 1970, the principle of this approach was that rather than policing from the outside, the police aimed at being embedded within the community, policing from the inside along with the people. This involved creating various forms of community-police cooperation organisations across the country and enlisting their help in monitoring student activity and supporting police interventions. The job of maintaining order was thus defused throughout society, with the ultimate goal being to bring about 'the emergence of a beautiful unity between the police and the people.'[11]

Superintendent General Hatano Akira argued that doing so required rejecting the opinion, which he saw as dominent in postwar Japanese discourse, that state power was, and always will be, stifling of democracy in Japan. Instead, buoyed by the successful police actions of 1969, he called for the public to see state authority as democracy's guarantor. In this regard, as well as the CR strategy, the relationship with the media must also be refashioned. 'In the 1970s,' he wrote, 'the police must be within the people and with the people; we cannot be outside the bounds of the people. As such the relationship between the police and the media must be one of cooperation, perhaps more than that, a relationship of cooperative collaboration (*kyōgyōteki kyōryoku*).' Should such cooperation with the people and media be secured, and through it 'human relationships built on trust' developed, Hatano wrote, 'I believe that a healthy path forward will be opened.'[12]

What of the 1970 Anpo uprising that had so animated Japan's security apparatus over the previous two years? In fact, coordinated by organisations such as Beheiren (the Citizen's League for Peace in Vietnam) the protests of 1970 were significantly larger than those of a decade earlier—at its peak on 23 June between 774,000 and 1.5 million people participated in demonstrations.[13] Yet the protests were never able to spark the sense of crisis seen in 1960, which had brought Japan's democracy to the brink of collapse. Part of the reason for this was simply the positive economic conditions of the 1970s, which many Japanese attributed to the security treaty having saved huge sums that could be reinvested productively into the economy and had brought about material wealth that would soon become the envy of the world. Scholars have also suggested that television, by bringing protests into the home, brought about a sense of 'protest fatigue.' The media reacted to this fatigue by focusing on ever-more sensational moments such as the Tokyo University struggle, which attracted the public to the spectacle but lacked analysis needed to elevate the images to more than just scenes of violence and as such alienated viewer from the movement.[14] There is no doubt truth to these explanations. But it should be added that it was in part the direct action—the violence—of the Bund in 1960 that brought about the sense of crisis seen in 1960. The state's pre-emptive policing, using mass arrest and prolonged detention had been successful in removing, in the words of the Public Security Intelligence Agency, those student pioneers who were ready to take on the role of 'the unfortunate protagonists of the Anpo Struggle.'[15]

As the 1970s progressed, violent confrontations between student factions, bombing campaings, and domestic and international direct action by various iterations of the Japan Red Army (Sekigun, JRA) served to strenghthen the legitimacy of this articulation of domestic state security, local organisations, and the media espoused by Hatano. By 1972, after a comprehensive strategy of searching apartments across Japan produced waves of arrests that crippled the leadership of the remaining New Left factions, the idea that revolution in Japan could be secured on the streets had been all but extinguished.[16] The February 1972 United Red Army incident, during which internal tensions claimed the lives of 10 members, and which resulted in a police siege that was watched by almost

90% of Japanese with televisions, cast a further pall over the movement that would shape memories for years to come.[17] Yet this moment of interrogation of order in Japan was carried on into new fields of activity such as the various organisations of the women's liberation (*ribu*) movement and the disabled rights movement.[18] And as Patricia Steinhoff has documented, the networks set up to support arrested activists also continued their work in the justice system through the 1970s and into the 80s and 90s. A significant aspect of this work was support for those sentenced to the death penalty, such as those convicted for the URA incident, who after their convictions are upheld by the Supreme Court are held in isolation and restricted from all contact with the outside world so as to 'calm their spirits'. In order to circumvent restrictions on communication with the outside world placed on prisoners awaiting death sentences, support groups members go as far as to marry prisoners or adopt them into their families, which then opens up a conduit for communication and support.[19] The knowledge and skills developed by those engaged in the support movement also enabled those who wished to support new legal causes, such as disability rights and cases of death by overwork among others.[20]

While the Tokyo University trial ended for students in 1978, for Yamane Jirō there was one last twist in the tale when in 1980 he suddenly found himself suspended from legal practice for four months. In December 1969 Tokyo District Court Chief Justice Niizeki (Shinzeki) Katsuyoshi had lodged a complaint with the Tokyo Bar Association (TBA) asking for sanctions against Yamane, asserting that 'setting aside his outward assertions, he is inwardly attempting to damage the authority of the Courts' and as such had transgressed Article 9 of the JFBA rules governing legal ethics.[21] The TBA investigated the court transcripts and recordings for a full two years before concluding in 1972 that Yamane's actions had been within the boundaries of legitimate legal practice, and as such disciplinary action was unwarranted. In their verdict the TBA noted the decision to sanction hinged on perspective. From the court's perspective Yamane may have been seen as undermining their authority and ability to process the students quickly. Yet the students wished for a 'rational unified trial', and as Yamane's duty as a lawyer was to his clients first and foremost, in pursuing a unified trial Yamane was being fundamentally truthful to his profession. To do otherwise, argued the TBA, would be contrary to a lawyer's responsibilities. The TBA were also worried about the potential chilling effect any such decision to sanction might cause. If sanctions were not limited to the most egregious dereliction of duty to their clients:

> ...it would force defence lawyers participating in vigorous exchanges in the courtroom to constantly be aware of the risk of disciplinary action in their minds. As a result, faithful duty towards their clients and their adversarial stance could be significantly weakened and compromised, leading to a potential decline in the effectiveness of their defence activities.[22]

Yamane continued to practice law, both in relation to the Tokyo University case, and also in taking up other politically sensitive cases which included that of Okuzaki Kenzō, who had in 1969 fired three pachinko balls at the emperor.[23] It came as a surprise then in 1980 when the Japan Federation of Bar Associations (JFBA) issued a statement overruling the TBA findings and suspended Yamane. Arguing that the TBA had been fundmentally mistaken in rationalising Yamane's actions in court, the JFBA argued that it should have been obvious to the Bengodan, as legal professionals, that a unified trial was impossible, and that in sticking rigidly to the logic set out in the Proposal and Opinion, Yamane had intentionally and of his own actions hampered the trial's progress and damaged the dignity of the courts.[24]

In response, a number of public intellectuals and activists, centred around writer Takenaka Rō and the film director Ōshima Nagisa, organised a campaign of support. As well as submitting documents asking for the disciplinary action to be repealed, members of the organisation attempted to raise the Yamane case at the JFBA's 7th Annual Symposium in 1980, which had as its theme 'self-governing lawyers for the people'. When representatives of Yamane's support group were effectively stopped from raising Yamane's case at the symposium, the group resolved to run its own 'anti-symposium' (*gyaku shinpojian*). Yamane's case, they argued in an appeal statement that also served as an announcement for the symposium, was symbolic of a new, terrifying era in which 'in the name of law-and-order, people are classified as 'citizens' and 'non-citizens.'[25] The appeal included the signatures of 280 members of the JFBA. After the symposium, which featured contributions from noted lawyers and left-wing intellectuals such as Hani Goro and Mononobe Nagaoki, was held and having in their eyes succeeded in their goal of 'manifesting socially' the significance of Yamane's treatment by the JFBA—through the symposium, a book, and by publishing materials relating to the disciplinary action—the support group called an end to their activities. And with this act of defiance, the Tokyo University trial finally came to an end.

Notes

1. "Tōdaijiken: 10-nen saiban ni keri," *Asahi Shimbun*, July 1, 1978.
2. Mukai Tetsujirō, "Tōkyō chihōsaibansho shōwa 44-nen (kei wa) 700-gō hanketsu," 1969, https://tinyurl.com/4ynd749f.
3. Tōdai tōsō tōitsu hikokudan jimukyoku, "Tōdaisaiban tōsō no kirihiraita chihei to wareware no ninmu," *Tōdaitōsō Hikokudan Nyūsu*, no. 5 (July 15, 1970): 1–3.
4. Sugimoto Shōjun, "Korekara no tōdai tōso saiban - hōtei tōsō," in *Tōdaisaiban Tōsō o Takakainuku Tame Ni*, ed. Tōdaitōsō tōitsu hikokudan and Tōitsu kyūtai (Tokyo: Jiritsu-sha, 1970), 16.
5. "Tōdaijiken: 10-nen saiban ni keri."
6. Takizawa Masahiro, "Kōsoshin o oete," *Mogura*, April 9, 1975.
7. Mitobe Takashi, "Tōdaisaiban o oete ima fukuu koto," *Mogura*, April 9, 1975.
8. Watanabe Hiroshi, "Tōdai saiban tōsō wo furikaette – kyūtaibu no tachiba kara," in *Shiryō: Tōdai Saiban Tōsō*, ed. Tōdaitōsō tōitsu hikoku-dan (jiritsu-sha) shiryō henshū iinkai (Tokyo: Tōdaitōsō tōitsu hikoku-dan (jiritsu-sha) shiryō henshū iinkai, 1978), 252–53.
9. Kawaguchi Kōtarō, "Tōdai jiken saiban no ato ni kuru mono," *Tsumi to Batsu* 7, no. 2 (1970): 2–5.
10. Ibid.
11. Ebashi Takashi, "70-nendaishakai to chiantaisei - shiryōkaidai ni kaete," *Hōritsu Jihō* 42, no. 8 (1970): 204.
12. Hatano Akira, "Kokka kenryoku wa aku ka," *Hōritsu Jihō* 42, no. 8 (1970): 223–24.
13. Jayson Makoto Chun, *"A Nation of a Hundred Million Idiots"? A Social History of Japanese Television, 1953–1973* (Abingdon: Routledge, 2006), 227.
14. Ibid., 230–36.
15. "1970-Nen o mezasu gakusei undō (kōanchōsachō shiryō 'wagakuni no kyōsan shugi undō no sho dōkō' yori)," *Keisatsugaku Ronshū* 21, no. 1 (January 1968): 178.

16. Peter J. Katzenstein and Yutaka Tsujinaka, *Defending the Japanese State: Structures, Norms and the Political Responses to Terrorism and Violent Social Protest in the 1970s and 1980s*, Cornell East Asia Series (East Asia Program, Cornell University, 1991), 20; Till Knaudt, "A Farewell to Class: The Japanese New Left, the Colonial Landscape of Kamagasaki, and the Anti-Japanese Front (1970–75)," *The Journal of Japanese Studies* 46, no. 2 (2020): 400.
17. For the United Red Army Incident see: Yoshikuni Igarashi, "Dead Bodies and Living Guns: The United Red Army and Its Deadly Pursuit of Revolution, 1971–1972," *Japanese Studies* 27, no. 2 (September 2007): 119–37, https://doi.org/10.1080/10371390701494135; Christopher Perkins, *The United Red Army on Screen: Cinema, Aesthetics and The Politics of Memory* (Springer, 2015), https://doi.org/10.1057/9781137480354; Patricia Steinhoff, *Shi e No Ideorogī Nihon Sekigun-Ha* (Tokyo: Iwanami Shoten, 2003).
18. Setsu Shigematsu, *Scream from the Shadows*, U of Minnesota Press (U of Minnesota Press, 2012). For crossovers between *ribu* and the disabled rights movement see: Anna Vittinghoff, "Reassessing Japanese Radical Feminism from the Vantage Point of Dis/Ability," in *Dis/Ability in Media, Law and History, Intersectional, Embodied and Socially Constructed?*, ed. Mickey Lee, Frank Rudy Cooper, and Patricia Reeve (London: Routledge, 2022), 119–33.
19. See Patricia G. Steinhoff, "Doing the Defendant's Laundry: Support Groups as Social Movement Organizations in Contemporary Japan," *Japanstudien* 11, no. 1 (January 27, 2000): 65–67.
20. See the examples in the various chapters of Patricia G. Steinhoff, ed., *Going to Court to Change Japan: Social Movements and the Law in Contemporary Japan* (Michigan: The University of Michigan, 2014).
21. Katsuyoshi Niizeki, "Chōkai seikyūsho," in *Shiryō (Gōhon): Bengoren, Yamane Jirō Bengoshi Chōkaishobun*, ed. Sendagaya sōgō hōritsu jimusho (Tokyo: Mugen Kōbō, 1980), 48–49.
22. Tōkyō dai-2 bengoshikai, "Giketsusho," in *Shiryō (Gōhon): Bengoren, Yamane Jirō Bengoshi Chōkaishobun*, ed. Sendagaya sōgō hōritsu jimusho (Tokyo: Mugen Kōbō, 1980), 109–10.
23. On leaving prison Okuzaki became the subject of Hara Kazuo's 1987 documentary The Emperor's Naked Army Marches On.

Hara Kazuo, *The Emperor's Naked Army Marches On* (Imamura Productions, 1987). Okuzaki's background and the film itself are discussed in Jeffrey Ruoff and Kenneth Ruoff, *The Emperor's Naked Army Marches On: Yukiyukite Shingun*, Flicks Books (Flicks Books, 1998).

24. Nichibenren / Chōkai i'inkai, "Giketsusho," in *Shiryō (Gōhon): Bengoren, Yamane Jirō Bengoshi Chōkaishobun*, ed. Sendagaya sōgō hōritsu jimusho (Tokyo: Mugen Kōbō, 1980), 130–31.
25. Takenaka Rō, *Hō o Sabaku: Nichibenren Yamane Shobun Kōgi Undō No Kiroku* (Tokyo: JCA shuppan, 1980), 126.

References

"1970-nen o mezasu gakusei undō (kōanchōsachō shiryō 'wagakuni no kyōsan shugi undō no sho dōkō' yori)." *Keisatsugaku Ronshū* 21, no. 1 (January 1968): 157–79.

Asahi Shimbun. "Tōdaijiken: 10-Nen Saiban Ni Keri." July 1, 1978.

Chun, Jayson Makoto. *"A Nation of a Hundred Million Idiots"? A Social History of Japanese Television, 1953–1973*. Abingdon: Routledge, 2006.

Ebashi, Takashi. "70-nendaishakai to chiantaisei - shiryōkaidai ni kaete." *Hōritsu Jihō* 42, no. 8 (1970): 199–204.

Hatano, Akira. "Kokka kenryoku wa aku ka." *Hōritsu Jihō* 42, no. 8 (1970): 223–24.

Igarashi, Yoshikuni. "Dead Bodies and Living Guns: The United Red Army and Its Deadly Pursuit of Revolution, 1971–1972." Japanese Studies 27, no. 2 (September 2007): 119–37.

Katsuyoshi, Niizeki. "Chōkai seikyūsho." In *Shiryō (Gōhon): Bengoren, Yamane Jirō Bengoshi Chōkaishobun*, edited by Sendagaya sōgō hōritsu jimusho, 48–49. Tokyo: Mugen Kōbō, 1980.

Katzenstein, Peter J., and Yutaka Tsujinaka. *Defending the Japanese State: Structures, Norms and the Political Responses to Terrorism and Violent Social Protest in the 1970s and 1980s*. Cornell East Asia Series. East Asia Program, Cornell University, 1991.

Kawaguchi, Kōtarō. "Tōdai jiken saiban no ato ni kuru mono." *Tsumi to Batsu* 7, no. 2 (1970): 2–5.

Kazuo, Hara. *The Emperor's Naked Army Marches On*. Imamura Productions, 1987.

Knaudt, Till. "A Farewell to Class: The Japanese New Left, the Colonial Landscape of Kamagasaki, and the Anti-Japanese Front (1970–75)." *The Journal of Japanese Studies* 46, no. 2 (2020): 395–422.

Mitobe, Takashi. "Tōdaisaiban o oete ima fukuu koto." *Mogura*, April 9, 1975.

Mukai, Tetsujirō. "Tōkyō chihōsaibansho shōwa 44-nen (kei wa) 700-gō hanketsu," 1969. https://tinyurl.com/4ynd749f.

Nichibenren / Chōkai i'inkai. "Giketsusho." In *Shiryō (Gōhon): Bengoren, Yamane Jirō Bengoshi Chōkaishobun*, edited by Sendagaya sōgō hōritsu jimusho, 113–36. Tokyo: Mugen Kōbō, 1980.

Perkins, Christopher. *The United Red Army on Screen: Cinema, Aesthetics and The Politics of Memory*. Basingstoke: Palgrave, 2015.

Ruoff, Jeffrey, and Kenneth Ruoff. *The Emperor's Naked Army Marches On: Yukiyukite Shingun*. Champaign: Flicks Books, 1998.

Shigematsu, Setsu. *Scream from the Shadows*. University of Minnesota Press. U of Minnesota Press, 2012.

Steinhoff, Patricia. *Shi e No Ideorogī Nihon Sekigun-Ha*. Tokyo: Iwanami Shoten, 2003.

Steinhoff, Patricia G. "Doing the Defendant's Laundry: Support Groups as Social Movement Organizations in Contemporary Japan." *Japanstudien* 11, no. 1 (January 27, 2000): 55–78.

———, ed. *Going to Court to Change Japan: Social Movements and the Law in Contemporary Japan*. Michigan: The University of Michigan, 2014.

Sugimoto, Shōjun. "Korekara no tōdai tōso saiban - hōtei tōsō." In *Tōdaisaiban Tōsō o Takakainuku Tame Ni*, edited by Tōdaitōsō tōitsu hikokudan and Tōitsu kyūtai, 15–16. Tokyo: Jiritsu-sha, 1970.

Takenaka, Rō. *Hō o sabaku: nichibenren yamane shobun kōgi undō no kiroku*. Tokyo: JCA shuppan, 1980.

Takizawa, Masahiro. "Kōsoshin o oete." *Mogura*, April 9, 1975.

Tōdai tōsō tōitsu hikokudan jimukyoku. "Tōdaisaiban Tōsō No Kirihiraita Chihei to Wareware No Ninmu." *Tōdaitōsō Hikokudan Nyūsu*, no. 5 (July 15, 1970): 1–3.

Tōkyō dai-2 bengoshikai. "Giketsusho." In *Shiryō (Gōhon): Bengoren, Yamane Jirō Bengoshi Chōkaishobun*, edited by Sendagaya sōgō hōritsu jimusho, 49–111. Tokyo: Mugen Kōbō, 1980.

Vittinghoff, Anna. "Reassessing Japanese Radical Feminism from the Vantage Point of Dis/Ability." In *Dis/Ability in Media, Law and History, Intersectional, Embodied and Socially Constructed?*, edited by Mickey Lee, Frank Rudy Cooper, and Patricia Reeve, 119–33. London: Routledge, 2022.

Watanabe, Hiroshi. "Tōdai saiban tōsō wo furikaette -- kyūtaibu no tachiba kara." In *Shiryō: tōdai saiban tōsō*, edited by Tōdaitōsō tōitsu hikoku-dan (jiritsu-sha) shiryō henshū iinkai, 251–53. Tokyo: Tōdaitōsō tōitsu hikoku-dan (jiritsu-sha) shiryō henshū iinkai, 1978.

Index

C. Perkins, *The Tokyo University Trial and the Struggle Against Order in Postwar Japan*, New Directions in East Asian History, https://doi.org/10.1007/978-981-99-7043-8

The manufacturer's authorised representative in the EU is Springer Nature Customer Service Centre GmbH, Europaplatz 3, 69115 Heidelberg, Germany. If you have any concerns regarding our products, please contact ProductSafety@springernature.com

Printed and bound by CPI Group (UK) Ltd, Croydon, CR0 4YY
30/09/2026
02225254-0007